C++ FOR GAME PROGRAMMERS

C++ FOR GAME PROGRAMMERS

NOEL LLOPIS

CHARLES RIVER MEDIA, INC.

Hingham, Massachusetts

Publisher: Jenifer Niles
Production: Paw Print Media
Cover Design: The Printed Image

CHARLES RIVER MEDIA, INC.
10 Downer Avenue
Hingham, Massachusetts 02043
781-740-0400
781-740-8816 (FAX)
info@charlesriver.com
www.charlesriver.com

This book is printed on acid-free paper.

Noel Llopis. *C++ for Game Programmers*.
ISBN: 1-58450-227-4

Library of Congress Cataloging-in-Publication Data

Llopis, Noel.
  C++ for game programmers / Noel Llopis.
    p. cm.
  ISBN 1-58450-227-4 (Paperback with CD-ROM : alk. paper)
  1. C++ (Computer program language) 2. Computer games—Programming.
I. Title.
  QA76.73.C153L62 2003
  005.13'3—dc21
                          2003004742

Printed in the United States of America
03 7 6 5 4 3 2

To my parents for all their love and
encouragement during all those years.
To Holly for everything.

CONTENTS

ACKNOWLEDGMENTS

First, I would like to thank Professor Sandy Hill from the University of Massachusetts Amherst, for doing such a fantastic job teaching computer graphics and motivating me to go further and learn new things. It was thanks to his classes and guidance that I eventually chose the career path I did, and ended up in the game industry.

Many thanks to Ned Way. Not only did he review parts of the manuscript and help out with some of the low-level details, but he also put up with me at work for four years, during which time I learned a lot from him.

Also, thanks to Tom Whittaker, Kyle Wilson, and Adrian Stone for their helpful comments and interesting discussions on different C++ topics that helped shape this book.

And thanks to all the game developers out there who are actively sharing information by writing books and magazine articles, giving talks, or even by participating in the game-development mailing lists. In particular, thanks to all the folks on the sweng-gamedev mailing list for a lot of interesting discussions, even if we do not always agree on everything. Without that spirit of sharing, we would all be stuck learning the same things over and over by ourselves, and not make much progress.

Most importantly, a big thanks to Holly Ordway, my wife. There is no way this book would have been possible without her encouragement and support, both moral and practical, since she tirelessly proofread every single chapter and offered many useful suggestions. Mipmap, our cat, helped in his own way by purring on my lap and not letting me get up, so I was forced to finish the book faster.

INTRODUCTION

WHY THIS BOOK?

There are a lot of C++ books out there. Hundreds. Some of them are excellent, classic books in the field, and you'll see them mentioned quite often here. Others are not quite so good, and memories of them quickly fade into mediocrity. So why add yet another C++ book to the mix?

Some months ago, I was reading an excellent book on the Standard Template Library (STL) that had just come out. I devoured it in a few days and was extremely impressed with it, so I started raving about it at work, recommending to all my colleagues that they should read it too. Then I thought, could this book have been any better? Surprisingly, I realized that the answer was yes: the book could have specifically dealt with game programming.

Those great C++ books all offer excellent advice; they will improve your C++ programming and your ability to design solid C++ programs. But for the most part, they offer nothing more than general advice, and while a lot of it applies to game programming, not all of it does. Not only that, but some of the advice will even be counterproductive for game development. By the time you realize this, you might be too far into your project to do anything about it.

That is where this book comes in. It does not intend to replace all the great C++ books out there. Instead, it supplements them by putting everything into perspective from a game-development point of view. This book will point out the most effective C++ practices and steer you away from the potentially dangerous ones. It will describe common C++ techniques to solve specific problems that most game developers have to face. It will be an experienced hand to guide you along the way and help you quickly become an experienced C++ game developer.

When in doubt, this book will take a pragmatic approach to C++ development. There are some recent books and articles expounding the cleverness of certain techniques and language tricks while glossing over the fact that there are hardly any compilers that actually support these techniques, and that they actually make the code more confusing. This book will focus on the techniques that have been proven in real project environments that resulted in shipping successful games, while steering clear of the more experimental and unproven approaches.

Is game development really any different than general application development? You can always find examples of applications that have some of the same requirements as games; but for the most part, the answer is a clear yes. These are some of the characteristics that games often have:

- Run at interactive speeds
- Maintain a minimum frame rate (30–60 frames per second)
- Take over the machine or a large part of it
- Use a lot of resources
- Employ cross-platform development

For example, it might be acceptable to spend 50 ms allocating some memory buffers in response to pressing a button to check your e-mail, but it is clearly not acceptable to do that in the middle of a game running at 60 frames per second (where every frame is at most 16.7 ms).

Those characteristics shape how we approach the development of games. It is a mix of shrink-wrapped application development, real-time development, and operating system development. To make things even more interesting, throw in the mix the need to create gigabytes of resources and the fact that game development teams are made up of very diverse people, and you end up with a truly unique development process.

C++ FOR GAME DEVELOPMENT

Just a few years ago in the mid to late 1990s, C was clearly the language of choice for game development. Nowadays, C++ has taken its place as the preferred language. It also happens to be really convenient, since C is just a subset of C++; so it offers an easy upgrade path.

Notice that just because a program has been written in C++ it does not mean it is object-oriented. There is a lot of code being written in C++ as just a 'better version of C.' Also, there are still platforms where C++ development is not the norm; these are usually severely limited environments, such as handhelds and cell phones.

There were two main reasons for the transition from C to C++. The first one was complexity. As programs got more and more complex, people looked for solutions that would allow them to deal with the added complexity. In a way, this is the same reason that motivated the change from assembly to C as the primary development language over a decade ago.

The second reason is maturity. During the 1990s, C++ finally reached a more stable state. The standard was completed, the compiler support improved, and more C++ compilers appeared for different platforms, including new game consoles.

So, those two reasons, along with faster computers and more easily available memory, made C++ an easy choice to transition to. However, it does not mean that C++ is perfect. Far from it! C++ has its share of problems. Some of them are due to the C baggage that it carries around for backward compatibility, and a few are due to poor design decisions. Even so, with all its problems, it is still the best tool that we have at hand today. This book is not intended as a language advocacy book; it will simply help you use C++ as effectively as possible for game development.

For all the bad things that can be said about C++, its strength is that it is extremely powerful. Using it effectively is difficult and requires a steep learning curve. However, the benefits that can be reaped are well worth it. C++ is one of the few languages that allows high-level programming while still allowing really low-level access to the computer when necessary. It is a perfect mix for systems programming, but it is also perfect for game development. The trick is to know how to avoid getting tangled up in little unnecessary details and look at the big picture. C++ programming is all about tradeoffs: there are many ways of implementing the same functionality, so successful programming and design is all about finding the right balance between efficiency, reliability, and maintainability.

Another great advantage of C++ is that it is quite platform-independent. Being able to develop for multiple platforms using the same source code is becoming more of an issue every year in light of the wide variety of game consoles as well as a significant PC market. There are good C++ compilers for all of the major game platforms as well as STL implementations and other major libraries. However, most of the low-level graphics, user interfaces, and sound APIs are still platform-specific; so abstracting out the details becomes a useful practice for development on multiple platforms.

AUDIENCE

This book is primarily intended for software engineers who are using C++ for game development or a similar field, such as real-time graphics or systems development. Both industry veterans with some C++ experience and people new to the industry who have a strong programming background will benefit from this book.

To get the most out of this book, you should have been using C++ for a few years, maybe even through a full project. You should have the C++ mechanics down and be ready to move on to the next step. If you have an extensive C background and are looking to move to C++, and you are ready to move at a fast pace, this book will also benefit you. Along with some basic C++ books, this book should shorten your learning curve by several years.

Specifically, as a minimum you should have written several C++ programs, be comfortable with the syntax, and be familiar with some of the basic object-oriented concepts, such as inheritance. If you are not at that point, it would be best to put this book aside for a few weeks, start with some of the introductory C++ references listed at the end of the Chapter 1 (see Suggested Reading), and then come back here. Though not necessary, a comfortable familiarity with the concepts of pointers, memory layouts, CPU registers, and basic computer architecture would be helpful for getting the maximum out of this book.

SOME GROUND RULES

Throughout this book, there will be certain terms that will be used over and over. These are terms that most C++ programmers will be familiar with, but which escape exact definitions. However, most of the time, their exact meaning will be very important in order to understand the concepts presented here. Instead of explaining them every time they come up, here is an explanation of the most important terms:

- **Class:** The abstract specification of a user-defined type. It includes both the data and the operations that can be performed on that data.
- **Instance:** A region of memory with associated semantics used to store all of the data members of a class. There can be multiples of these for each class.
- **Object:** Another name of an instance of a class. Objects are created by *instantiating* a class.

```
// This is an object of the class MyClass
MyClass object1;
// This is another one
MyClass object2;
// The pointer points to an object of the class MyClass
MyClass * pObj = new MyClass;
```

- **Declaration:** The part of the source code that introduces one or more names into a program. The following code is the declaration for a class:

```
class MyClass {
public:
    MyClass();
    void MyFunction();
};
```

- **Definition:** The part of the code that specifies the implementation of a function or class. The following code defines the function `MyFunction` from the previous declaration:

```
void MyClass::MyFunction() {
    for (int i=0; i<10; ++i) {
    // Do something...
  }
}
```

ON THE CD

There are small code snippets in almost every chapter, in addition to the full source code on the CD-ROM. I have tried to maintain a plain, consistent style, with as few distractions as possible from the concepts that the code is trying to present. You will see all variables and function names using the MixedCaseApproach. In addition, I have used some basic prefixing in variable names that I think greatly increases readability (no, do not run away, it is not a full Hungarian notation!).

Scope prefixes:

- **m_:** Class member variable. Hence, it is possible to, at a glance, distinguish a member variable from a local (stack) variable—for example: `m_HitPoints`.
- **s_:** Class static variable—for example: `s_HeapName`.
- **g_:** Global variable. Hopefully, you will not see many of those around—for example: `g_UserInfo`.

Type prefixes:

- **b:** Boolean variable—for example: `bAlive`.
- **p:** Pointer—for example: `pItem`.

The scope and type prefixes can be combined to create variables, such as `m_bCanFly` and `s_pHeap`.

SOURCE CODE

This is primarily a book about ideas and concepts. This is not a source of C++ code that you can just drop into your game project without knowing what it does. Instead, this book covers how things work in detail, what tradeoffs are involved, and what are some good rules to follow.

ON THE CD

The source code on the CD-ROM that accompanies this book is intended to illustrate the concepts explained in the chapters. It is one thing to talk about a construct and show a few code snippets, and another to actually see a small program working in tandem to illustrate that specific construct.

In order to keep the source code as clear and to the point as possible, it is implemented in a very straightforward way. It will usually have no error-handling support or a clear abstraction between different layers. It is not the type of code you want to drop straight into a commercial product.

However, you can use it as a starting point. Modify it, experiment with it, and eventually adopt it to fit your needs, or rewrite it from scratch to fit into your game engine with the knowledge you acquire from this book.

I

TAPPING THE POWER OF C++

Ask your favorite basketball player what the secret of his success is. Chances are, he will say it is all due to the basics. He took the time to practice the basics over and over: dribbling with the right hand, dribbling with the left hand, making jump shots—over and over for many years. By learning those basic moves and concepts to the point that they became second nature to him, he is then able to put together some of the most effective and spectacular plays on the court.

In that respect, C++ is fairly similar to basketball or any other skill-based activity. It is possible to create large, breathtaking programs in C++, but that requires a very solid foundation rooted in a knowledge of the basic elements of C++. Before we can jump into creating full-blown games in C++ that awe players with their silky smooth animation at 60 frames per second and their efficient use of the hardware, we need to learn the ins and outs of the language.

In this first part, we will cover the major new features that differentiate C++ from C. We will see how they are used, how they are implemented internally, and most importantly, what their tradeoffs are and when they should be used. Knowing when not to use a specific feature is just as important as knowing the mechanics of how to use it.

1

INHERITANCE

IN THIS CHAPTER

- Classes

- Inheritance

- Polymorphism and Virtual Functions

- To Inherit or Not to Inherit?

- When to Use and When to Avoid Inheritance

- Inheritance Implementation (Advanced)

- Cost Analysis (Advanced)

- Alternatives (Advanced)

- Program Architecture and Inheritance (Advanced)

nheritance is a fundamental concept that will be used often in advanced C++ topics, and it will appear repeatedly throughout this book. Inheritance allows us to create new classes based on an existing class. Understanding exactly how inheritance works, how it is used, and what its consequences are is an important step toward effective game development in C++.

CLASSES

To a beginner, the main difference between C and C++ is usually the concept of classes. C++ code written by an experienced C programmer with little exposure to C++ will often be referred to as "C with classes." But classes, in themselves, are little more than syntactical sugar.

In a nutshell, classes are ways of associating data with functions. Objects are specific instances of a class, each holding its own data, but with all objects of the same class sharing the same functions.

The data part of a class is no different from a plain C structure. The only thing new is that C++ offers three levels of access: public, protected, and private. Additionally, by default, the items of a class are private, while the items of a structure are public. The following data structures are exactly the same. Notice how we had to explicitly add the `public` keyword to the class in order to make the member variables accessible from the outside.

```
struct Point3d
{
    float x;
    float y;
    float z;
};

class Point3d
{
public:
    float x;
    float y;
    float z;
};
```

As we will see later on, compilers vary a fair amount among themselves and from one platform to another in their code generation rules.

They also vary in the types of optimizations they will perform. In spite of this, both the `struct` and the `class` shown above will generate an identical assembly sequence, and will have the same performance characteristics on just about any platform.

What about being able to associate functions and data as part of the same data structure? That is where the syntactical sugar that makes classes unique comes in. It is certainly a very nice feature to have; it allows us to clearly express what operations we want to perform on a set of data. For example, to get the length of a vector, it's much more natural to write `objToCamera.Length()` than `Length(objToCamera)`.

But this is nothing more than an illusion. Internally, the C++ compiler quickly rewrites member function calls as plain C function calls, with the difference being that the first parameter passed to the function is a pointer to the object to which the function is applied. The following code shows a member function call, and how the compiler interprets it internally.

```
Vector3d objToCamera = object.GetPos() — camera.GetPos();

// This function call
float fDist = objToCamera.Length();

// Would be transformed to something like this
float fDist = Vector3d_Length(&objToCamera);
```

This is not to say that classes are not important. They are the basis for some other C++ features that allow us to do object-oriented programming in a very natural way. They are also a pleasure to work with—our taste of syntactical sugar. To really see where the power of C++ comes from, we must look at inheritance.

INHERITANCE

Inheritance allows us to easily create new classes that are variations on an existing class. This is achieved with minimum work and without having to modify the original class in any way.

Inheritance comes in really handy for representing concepts in a very intuitive way. For example, we might have just finished creating a class that represents a normal enemy character in our game. The class takes care of animating the character on the screen, keeping track of its hit points, running the AI (Artificial Intelligence) for that character, and so forth.

```
class Enemy
{
public:
    void SelectAnimation();
    void RunAI();
    // Many more functions
private:
    int m_nHitPoints;
    // Many more member variables here
};
```

When it comes time to add bosses to the end of the level, we are faced with a tough decision: we would like to reuse a lot of the functionality of the Enemy class (e.g., tracking hit points, running animations, etc.), but the boss character is going to do a lot more than a regular enemy unit. We could move a lot of the functions out of the Enemy class and write a Boss class that also uses them. Unfortunately, that would mean breaking up the nice, encapsulated class that we just created, which will result in more maintenance headaches down the line.

This is where inheritance comes into play. We can create a new Boss class that inherits from the Enemy class. That means that it is going to adopt all the functionality of the Enemy class by default, but in addition, we can override particular sections to give the boss the unique behavior we want. In this case, we can override the AI to do something completely different and give the boss his unique character. This is how the Boss class would look using inheritance:

```
class Boss : public Enemy
{
public:
    void RunAI();
};
```

In a situation like this, Enemy would be called a parent class, and Boss would be a child class, because Boss inherits from Enemy. Now we can use both enemies and bosses like this:

```
Enemy enemy1;
Boss boss;

// Do other things for this frame
enemy.RunAI();
boss.RunAI();
```

The variables and functions in a public section in a class are exposed to everybody using that class. The protected section can only be used by the class itself and all the classes that derive from it. Finally, the private section is only available to that class, not even to the ones that derive from it. Refer to one of the C++ references at the end of the chapter for the specific syntax details of those keywords if you are not already familiar with them.

Sometimes we do not want to completely override a particular function in the parent class; instead, we just want to add some functionality to it. For example, we might want the Boss class to still behave like an enemy, but we want it to do some extra AI computations on top of that. The implementation of `RunAI()` would look like this:

```
void Boss::RunAI()
{
public:
    // First run the generic AI of an enemy
    Enemy::RunAI();
    // Now do the real boss AI on top of that
    // ....
}
```

As you can see from the code, in order to call a function in the parent class that we are overriding, we need to prefix the call by the parent's class name followed by two colons (::). That is the C++ scope operator, and it specifies where a function, variable, or class resides. In this case, we are saying we want to call the `RunAI()` function in the parent `Enemy` class, not in the current `Boss` class.

There is nothing stopping us from inheriting from a child class to create a new child class. For example, we might want to create a really special boss for the end of the game, so we create the `SuperDuperBoss`. A derived class is not limited to overriding functions from its immediate parent class; it can override public and protected functions from any of its parent classes. In this case we will override another function from the `Enemy` parent class.

```
class SuperDuperBoss : public Boss
{
    public:
        void RunAI();
};
```

It quickly gets cumbersome to talk about classes inheriting from each other and from other classes in turn just by trying to describe how they are connected. Sentences quickly become a mouthful of the words parent, child, and derived mentioned over and over, making very little sense. This is not all that different from trying to explain a distant family relation: "It was my stepsister's twice-removed cousin's brother who..." Just like a family tree, class diagrams can be used to give the same information in a much more concise way. The diagram in Figure 1.1 shows the relationship between the three classes we have constructed so far.

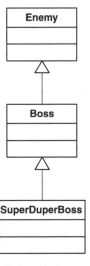

FIGURE 1.1   Inheritance relationship between three enemy classes.

We will be using the type of diagram shown in Figure 1.1 throughout this book. You will find similar diagrams used extensively in other C++ literature.

POLYMORPHISM AND VIRTUAL FUNCTIONS

So far, the inheritance examples we have covered are very simple but already very useful. However, if we were to begin using inheritance in a real project in the way described, it will quickly become limiting and cumbersome. The main drawback is that pointers to objects have to be of the exact same type as the object to which they point. It sounds strange, doesn't it? After all, an int has always been of the type int, and nobody has complained about not being able to use a float pointer to refer to it. Read on.

If in the example from the previous section we have 20 different types of enemies and 5 different bosses, and we want to call the `Execute-Frame()` function once for all the enemies currently in the level, we need to keep track of the type of each enemy unit. That means keeping a list for each type of enemy and boss, and then iterating through each list. Every time we add a new unit type, we have to remember to add a new list and iterate through it. This could prove quite cumbersome. Wouldn't it be nice if there were a way to just keep a list of enemy units and call the `ExecuteFrame()` function in all of them, regardless of what type they really are?

That is exactly what *polymorphism* gives us: the ability to refer to an object through a reference or a pointer of the type of a parent class of the object itself. This may seem intimidating, but it sounds worse than it is. Read it again, and it will start to make sense. It is a fundamental concept that is extremely important to understand in order to be able to follow this chapter and the rest of the book, as well as for any work you do in C++. Here is a short example of what polymorphism allows us to do:

```
class A {
//...
};

class B: public A {
//...
};

// We create an object of type B
B * pB = new B;
// But now we use a pointer of type A to refer to it
A * pA = pB;
```

Even though it does not sound all that impressive, polymorphism is an extremely powerful feature. It allows us to forget about the true type of the object we are manipulating and decouple the code that deals with those objects from the specific implementations of each derived class. For instance, we could have a function that takes an enemy as a parameter, and figures out whether or not we can shoot at it. This function could look something like this:

```
bool CanShootAt ( const Enemy & enemy ) const;
```

Do not worry if you are not familiar with those const keywords. We will look at them in detail in Chapter 3. As soon as we add a boss to the game, we need to determine whether or not we can shoot at it. Without polymorphism, we are either forced to write a similar function that takes an object of type Boss as a parameter, or do something very dangerous, like passing a void pointer and a flag indicating what type of variable it is. Things can only get worse once we add new types of enemy classes. Polymorphism helps us by allowing us to have only one function that takes a reference to an enemy class, regardless of what type of enemy it is. This is also the mechanism we will use later on to write plug-ins, and to extend the functionality of the game without recompiling it (great for patching or even user-created 'mods').

Going back to the enemy example, we can take advantage of polymorphism to make our program a lot simpler by keeping all the enemy units in one array, regardless of whether they are plain enemies, bosses, or the final special boss. That way, we can treat them all the same way.

But there is potential for trouble here. Remember that we wrote a RunAI() function for both the Enemy class and the Boss class (which inherits from Enemy). Consider the following code snippet that uses polymorphism:

```cpp
Enemy * pEnemy = new Enemy;
pEnemy->RunAI(); // Enemy::RunAI() gets called
Enemy * pBoss = new Boss;
pBoss->RunAI();    // Which function gets called??
    // Boss::RunAI() or Enemy::RunA()
```

When both the pointer and the object are of the Enemy type, then calling RunAI() clearly calls Enemy::RunAI(). But what happens when the pointer is of the Enemy type, and the object is of the Boss type? The answer is, it depends on whether RunAI() is a *virtual function* or not.

A function marked as virtual indicates that the type of the object should be used to determine which function should be called in case inherited classes override that function. Otherwise, the type of the pointer will always be used.

In our example, we want the bosses to run the Boss AI, and we want each enemy to run the correct type of AI based on its object type; so we should make the RunAI() function virtual. Here is the revised Enemy class:

```cpp
class Enemy
{
public:
    void SelectAnimation();
    virtual void RunAI();
    // Many more functions
```

```
private:
    int m_nHitPoints;
    // Many more member variables here
};
```

Now we can finally treat all the enemies with the same code, independent of whether they are a boss or not.

```
Enemy * enemies[256];
enemies[0] = new Enemy;
enemies[1] = new Enemy;
enemies[2] = new Boss;
enemies[3] = new FlyingEnemy;
enemies[4] = new FlyingEnemy;
// etc...

{
    // Inside the game loop
    for ( int i=0; i < nNumEnemies; ++i )
        enemies[i]->RunAI();
}
```

TO INHERIT OR NOT TO INHERIT?

When you have a hammer, everything looks like a nail. Inheritance is a very powerful tool. A natural, initial reaction is to try to use it for everything. However, used incorrectly, inheritance can cause more problems than it solves, so you should consider using it only when appropriate, and when there is no other, simpler solution. Without getting into a whole thesis on object-oriented design, there are two rules of thumb to consider when using inheritance. For more detail on this, read some of the Suggested Reading references at the end of this chapter.

Rule 1: Containment vs. Inheritance

Usually, creating a new class that inherits from another class models the 'is a' relationship. If class B inherits from class A, it means that an object of type B is also of type A. In our previous example, the Boss 'is an' Enemy, so it follows the rule correctly.

Imagine someone suggests that the Enemy class should in turn inherit from the Weapon class; that way, the enemy can shoot and do all the things that a weapon does. Tempting, but does it follow the rule? Is an enemy a weapon? Clearly not. An enemy 'has a' weapon is a more accurate statement. This is called *containment,* and it means that the Enemy class should probably have a member variable of type Weapon, but it should not inherit from it. The first rule is: *Inheritance must model the 'is a' relationship.*

Why bother making the distinction? The program will compile and run correctly even if Enemy inherits from Weapon. It might even save us some typing in the short term. The problems will arise later when we try to maintain it or make changes to it. What if enemies can switch between different weapons? What if they can have multiple weapons? What if some of them have no weapons at all? A good, logical design makes all of these changes a breeze. Using inheritance incorrectly will make your life much more difficult.

When in doubt about whether to use inheritance or not for a particular situation, avoid it—especially at the beginning, when you are still learning its long-term effects on a large project. Many more projects were ruined by badly used inheritance than by using it too conservatively.

Rule 2: Behavior vs. Data

Armed with the inheritance tool and our previous rule, an eager programmer creates a new class, EnemyTough, which inherits from Enemy, but which has twice as many hit points. It fits the previous rule perfectly: EnemyTough is an Enemy. So is there anything wrong with this?

Things will probably start looking strange when the EnemyTough class is fleshed out—the class is almost empty. The only content is going to be in the constructor, which assigns more hit points than the Enemy class. It looks useless, and it is rather useless.

The reason that EnemyTough should not be a new class is that the only thing that changed is data, not the behavior of the object. If EnemyTough is not going to have any different behavior, then it is no different than an Enemy object that was initialized with more hit points.

Our second rule then becomes: *only inherit from a class to modify the behavior, not to change the data.*

Apart from not doing anything that could not be accomplished in a much easier way, one of the main drawbacks of inheriting from classes in order to change data is the combinatorial explosion that can occur. Maybe we have an invulnerable enemy. If instead of using a flag in the Enemy class, we create a new class, EnemyInvulnerable, what if we want a tough, invulnerable enemy? What about bosses and tough, invulnerable bosses? Also, data is something that can change easily during the course of the game. Maybe the enemy can use special powers and become invulnerable for a short period of time, or perhaps the enemy can get extra hit points and become 'tough.' If you have modeled those concepts through classes instead of through data, it will be very cumbersome to change the enemy object type while the game is running.

WHEN TO USE AND WHEN TO AVOID INHERITANCE

The previous section explained when it is correct to use inheritance as opposed to other types of construction. Normally, that is all you need to know, and that is as far as most other books take the subject.

What you also need to be aware of is that there is a slight performance penalty associated with virtual functions. The gory details are covered in the following section, Inheritance Implementation (Advanced), which deals with how inheritance and virtual functions are implemented. For the time being, though, let's just say that our program will run a bit slower when using virtual functions.

The first consequence is that we should not use virtual functions unless we have to. This might sound really obvious, but sometimes people will be tempted to make every function a virtual one just in case somebody, sometime, somewhere decides to inherit from that class and extend it. Planning for the future like that is commendable, but in most cases it is better not to. Maybe no object will inherit from those classes and will not override those functions. It would be great if compilers were smart enough to optimize virtual functions into plain functions when the virtual mechanism is not needed, but the C++ language was not designed that way. So for now, every time there is a virtual function call, we are paying a small penalty in performance.

Apart from that, there are still really good reasons not to make every function virtual. We cannot predict the future; so unless we are aware of a pressing need to derive from a particular class, by the time somebody decides to do it, things might have changed enough that the class needs to be rewritten anyway. Also, it is much easier and faster to create a class without thinking of future extensibility, private functions, and member variables. As soon as we make them protected or public, and virtual, we need to start worrying about how they are going to be used, split them correctly, and maintain a consistent state. In other words, do not make a function virtual unless you are aware of a reason to do so right now.

Most of the time, this is all we need to worry about. With current hardware, the overhead of virtual function calls is pretty small, so we can almost forget about it.

As it happens, sometimes we just cannot afford for a particular function to be virtual. Maybe it is a function deep inside an inner loop that gets called thousands and thousands of times per frame. This can be particularly true if it is a simple function that could otherwise be inlined (see Chapter 6 for more information on inlining functions and dealing with performance). Before we get ready to replace this function with something else, we should really check to see that the fact that it is virtual (or not inlined) is hurting performance. If that is the case, we should replace it with a nonvirtual function. Remember that just putting in an `if` statement and calling separate nonvirtual functions probably will not be any faster. We might need to make several copies of our inner loop, one for each function called. Even better, we might want to consider moving that inner loop into a class, and the correct loop gets called based on a virtual function; that way there is only one virtual function call's worth of overhead for the whole loop.

Another potential performance drain is when the program crosses the virtual boundary many times. This is different from the case described before in that it is not just one virtual function that gets called over and over again, but a whole set of functions. For example, imagine a virtual interface to a graphics renderer module. All the functions in the interface are virtual functions.

```
class GraphicsRenderer {
public:
    virtual void SetRenderState(...);
    virtual void SetTextureState(...);
    virtual void SetLight(...);
    virtual void DrawTriangle(...);
    //...
};
```

Unfortunately, the abstraction for the renderer class was not chosen at the correct level, so every time we want to draw a triangle on the screen, we end up calling the sequence of virtual functions: `SetRenderState()`, `SetTextureState()`, `SetLights()`, and `DrawTriangle()`. Repeat that by the amount of triangles we are rendering per framethese days, and the virtual function overhead will quickly add up.

That is an extreme example, and the performance of drawing one triangle at a time on current PC graphics hardware would kill the game right there, but imagine for a moment that the main cost comes from the virtual function calls. How can we solve this problem? We can solve this by moving the abstraction to a bit higher level. Instead of the previous interface, we can come up with a new abstract interface that draws an initial mesh (set of triangles), like this:

```
class GraphicsRenderer {
public:
    virtual void SetMaterial(...);
    virtual void DrawMesh(...);
    //...
};
```

Now, to draw a set of triangles, we call only two functions: `Set-Material()`, and `DrawMesh()`. We have reduced the number of virtual functions called from four or five per triangle to only two per hundreds or thousands of triangles. Notice how the change we had to make was a major one. Completely changing such an interface has major consequences in all the code that calls it as well as in the program architecture in general, so this is something we should carefully consider when we design the interface for the first time.

INHERITANCE IMPLEMENTATION (ADVANCED)

In order to go any further in our understanding of the tradeoffs of inheritance, it is imperative to learn exactly how inheritance is implemented under the hood. Compiler writers have a fair amount of freedom in how they decide to implement inheritance; as long as they comply with the standard, they can pretty much do anything they want. Fortunately, just about every compiler we will come across in the PC and modern consoles will implement inheritance in roughly the same way, and with only minor differences.

First let's start with nonvirtual functions. These are the easy ones, since a particular function call will always map to a particular part of the code. The compiler can calculate the address of that function at compile and link time; at runtime, all it does is call to a fixed address.

Virtual functions are tricky, because the code called depends not only on the specific function call made, but on the type of the object that the function is called on. Usually, this is solved through the use of *virtual tables*, which are more often referred to as "vtables." The vtable is nothing more than a table of pointers to functions. Every class with at least one virtual function has one of these vtables, and indexing into the correct slot of the table will determine what function needs to be called at runtime.

A few important things to note about the the vtable are that it only contains pointers to virtual functions; nonvirtual function addresses are still computed at compile time and called directly in the code. That means that we only pay a few extra bytes and a small performance penalty per virtual function, but we are not affecting the performance of nonvirtual functions. This has been one of the guiding design principles of C++ from the start—you do not have to pay for features you are not using.

It is also important to notice that there is only one vtable per class, not per object. This is extremely important, since we will typically have many instances of objects for a single class. For example, if we have a tile-based terrain, we might have a class that represents a terrain tile. If the map is 256×256, we will have 65,536 objects, but fortunately only one vtable (assuming all those terrain tiles are of the same class and have at least one virtual function).

The vtable for all the objects of a particular class will be the same, so instead of each object having a vtable of its own, each object has a pointer to the vtable for that class. Otherwise, how is the program going to know what class that object belongs to at runtime? Usually, this pointer will be the first entry of the object. Consequently, the size of an object containing at least one virtual function will increase by the size of a pointer. In current platforms, a pointer is usually four bytes. In the previous terrain example, that means we will be using an extra 64 KB just in vtable pointers, plus a few bytes for the vtable itself. That is a rather modest memory consumption considering the benefits we get out of it, but it is something we should be aware of nonetheless, especially in platforms with more limited memory.

To be correct, not every object has a pointer to a vtable, not even every object that belongs to a class with inheritance. Only objects that belong to a class with virtual functions will have a vtable. It is a small, but important distinction. It means we are free to use inheritance for small, basic classes, such as a vector or a matrix, as long as we do not have any virtual functions. Again, the same design principle is at work: if we are not using a feature, we are not paying any performance or memory penalties for it.

Figure 1.2 shows roughly how the memory layout looks for a class with virtual functions. For all of the gory details of virtual function implementation, refer to the Suggested Reading.

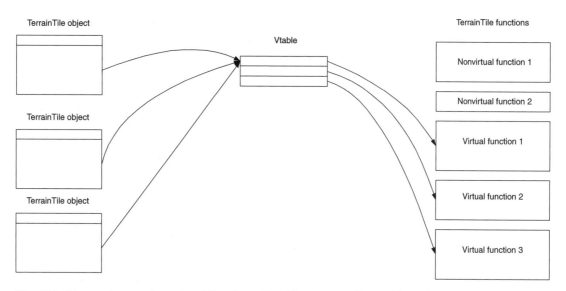

FIGURE 1.2 Memory layout of nonvirtual functions, virtual functions, a class vtable, and objects from that class.

COST ANALYSIS (ADVANCED)

Throughout this chapter, we have talked about a performance penalty for using virtual functions. We have been waving our hands, saying that it is not too much; but this penalty is not something we can totally ignore at all times, either. How much of a penalty is that exactly? Do you pay it every time you call a virtual function? How does it vary from platform to platform? Here is what happens at runtime when we call a virtual function through a pointer of a base class:

Step 1. Everything starts with an innocent-looking function call.
```
pEnemyUnit->RunAI();
```

Step 2. The vtable pointer of that object is fetched (see Figure 1.3).

Step 3. The entry at the offset corresponding to the function we are calling is fetched from the vtable (see Figure 1.4).

Step 4. A function call is made to the address specified by the vtable entry (see Figure 1.5).

Step 4 is the same as for a nonvirtual function, so the added cost comes from Step 2 and Step 3. Those steps make the sequence look more expensive, but exactly how expensive is it? Unfortunately, it is very hard

FIGURE 1.3   The vtable pointer of the object is fetched.

FIGURE 1.4   The correct entry in the vtable is fetched.

FIGURE 1.5   The function pointed to by the vtable entry is called.

to answer that question accurately these days. Not only will the cost greatly vary from platform to platform, but different cache levels, specular execution, and deep pipelining make it almost impossible to come up with a good answer.

We could just ignore any performance penalties, write the game, and then profile it to find out if we have a bottleneck caused by virtual functions. Even though leaving optimizations for the end is a very good general rule, it falls short here. First of all, it is difficult to determine that things are being slowed down by virtual functions. Unlike an expensive inner loop, these are not going to show up as hot spots in the profiler output. The consequences of virtual function overhead are going to be much more subtle and much more widespread. Most important, even if we narrow it down to virtual function overhead, it might be too late to change it. If the whole game is architected to use inheritance and virtual functions to override specific behaviors, it is going to be extremely difficult to radically change this structure and remove all of the virtual function calls that are slowing us down.

The best approach is to have some reasonable expectations of the impact virtual function calls have on our program, and keep those in mind when writing the game. Still, theoretical knowledge of virtual functions is no substitute for getting our hands dirty once the game is running, doing some real profiling, and making sure our assumptions were in the ballpark.

Most of the time the added cost will be negligible. Sometimes it will not be any slower (assuming the CPU was waiting for some other results to complete in the FPU unit, for example). Yet at other times in very deep, frequently called loops, we might feel the extra performance hit.

The greatest performance penalty often comes from what we do not get, rather than from the overhead of Steps 2 and 3. Virtual functions are usually not inlined, so if the function could have been otherwise inlined, that might amount to a significant hit. We should avoid making functions virtual that we want to be inlined; it probably means we are trying to set an interface at too low a conceptual level anyway, so it is probably time to rethink that design.

Another big issue is the impact of the vtable lookup in the data cache. If we have many different types of classes, and all are being executed in a random order, we will end up looking up entries in many different vtables during the course of a frame. This could cause the data cache to eject some other data we need, or even to consistently have cache misses for vtables we need to look up. In a this situation, or in a platform with little or no data cache, the penalty added by virtual functions is much more noticeable and can lead to significant performance degradation of the game.

Do we always pay the cost of the extra indirection for virtual function calls? Surprisingly, not always. Compiler writers are very crafty and will go out of their way to make sure our programs run as fast as possible. So if there is a shortcut they can take to make our program faster, they will usually do it.

As it turns out, we only need to go through the vtable jumps for the most general (but also most common) cases. It is possible that we will be calling a function marked as virtual on an object directly (instead of through a pointer or a reference). In that case the compiler will notice it and will invoke a nonvirtual function call. A similar case happens if we are using a pointer or reference of the same type as the object itself; the compiler will be able to optimize away the vtable jump and call the function directly.

```
Enemy * pEnemy1 = new Boss;
pEnemy1->RunAI(); // We pay the virtual function cost

Boss * pEnemy2 = new Boss;
pEnemy2->RunAI(); // Virtual function call optimized out
```

ALTERNATIVES (ADVANCED)

You have reached this point, and you are still not convinced you want to use inheritance. The extra memory overhead and performance hit really look like too much for what you are trying to do. Besides, you have managed to program perfectly fine in C without using inheritance, so why would you need it now?

That is a fair question. The best way to address it is to think about how we would go about doing a similar implementation in C without the help of inheritance. There are a variety of ways to do it.

- **One structure and many conditional statements:** We could create one C structure containing all possible data we might need for all inherited classes, add a type field, and everywhere we use it, have many conditional checks on the type field, doing different things depending on the type. Apart from how ugly the code will get and the maintenance nightmare, memory is wasted because all of our structures are the same size (the size of the largest set of data we want to represent). Performance will also be much worse than using virtual functions as soon as there are more than a few if statements, since the performance cost of several conditional jumps will quickly add up.
- **One structure, but use switch statements instead of conditional statements:** The source code will look a bit tidier, but chances are the compiler will produce the same code as for the if statements, resulting in the same drawbacks. In some very rare instances, the compiler might be able to replace all the conditional

jumps with a jump table. In that case, at best, performance will be the same for virtual functions. Unfortunately, there is usually no easy way to reliably coerce the compiler into generating a jump table out of switch statements.

- **Tables of pointers:** We could create a table of function pointers for each type of object, and then put a pointer to the appropriate table in each structure. We would have to take extreme care to fill it correctly for each structure, and it would not be particularly easy read or pleasant to debug. Does this approach sound familiar? Of course it does; we are just re-implementing virtual functions, except that we are not getting any of the other benefits of inheritance (different object sizes, private-protected members, etc.). Performance will be the same as when using virtual functions and inheritance, except that it will require a lot of work. Let the compiler do the busy work for you instead.

The conclusion we should take away from this is that if we need the features of inheritance and virtual functions, we should just use them instead of trying to re-implement them all from scratch. Chances are the compiler will do a better job than we could at optimizing the code and doing all the bookkeeping.

PROGRAM ARCHITECTURE AND INHERITANCE (ADVANCED)

You might recall some warning comments in an earlier section mentioning the potential dangers of inheritance. The problem goes way beyond 'little' things such as unnecessary performance penalties or increased memory consumption. The real problem is what extensive use of inheritance will do to your source code.

The purposes of classes is to be able to model self-contained concepts and to abstract out their implementation. This is done by providing the smallest public interface that is necessary, and hiding all the complexity inside private functions and member variables. Keeping that in mind, creating a class with a clean public interface is a challenge. Decisions need to be made about what should be exposed and what should be hidden; we must decide how to minimize the interface while providing all the flexibility we need. It is not an easy or straightforward job.

Adding inheritance to that mix is like fighting a war on two fronts. Not only do we have to worry about the current users of the class, but we also have to worry about future extensibility and the protected interface we should expose. Things just got a lot more difficult all of the sudden.

The other major problem with inheritance has to do with its effect on the overall architecture of the program. Use of inheritance can quickly turn into deep inheritance chains—whole inheritance trees spanning dozens or hundreds of classes, some of them five, six, or more levels deep. Even though each class might have been modeled correctly, and they follow all the rules for what a correct inheritance is, this situation is still undesirable. Large inheritance trees with many levels of inheritance make it hard for the programmers to understand what the code is doing. Function calls need to be traced up and down the inheritance tree, and it might be difficult to exactly know what function is being called, depending on which functions specific classes override.

Worst of all, inheritance tends to 'harden' the program design. Software in general (and games a bit more so) needs to be flexible. Things change—new requirements come from the publisher, new features need to be added to stay competitive, or something needs to be changed to make it more fun. Having a code base that can easily adapt to change is a worthy goal. The last thing we want to happen is to be two weeks away from shipping the game and not be able to make a crucial change that *should* have been trivial, but it is not.

What are our alternatives? We previously mentioned containment as being different from inheritance. Containment models the 'has a' relationship, while inheritance models the 'is a' relationship. Inheritance should never be used to model the 'has a' relationship. However, sometimes we might want to use containment when inheritance would have been appropriate.

Containment, unlike inheritance, does not have the tendency to harden the program design. Things stay flexible and malleable. Because objects are contained within objects, they do not need to know anything about who is holding them; they just need to worry about doing their job when they are told to do it. In a way, we are back to pure encapsulation. And the simpler the classes can be, the easier they will be to use, develop, maintain, and change over time.

This does not mean that we should replace all inheritance with containment, only problematic uses of inheritance. In a situation with a really deep inheritance chain, we might want to consider using containment judiciously in a few places just to break that chain into two or three much smaller chains.

Look at the diagram in Figure 1.6 for an example of such a transformation. A deep inheritance chain six levels deep was transformed to use containment, and now the largest inheritance chain only has three levels. Notice how the arrows for inheritance are different than the arrows for containment.

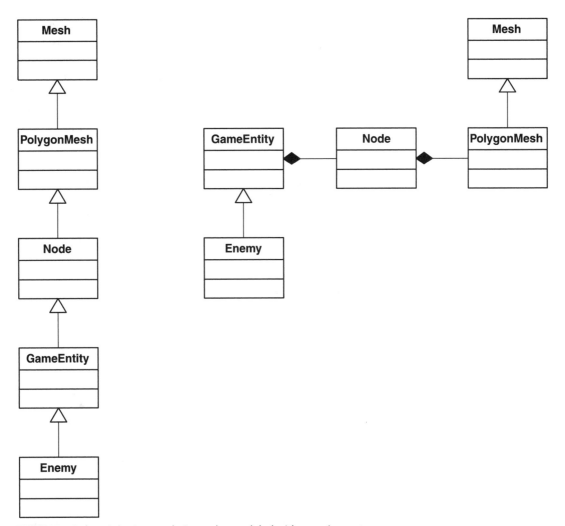

FIGURE 1.6   A deep inheritance chain can be modeled with containment.

CONCLUSION

After a quick review of C++ classes and objects, we saw how to create new classes based on existing classes through the use of inheritance. Then we saw a key concept behind object-oriented programming: polymorphism, the ability to refer to different types of objects through a pointer of the type of one of their parent classes. Virtual functions go hand in hand with polymorphism, because they let us specify whether we want to call a function based on the pointer type or on the object type.

We then examined how and when inheritance should be used, what the correct use of inheritance was, presented alternatives, and looked at the potential drawbacks of inheritance. Specifically, we covered in detail how inheritance and virtual functions are implemented and what performance penalties they can cause.

SUGGESTED READING

These are some excellent introductory C++ texts. You might want to browse through them as a refresher for some of the concepts in this chapter or as a starting point if you have no previous C++ experience.

Eckel, Bruce, *Thinking in C++*. Prentice Hall, 2000. Also available online at http://www.mindview.net/Books/TICPP/ThinkingInCPP2e.html.
Lippman, Stanley B., *C++ Primer*, Addison-Wesley, 1998.
Cline, Marshall, *C++ FAQ Lite, http://www.parashift.com/c++-faq-lite/*.

These books give some good advice on how to use and not use inheritance.

Cargill, Tom, *C++ Programming Style*, Addison-Wesley, 1992.
Murray, Robert B., *C++ Strategies and Tactics*, Addison-Wesley, 1993.

For a really in-depth look at how inheritance and virtual functions are implemented, this is one of the best references out there.

Lippman, Stanley B., *Inside the C++ Object Mode*, Addison-Wesley, 1996.

2

MULTIPLE INHERITANCE

IN THIS CHAPTER

- Using Multiple Inheritance
- Multiple Inheritance Problems
- When to Use Multiple Inheritance and When to Avoid It
- Multiple Inheritance Implementation (Advanced)
- Cost Analysis (Advanced)

M*ultiple inheritance* is another concept that is new to C++. Single inheritance allowed us to create new classes from a parent class; multiple inheritance extends that by allowing us to create a class based on two or more parent classes. It is not as widely used as single inheritance, and it has its share of problems; when used properly, it can be an effective tool in your design repertoire. In particular, specific idioms of multiple inheritance, such as abstract interfaces, can be very useful.

USING MULTIPLE INHERITANCE

Let us consider a simple design scenario, how we would implement it with the different tools we have at hand, and how it could be solved with multiple inheritance. For this example, we are designing the basic `GameObject` class. This is the class that all of our game types will inherit from: enemy units, items, triggers, cameras, and so forth. In particular, there are two requirements that we must implement; all game objects must be able to receive a message, and all game objects must be able to be linked as part of a tree. Forgetting about all other aspects of the `GameEntity` class, how can we go about implementing those two requirements?

The All-in-one Approach

The most obvious approach is to implement those requirements as part of the `GameEntity` class itself. There we can add the functions to receive messages and to link the game object to any part of the tree.

As usual with C++, there are many different ways to skin a cat and implement the same solution. Unfortunately, the first one that comes to mind, or the one that requires the least amount of typing, is not always the best approach. The all-in-one approach is clearly very simple and straightforward, which is a big plus, but it also has some major drawbacks.

The class' simplicity is a double-edged sword. Yes, on the one hand, it is very simple to add functionality without having to create new classes, change inheritance chains, or make any other structural changes; but on the other hand, the `GameEntity` class will continue to grow in size and complexity every time a new concept is added. Soon, a fundamental base class like `GameEntity` could balloon to an unmanageable size and a tangle of functions, difficult to both use and maintain. In our attempt to keep things simple in the short term, we have made things much more complicated over the long term.

Another problem with that approach is code duplication. Is GameEntity the only class that will receive messages? Maybe the Player class will also receive messages without being a game object itself. What about being part of a tree? Probably, other objects, like scene nodes or animation bones, might be organized in a similar way. It would be a pity, as well as bad software engineering practice, not to reuse that code. Simply copying the relevant code everywhere it is needed is not a viable solution, since it will lead to major headaches as the program changes and during future maintenance.

Containment Considered

It is clear that each of those concepts should be represented by its own class. In this case, we could have MessageReceiver and TreeNode classes. The question remains: how should these classes be related to the GameEntity class?

The game object class could contain one of each of those objects and provide functions in its interface to use them. This approach is called containment (see Chapter 1), because a GameEntity object contains a MessageReceiver and a TreeNode object. As we will see in a later section, this is often an excellent solution. It leads to great reuse, without adding too much complexity to the classes that are extended in this way.

Its only drawback is that many interface functions, whose only purpose is to call a member function of another object, must be created and maintained. Those functions are tedious to maintain, particularly if the interfaces change often, and will slightly degrade performance because of the extra function call overhead. This is how the class looks with containment:

```
class GameEntity {
public:
    // MessageReceiver functions
    bool ReceiveMessage(const Message & msg);

    // TreeNode functions
    GameEntity * GetParent();
    GameEntity * GetFirstChild();
    // ...

private:
    MessageReceiver m_MsgReceiver;
    TreeNode        m_TreeNode;
};
```

```
inline bool GameEntity::ReceiveMessage(const Message & msg) {
    return m_MsgReceiver.ReceiveMessage(msg);
}
inline GameEntity * GameEntity::GetParent() {
    return m_TreeNode.GetParent();
}
inline GameEntity * GameEntity::GetFirstChild() {
    return m_TreeNode.GetFirstChild();
}
```

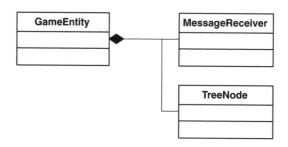

FIGURE 2.1   GameEntity class using containment.

We could use containment, as in the first example, but instead of providing member functions to interact with the objects inside GameEntity, we
could just expose the objects themselves. That would certainly cut down
on the maintenance of the dummy interface functions, but it exposes
more information than necessary about how GameEntity is really implemented. If later on we were to change its implementation to a more efficient way that did not use one of those classes, all the code that used
GameEntity would have to be changed. This is not an attractive prospect,
so let's keep them private for the moment (see Figure 2.1).

The Single Inheritance Approach

Let's approach the problem using a technique we learned in Chapter 1:
single inheritance. We saw that it very easily allows us to create a class
that is a variation of a parent class. We could declare that a GameEntity is
a MessageReceiver and that it inherits from MessageReceiver. But what
about TreeNode? In a way, GameEntity also is a TreeNode. This concept
cannot be modeled easily with single inheritance. We might be tempted
to create an inheritance chain like the one shown in Figure 2.2.

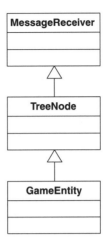

FIGURE 2.2   Single inheritance is not always enough.

On the surface, this solution seems to work. The program will run correctly, but it is a really ugly design that will only cause trouble later on. Is a `TreeNode` a `MessageReceiver`? It does not have to be, so why does it inherit from it? The other way around does not seem right, either. Besides, doing such an inheritance tree would prevent us from reusing `TreeNode` elsewhere without it being a `MessageReceiver` as well. So, we'll have to come up with a better idea.

Multiple Inheritance to the Rescue

Multiple inheritance is the solution to our problem. It works just like single inheritance, but a class is allowed to inherit from multiple parent classes. In our case, we can have `GameEntity` inherit both from `MessageReceiver` and `TreeNode`, and it will automatically have the interface, member variables, and behavior of all of its parent classes. This is how we would do it in code:

```
class GameEntity : public MessageReceiver, public TreeNode
{
public:
    // Game entity functions...
};
```

The corresponding inheritance diagram is shown in Figure 2.3.

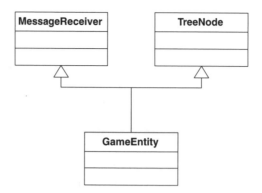

FIGURE 2.3 GameEntity modeled with multiple inheritance.

This type of object can be used just as if it had been implemented using single inheritance:

```
GameEntity entity;
//...
GamEntity * pParent = entity.GetParent();
```

MULTIPLE INHERITANCE PROBLEMS

As usual, introducing new functionality and new features also introduces new complexities and problems. Multiple inheritance is no exception. As a matter of fact, some people might argue that multiple inheritance introduces more problems than it solves. Let's consider some of the main problems.

Ambiguity

The first problem is ambiguity. What happens if two classes we inherited from contain a member function that has the exact same name and parameters? In our previous example, imagine that both MessageReceiver and TreeNode have a public member function called IsValid(), which is used for debugging, that checks whether the object is in a correct state. What is the result of calling IsValid() on a GameEntity object? The result is a compile error because the call is ambiguous.

To solve the ambiguity, we need to prefix the function call with the class name of the function we want to call. If we want to call those functions from within the GameEntity class, we would need to use the scope operator and write it like this:

```
void GameEntity::SomeFunction() {
    if (MessageReceiver::IsValid() && TreeNode::IsValid()) {
        //...
    }
}
```

Things get worse if we want to call those functions from outside the GameEntity class. We also need to prefix them with the class they belong to, so now the calling code needs to know about the parent classes of GameEntity.

```
bValid = entity.MessageReceiver::IsValid() &&
         entity.TreeNode.IsValid();
```

Topography

An even larger problem is the topography of some of the possible inheritance trees that can be created with multiple inheritance. Consider the following situation: we have an AI class that deals with moving entities on land (LandAI), and another class that deals with moving them through the air (FlyingAI). Our game designers just came up with a new type of hybrid entity that needs to move both on land and through the air, and we need to create an AI class for it. A possible solution would be to inherit from both LandAI and FlyingAI (see Figure 2.4).

Everything goes well until we realize that both LandAI and FlyingAI inherit from the same base class. The inheritance tree we have created without realizing it is shown in Figure 2.5.

In code the same class structure would be represented by:

```
class MovingAI {
    // ...
protected:
    int m_Counter;
};

class FlyingAI : public MovingAI {
    // ...
};

class LandAI : public MovingAI {
```

```
    // ...
};

class HybridAI : public FlyingAI, public LandAI {
    // ...
};
```

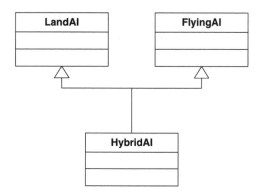

FIGURE 2.4   An innocent-looking multiple inheritance tree.

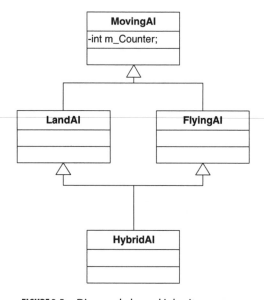

FIGURE 2.5   Diamond-shaped inheritance tree.

This is the dreaded diamond-shaped inheritance tree, also referred to as the DOD (Diamond Of Death). `MovingAI` is a parent class for `HybridAI`, but through two different paths. This arrangement has several unexpected consequences:

- The contents of `MovingAI` appear twice in `HybridAI` because `HybridAI` is created from two different classes, each of which already contains `MovingAI`. So, surprisingly, `HybridAI` will contain two `m_Counter` variables.
- Trying to use a member variable of `MovingAI` from within `HybridAI` is ambiguous. We need to specify the inheritance path through which we want to access the member variable. It sounds redundant, since both paths seem to lead to the same variable, but as we saw in the previous point, this is not the case.

A representation of a `HybridAI` object, showing how it is composed of different sections from its parent classes, is shown in Figure 2.6.

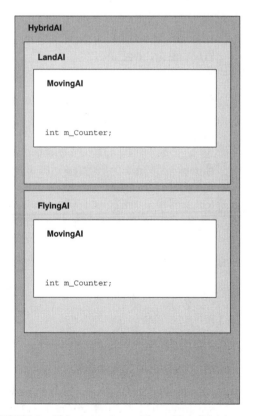

FIGURE 2.6   Object structure with multiple inheritance.

To solve this problem, C++ introduces a new concept: *virtual inheritance*, which is a totally different concept than 'virtual functions.' Virtual inheritance allows a parent class to only appear once in its children's object structures, even in the presence of the diamond inheritance hierarchy. But virtual inheritance comes with a runtime cost, as well as a small space cost. There is a lot of pointer fix up and table dereferencing that needs to happen under the hood for everything to work as expected at runtime. In addition, virtual inheritance introduces its own share of problems and complexity.

So, what is the best solution? It is best to avoid the diamond inheritance hierarchy at all costs. Usually, it is the sign of a bad class design, and it will cause more problems in the long run than it will solve. If you are absolutely convinced that a diamond-shaped hierarchy is the best design for your program, then make sure you and your team are aware of all the details and side effects of virtual inheritance. The Suggested Reading section at the end of this chapter is a great place to start. As for the rest of this book, we will avoid both virtual inheritance and the diamond-shaped hierarchy.

Program Architectures

As if that were not enough, multiple inheritance presents one last, fundamental problem; its correct but careless use could lead to a horrible program architecture. Over-reliance on multiple inheritance, and to a lesser extent single inheritance, ends up causing deep inheritance hierarchies with large objects, bloated interfaces, and very tight coupling between classes. All this translates into not being able to easily reuse individual classes in different contexts, difficulty in maintaining and adding new features to existing code, and increased compile and link times.

Multiple inheritance is a complex, difficult tool to use. Whenever possible, it is best to look for alternative solutions, such as composition, and only use multiple inheritance whenever it is the best of all alternatives. Later in this chapter, we will examine in more detail some specific cases where multiple inheritance is the preferred solution.

POLYMORPHISM

Just as with single inheritance, it is possible to refer to an object through a pointer of the type of a parent class. However, unlike single inheritance, we have to be much more careful in how we obtain and manipulate those pointers.

We can always cast a pointer to a class further up the hierarchy, as in the case of single inheritance. We can use the old-style C casting or the preferred C++-style casting.

```
GameEntity * pEntity = GetEntity();
MessageReceiver * pRec;
pRec = (MessageReceiver *)(pEntity); // C cast
pRec2 = static_cast<MessageReceiver *>(pEntity); // C++ cast
```

However, things are more complicated when casting down or across the hierarchy. With single inheritance, all we had to do was to make sure that object we were pointing to was of the right type, and do a cast as usual. With multiple inheritance, this approach will not work. The reason is the structure of the object with multiple inheritance—specifically, of the vtable. With single inheritance, the beginning of the vtable was the same for all the classes in the hierarchy, but derived classes would use entries further down in the vtable. With multiple hierarchy, different base classes will have different entry points in the vtable, so the cast will actually return a different pointer than the one from which it was cast. This is covered in more detail in Multiple Inheritance Implementation, later in this chapter.

How is this casting accomplished? It is typically accomplished through the use of dynamic_cast, one of the new casting styles. Unlike the other forms of casting, dynamic_cast will introduce some runtime code to actually do any necessary pointer arithmetic and adjust for different vtable offsets. Additionally, dynamic_cast will return NULL if our casting is not legal given the object or the inheritance hierarchy.

```
GameEntity * pEntity = GetEntity();
// Normal dynamic cast. Works fine.

MessageReceiver * pRec;
pRec = dynamic_cast<MessageReceiver*>(pEntity);

// Also works fine, but pNode will have a different value
// than pEntity
TreeNode * pNode;
pNode = dynamic_cast<TreeNode*>(pEntity);

// This is not a valid cast because the entity we have is not
// actually a player object. It will fail and return NULL.
Player * pPlayer;
pPlayer = dynamic_cast<Player*>(pEntity);
```

Unfortunately, not only does `dynamic_cast` introduce a slight performance penalty, but it also requires RTTI (Runtime Type Information) to be enabled in the compiler settings. That means that the compiler will create and keep information at runtime about all the C++ classes, enough to be able to perform `dynamic_cast` correctly. It is not a huge amount of memory per class, but every single class will have that information, which can add up to a fair bit of memory. That is particularly unfortunate, since we probably do not need that information in every single class, especially not in simple, lightweight classes such as matrices or vectors. In Chapter 12 we will examine the default RTTI system in detail and present a custom-made alternative that might be better suited to games.

WHEN TO USE MULTIPLE INHERITANCE AND WHEN TO AVOID IT

So far, the picture we have presented of multiple inheritance has not been particularly promising. You might even be wondering why there is a whole chapter dedicated to it. After all, the conclusion so far seems to be that it is better to avoid it as much as possible. However, if applied carefully, multiple inheritance can be a useful tool.

The most important thing to remember is not to use multiple inheritance indiscriminately. Just because it is the first solution that comes to mind, it does not mean it is the best one. We saw that multiple inheritance carries several potential problems with it: it can cause ambiguities, increasing the complexity of the program, and it can also cause a small performance hit.

Whenever possible, consider using containment as an alternative to multiple inheritance. Most often, it will a better solution for our intended design. If containment is not possible or is really cumbersome, do not apply single inheritance unless it fits right in. Trying to twist a single inheritance chain to solve a problem that requires multiple inheritance is even worse. It will create useless temporary classes without real meaning, and it will make the program even harder to understand and maintain.

As we will see in more detail in Chapter 10, abstract interfaces are a great application of multiple inheritance. By putting a few restrictions on the type of classes we can inherit from, abstract interfaces can use multiple inheritance without any of the problems seen in this section. Abstract interfaces are the basis for switching implementations at runtime, extending the game after it has shipped, and for creating plug-ins, which is the topic of Chapter 11.

Avoid multiple inheritance in deep, complex hierarchies. Single inheritance makes things confusing enough when you are trying to find out where things are implemented and what the flow of the program is. Multiple inheritance makes that much harder. Also, with deep, complicated hierarchies, it is very easy for the dreaded diamond-shaped hierarchy to rear its ugly head. That should be avoided at all costs until you are absolutely sure you need it to be that way, and are very familiar with its consequences and virtual inheritance.

Some good examples of multiple inheritance that have come up in the past in game development are simple, general extensions to a class. A reference-counted class is a good example of a function that can be used freely with multiple inheritance. Any function that inherits from it will become reference counted through `AddRef` and `Release` functions. Such a class is usually perfectly fine to inherit from because it is very simple, and it does not inherit from any other classes in turn.

MULTIPLE INHERITANCE IMPLEMENTATION (ADVANCED)

Multiple inheritance is implemented in a very similar way to single inheritance, but with some added complexity. Unfortunately, multiple inheritance does not result in nearly as neat and efficient an implementation as single inheritance does.

One of the most elegant aspects of single inheritance implementation is that objects are always backward-compatible with objects of parent classes. This is due to the fact that only one vtable pointer is needed, and all extra elements added by derived classes are tacked on at the end, so a parent class will simply ignore them. This allows us to easily cast up and down the inheritance hierarchy as long as we know the types of the objects (see Figure 2.7).

Under multiple inheritance, things are a bit more complicated. Because of polymorphism, a derived class should be able to be addressed like any of its parent classes after it has been correctly cast. Just appending the member variables and keeping one vtable, like in the case of single inheritance, does not work because we cannot make it look like all of its parent classes, no matter how hard we try.

Instead, along with the data, we must also append one vtable for each of its parent classes. Now it becomes possible to cast a derived object to any of its parents by adding an offset to the pointer (see Figure 2.8).

From a memory standpoint, multiple inheritance will add an extra pointer to every object for every parent class. This is usually not a big deal with today's large amounts of RAM, but it is something to keep in mind. There can be some objects that are created many thousands of times, and we should be aware of this extra space requirement. As in the

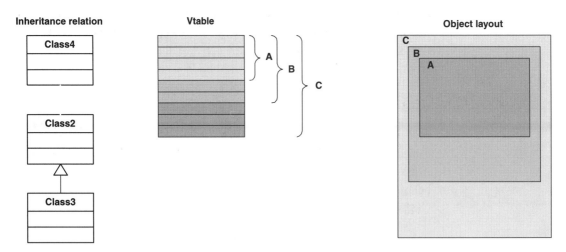

FIGURE 2.7   Parent class and derived class using single inheritance.

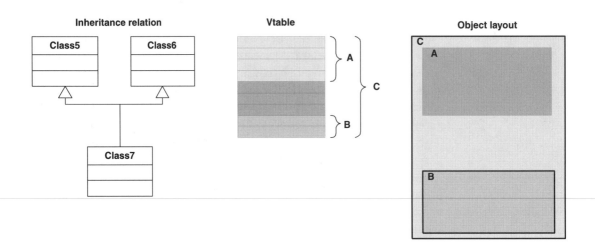

FIGURE 2.8   Two parent classes and a derived class with multiple inheritance.

case of single inheritance, the vtable pointer is only necessary if there are some virtual functions in the parent class that we are inheriting from. Otherwise, only the member variables are appended.

One last thing to notice is that the order in which those classes are appended to create the derived class is completely implementation-dependent.

Most compilers will append them in the order in which they are declared in the inheritance statement, but some others will shuffle classes around a bit to gain a slight performance improvement.

COST ANALYSIS (ADVANCED)

Multiple inheritance has the same performance characteristics as single inheritance except for two cases. These include casting and virtual functions of the second parent class.

Casting

In the case of single inheritance, casting a pointer up and down the hierarchy is a free operation. Casting just identifies an object as being of a particular class to the compiler. The compiler makes sure that all operations on that pointer are legal and that any virtual functions are using the correct vtable.

With multiple inheritance, things are more complex. Because the derived object is made out of multiple concatenated objects, each of them with its own vtable, some pointer adjustment is needed when casting between different types. Specifically, when casting a pointer from a derived class to the second (or later) parent class, or vice versa, a small offset is added to the pointer to point to the 'correct' part of the object.

Casting to and from the first parent class has no effect on the pointer; it is a free operation, just like with single inheritance. Casting from the derived class to the first parent class is a similar operation without any effect on the pointer (see Figure 2.9a).

```
Parent1 * pParent1 = new Child;
Child * pChild = dynamic_cast<Child*>(pParent1);
assert (pParent1 == pChild);    // Unchanged
```

Casting from a parent class other than the first to the derived class will change the pointer. In this case, it will add a negative offset to point to the 'real' beginning of the object (see Figure 2.9b).

```
Parent2 * pParent2 = new Child;
Child * pChild = dynamic_cast<Child*>(pParent2);
assert (pParent2 != pChild);    // Not the same!
```

Finally, casting from the derived class to the second parent class will also change the pointer. Now it will add a small offset that points to the subsection of the object that corresponds to that parent class (see Figure 2.9c).

```
Child * pChild = new Child;
Parent2 * pParent2 = dynamic_cast<Parent2*>(pChild);
assert (pChild != pParent2);    // Not the same!
```

How much of a performance hit can that extra pointer offset cause? Not much. The offset needed to add or subtract from the pointer is known at compile time, so it does not even require a data access somewhere else in memory (with potential data cache thrashing problems). The overhead of the vtable access and eventual function call more than overshadow the cost of adding an offset.

The more serious performance hit comes from the dynamic_cast<> call itself. At runtime, the program needs to determine if it is possible to cast between the original pointer type and the class we are trying to cast to. For that, it needs to take into account the type of the pointer we are casting, the type of object referenced by the pointer, and the final class type we want to cast to. Depending on the implementation, the larger and more complicated the inheritance tree becomes, the slower the operation will be. In Chapter 12, we will examine dynamic casting and runtime type information more closely, and implement a custom version with better performance characteristics.

Virtual Functions of the Second Parent Class

The extra performance cost of multiple inheritance is not limited to dynamic_cast. There will be a small performance cost involved whenever a virtual function is invoked that belongs to a parent class other than the first one.

Look again at Figure 2.8 and notice how the derived object has multiple vtables. Whenever one of the functions in a vtable other than the first one is called, the pointer needs to be adjusted accordingly before the call. As it turns out, the pointer adjustment is exactly like what happens during the casting, as we described it in the previous section. Fortunately, this time there is no need to involve dynamic_cast<>, so the actual performance cost is negligible and can easily be ignored most of the time.

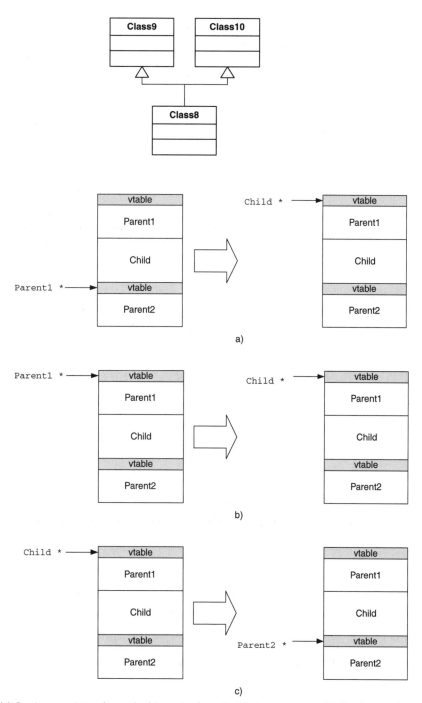

FIGURE 2.9   (a) Casting a pointer down the hierarchy from the first parent class. (b) Casting a pointer from the second parent class to the derived class. (c) Casting a pointer from the derived class to the second parent class.

CONCLUSION

In this chapter, we examined the concept of multiple inheritance. It allows us to create a new class based on two or more parent classes and works very similarly to single inheritance, but with more than one parent class.

Unfortunately, multiple inheritance has many problems: the ambiguity introduced by diamond-shaped inheritance trees, the need for virtual inheritance to solve that problem, a slight performance penalty, and worst of all, a lot of complexity in what should be a simple building block.

Because of these problems, it is often better to look elsewhere for other constructs when designing our programs. However, one good use of multiple inheritance is in abstract interfaces and their applications, such as plug-ins. We will cover those in detail in later chapters.

SUGGESTED READING

General advice about multiple inheritance, its uses and abuses:

Cargill, Tom, *C++ Programming Style*, Addison-Wesley, 1992.
Meyers, Scott, *Effective C++ Second Edition*, Addison-Wesley, 1997.
Meyers, Scott, *More Effective C++*, Addison-Wesley, 1995.
Murray, Robert B., *C++ Strategies and Tactics*, Addison-Wesley, 1993.

All the gory details about how multiple inheritance is implemented, including a discussion of virtual inheritance:

Lippman, Stanley B., *Inside the C++ Object Mode*, Addison-Wesley, 1996.

CONSTNESS, REFERENCES, AND A FEW LOOSE ENDS

IN THIS CHAPTER

- Constness
- References
- Casting

T his chapter deals with some of the new concepts introduced in C++ that are not present in C. They are not fundamental concepts with major consequences, such as inheritance or templates, which will be covered in Chapter 4. Rather, they are concepts with a more limited scope, and they are not going to radically affect the program architecture. This chapter should be a nice interlude after dealing with the complexities of multiple inheritance and before tackling the mind-bending subject of templates.

Specifically, the concepts covered in this chapter are: constness, which allows us to mark objects as read-only; references, which are a safer, nicer form of pointers; and the new casting operators, which even though they are a bit verbose, have some clear advantages over the brute-force approach of C-style casts.

All these concepts are very useful in everyday programming. They will be used throughout this book and in most C++ code written today. Becoming familiar with these new concepts and knowing how to use them effectively is the focus of this chapter.

CONSTNESS

The const keyword is not new to C++, but you will see it a lot more often than in plain C programs. In addition to its old meaning, it has been extended to work on references and member functions.

Concept

The concept of const is very straightforward; it indicates that the "part" marked const cannot be changed (will be constant) during program execution. The extremely vague word "part" was used on purpose to leave the definition sufficiently general to deal with all the different things that we will be able to flag as const, as we will see shortly.

By itself, const is only moderately useful. What makes it really an outstanding feature is that the compiler will enforce that rule in a very similar way to flagging parts of a class as private or protected. If anybody tries to modify the contents of an area marked as const, the compiler will report it right away as a compile-time error. Compile time is the best possible time to find out about these errors, and the sooner we find them, the sooner they can be corrected. Let's start by reviewing const variables.

```
const int MAX_PLAYERS = 4;
const char * AppName = "MyApp";
```

The variables are marked as const, so any attempt to modify them will result in a compile-time error.

```
MAX_PLAYERS = 2;    // Error, MAX_PLAYERS is declared const
```

Experienced C programmers will no doubt wonder what the advantage is over using the `#define` preprocessor directive. Functionally, they are very similar, but using a `const` variable allows the compiler to apply the usual C++-type safety, which might help catch errors and potential problems. Using `#define` just results in a straight substitution with no type checking whatsoever. As a general rule, we should try to rely on the compiler as much as possible to check things for us. If the compiler can handle this busy work, our time is better spent elsewhere, rather than in tracking down strange type-casting problems.

Another added advantage of using `const` variables is that they will be entered in the symbol table as they are compiled, which means they will be available in the debugger. It makes debugging a lot easier to see the symbolic name of the constant in the debugger as opposed to trying to guess what `#define` a certain number belongs to. Anyone who's had to debug and make sense of Win32 error codes and flags will immediately appreciate this advantage.

Pointers and Const

Pointers are always a bit tricky when combined with const. Consider the four possibilities:

```
int * pData1;
const int * pData2;
int * const pData3;
const int * const pData4;
```

The easy ones are the first and last lines. Clearly, `pData1` is a non-const pointer to non-const data, meaning you are free to modify either one. The last one, `pData2`, is the opposite; you cannot modify either the pointer or the data pointed to by it. But what about the other two?

The `const` refers to what follows immediately to the right of it. So `pData2` is a non-const pointer to `const` integers. On the other hand, `pData3` has a `const` immediately to the left of the pointer variable, so the pointer is a `const`, but not the data it points to. Drawing mental parentheses to group the `const` keyword and what it affects helps make things clearer.

```
// Not C++ code, just a mental aid
(const int *) pData2;
int * (const pData3);
```

As if this were not complex enough, C++ adds yet another syntax variation to express the same concept. Otherwise, it would be hard to come up with tricky interview questions. What do you think this third form means?

```
int const * pData5;
```

It is a syntactically correct statement, but the const is between the data type and the asterisk. Drawing mental parentheses as before, we get (int const *) pData5, which should give us the right answer. This is a non-const pointer to const data. It is no different than pData2; it just has the const in a slightly different place. This style is not as common, but you might come across it sometime, so it is a good idea to at least be aware it exists as an alternate form.

Functions and Const

One of the most useful applications of const is to flag function parameters and result values. Whenever we need to pass a function parameter that is large or expensive to copy, we usually pass a pointer to it instead (or a reference, as we will see in the next section). Using a pointer will avoid any copying costs and is very efficient. However, doing so has changed the behavior of the program. We initially intended to pass a copy of the original data, but now, to make things faster, we are passing the original data itself. We have changed from passing parameters by value to passing them by reference, purely for performance reasons.

Without using const, we have no way of distinguishing when a pointer to data is passed because of performance reasons and when it is passed so the function can modify the original data. This distinction is extremely important when maintaining a large code base. Even worse, a function might originally just read the data passed to it, but somewhere down the line the function can be changed to actually modify that data. That could be disastrous if other parts of the program assume that the data will not change.

Using const solves all of those problems. It removes any assumptions about when data changes and makes it totally explicit. Not only does const help us by flagging violations of the rule as a compile error, but it lets a human reader of the source code quickly see the intent of a pointer (or a reference) parameter.

```
// Clearly pos is read-only
void GameEntity::SetPosition (const Point3d * pos);

// Vector entities will not be modified
int AI::SelectTarget (const vector<GameEntity*> * ents);
```

If a parameter is passed by value to a function, there is no need to use const at all. We are already passing a copy of the data, so there is no point in preventing the function from modifying that data if it wants to for its internal computations. That is an implementation detail, and the code that calls it should not have to care about it.

The same concept is applied to return values. Imagine a function that returns a rather expensive object to copy, such as a string or a matrix. The normal optimization is to return a pointer to the object instead of a new copy. Now the object can be modified directly through the pointer that was returned by the function. If that was our original intent, then all is well and good. However, maybe in our design we did not want people to be able to modify it in such a direct fashion. In that case, we have created a potential loophole in our design. Consider the following Player class as an example:

```
// Player class with some constness problems
class Player
{
public:
    void SetName (char * name);
    char * GetName();
    //...
private:
    char m_name[128];
};

void Player::SetName (char * name)
{
    ::strcpy(m_name, name);
}

char * Player::GetName()
{
    return m_name;
}
```

At first glance everything looks good. We can set the name (probably in response to the player typing his or her name on the user interface), and we can retrieve the name to print it on the scoreboard or to send it along with chat messages over the network. The class will work as it stands.

However, as it is written, it has the potential for many problems. Anybody can call GetName, retrieve the pointer to the actual character array in the player object, and not only read from it, but modify it with impunity. Is that a problem? Most likely, yes. Chances are the class was designed to expect any player name changes to happen by calling the SetName member function. Maybe the new name is set to all the other players over the network, or maybe the new name is changed on the user interface. In either case, changing the name directly on the pointer we got from calling GetName will not cause the desired effects. It can also be a hard bug to track down, because it does not result in a crash or in any immediately apparent problem. Things that just get mysteriously out of synch are some of the hardest bugs to track down.

A way to get around that potential problem would be to check every frame for whether the player name has changed, and if so, do whatever we need to in response to that change. But this is a lot of work and complexity for something that should be much simpler.

We could document the function profusely and explain that the pointer to the character array returned by GetName is not supposed to be modified directly. But there is always the potential that someone will misuse the function, especially when people are in a hurry to meet their approaching deadlines.

A much better approach is to let the compiler enforce the fact that the object cannot be modified. We can do that by using const as part of the type of the return value of the function.

```
// A better Player class without const problems
class Player
{
public:
    void SetName (const char * name);
    const char * GetName ();
    //...
private:
    char m_name[128];
};

void Player::SetName (const char * name)
{
    ::strcpy(m_name, name);
```

```
}

const char * Player::GetName()
{
    return m_name;
}
```

Now, the only way to change the `Player` name is to go through `Set-Name`, and the code should be greatly simplified. If somebody forgets and tries to write on the pointer returned by `GetName`, they will get an immediate reminder from the compiler.

Incidentally, the `Player` class still leaves much to be desired, even in the previous two functions. A cleaner implementation would use references instead of pointers (which are covered in the next section), and it would use a string class instead of a character pointer (see Chapter 9, The String Class). Even with these changes, the use of `const` will remain the same.

Classes and Const

So far, this chapter has been a recap of how the C keyword `const` should be used but this is a book on C++, so why the recap? First, because `const` is not widely used in C code, or not as often as it is in C++ code, anyway. Second, C++ extends its meaning to deal with class member functions, so it is a good idea to be familiar with the `const` concept before covering new ground. C++ allows us to flag a class member function as a `const`. For example:

```
// An even better Player class
class Player
{
public:
    void SetName (const char * name);
    const char * GetName() const;
    //...
private:
    char m_name[128];
};

const char * Player::GetName() const
{
    return m_name;
}
```

Notice that both the declaration and the implementation of the member function `GetName` were flagged as `const`. A member function marked as `const` indicates that executing it will not change the state of the object to which it was applied.

In our example, by flagging `GetName` as `const`, we are telling the readers of the program (and the compiler) that nothing will be changed in the `Player` just by calling that function. And it is true, notice that all we do is return a pointer. On the other hand, the `SetName` function is not marked as `const`. This is because `SetName` changes the internal state of that `Player` object by changing its name.

This is important for the same reasons that it was important to flag variables or function arguments as `const`—actually, even more important. We are adding more information about the intentions of a function to the source code. It will make things more readable for other programmers, and it will let the compiler enforce the rules.

The compiler is actually pretty smart. If we had tried to implement the `GetName` function returning a non-const character pointer, it would have detected that as a compile error because a member function that is marked as `const` is making an internal variable available to the caller without any guarantees of constness. So the `const` in the `return` value and the `const` in the member function go hand in hand.

The same thing applies to calling other functions. A member function flagged as `const` may not call a member function of an member object that is non-const. In other words, a const function may not modify data in the object it is applied to or call any non-const functions in other objects.

The consequences of this rule are very important. It means that to use `const` effectively, it must be used everywhere possible. If only some classes mark const functions correctly, those functions will not be able to call other parts of the program that are not marked as `const`, even though they should have been marked that way. This will make interacting with older libraries that do not use `const` correctly somewhat annoying. Fortunately, the constness can be cast away (more on this later in this chapter). Needless to say, it should only be cast away when it is absolutely necessary; otherwise we are just defeating the whole point and foregoing all the advantages that the compiler-checking provides us.

Const, but not Const

Notice that throughout this discussion, we have talked about the 'status' of an object, but we were never more specific about what that meant. The compiler takes the literal meaning, and it interprets 'status' as any member variable of that object changing. Usually, that interpretation matches exactly with what we mean, so everything will work as it should.

However, sometimes there are some member variables that do not reflect the status of an object at all, or at least not the logical state. This situation arises most often when an object keeps some internal information about its physical implementation. A simple example is an object that keeps track of how many times a certain query function has been called.

In our `Player` example, maybe each `Player` object wants to keep track of how many times the function `GetName` has been called. The first thought would be to simply increment an internal counter every time the function is called. But the `GetName` function is marked as `const`, so any attempt to change a member variable will result in a compile error. We could demote the function and not mark it as `const`, but this does not make any sense. For all intents and purposes, the `Player` object has the same state that it did before the function was called. Why should someone using the `Player` class care whether or not we are keeping some statistics inside?

Another, more complex example could be caused by the object caching some data. Maybe the object has a large amount of data and wants to load and unload it explicitly whenever necessary. To the outside world, the object should always appear to be present, with all its data; so a simple query function should clearly be marked as `const`, even though we will be loading a lot of data inside.

Fortunately, C++ has a clean solution to this problem—the keyword `mutable`. A member variable marked as `mutable` can be changed from any member function, whether it is marked as `const` or not. So we can mark any member variable that does not represent the object's logical status as `mutable`, and this would solve our problem of changing them from a const function.

Going back to the Player class example, let's add a `mutable` variable that keeps count of how many times the function GetName has been called.

```
class Player
{
public:
    void SetName (const char * name);
    const char * GetName() const;
    //...
private:
    char m_name[128];
```

```
        mutable int m_TimesGetNameCalled;
};

const char * Player::GetName() const
{
    ++m_TimesGetNameCalled; // OK because it is mutable
    return m_name;
}
```

Const advice

The best advice with respect to const is to use it as much as possible—everywhere: variables, arguments, return values, and member functions. The more extensively it is used, the more useful it becomes, and the easier it is to enforce.

There are no drawbacks at all for using const. It makes the intent of our code clearer for other programmers and lets the compiler enforce some added rules. The only time it can become a bit of a chore is when we start to use const with an existing code base. Until enough parts of the code have been correctly labeled as const, we will have to do a fair amount of casting away of constness. But it will all be worth it once most of the code has been converted to using const correctly.

REFERENCES

A *reference* is simply an alternative name for an object. Any operations done on a reference will affect the original object to which it is referring. Surprisingly, such a simple concept can become an extremely useful tool to manage complexity.

The syntax for references is very simple. Other than the & symbol used to indicate that they are references, they behave almost completely like regular objects. References work the same way with built-in data types and with objects.

```
int a = 100;
int & b = a;     // b is a reference to a
b = 200;         // both a and b are 200 now

Matrix4x4 rot = camera.GetRotation();
Matrix4x4 & rot2 = rot; // rot2 is a reference to rot
rot2.Inverse();         // inverses both rot and rot2
```

References are very much like pointers. They refer to an object, and all the operations will affect the object that is pointed to by the reference. Also, creating a reference to an object is a very efficient operation, just like creating a pointer.

References vs. Pointers

However, there are several major, very important differences between references and pointers:

- Working with a reference has the same syntax as working with an object. Instead of using the operator -> to dereference the pointer and access member functions and variables, a reference uses a dot (.), just like a regular object.
- References can only be initialized once. A pointer can point to a certain object and then, at any time, be changed to point to a different object. References are not that way. Once they have been initialized to refer to an object, they cannot be changed. In that sense, they behave like const pointers.
- References must be initialized as soon as they are declared. Unlike a pointer, we cannot create a reference and wait until a later time to initialize it. The initialization must happen right away.
- References cannot be NULL. This is a consequence of the first two points. Since references must be initialized right away with a real object, and they cannot be changed, they can never be NULL like a pointer. Unfortunately, this does not mean that what they point to is valid. It is always possible to delete the object a reference is pointing to or 'trick' a reference through some casting to point to NULL.
- References cannot be deleted or newed like a pointer. In that sense, they are just like an object.

References and Functions

Two of the main uses of references are to pass arguments and to return values from functions. In the previous section about const pointers as function arguments, we saw how, for efficiency's sake, it was advantageous to pass a pointer to large objects instead of passing a copy of the object. While using a const pointer solved all the potential problems, having to change an object for a pointer just because of performance is awkward. References solve that problem. By passing a const reference as a parameter into a function, we accomplish the same goal as passing that object by value, without incurring any of the performance costs and with the same syntax. Notice that all the advice about using const pointers applies to using references, also.

```
Matrix4x4 rot; // Relatively expensive object to copy
//...
entity.SetRotation(rot); // Cheap call. No copying

void GameEntity::SetRotation (const Matrix4x4 & rot)
{
    if (!rot.IsIdentity)
        // ...
}
```

References can also be used to return objects from a function in an efficient manner. We need to be careful what we do with the returned reference however, because if we assign it to an object, a copy will take place. If we just want to keep that reference around while we do some calculations, we must save it into a reference itself.

```
const Matrix4x4 & GameEntity::GetRotation() const
{
    return m_rotation; // Cheap. It's just a reference
}

// Watch out. This is making a new copy of the matrix
Matrix4x4 rot = entity.GetRotation();

// This just holds the reference. Very cheap.
const Matrix4x4 & rot = entity.GetRotation();

// We can pass the reference straight from a return
// value into a parameter too. Very efficient also.
camera.SetRotation (entity.GetRotation());
```

As with pointers, however, we have to make sure that the object we are returning a reference to does not go out of scope when the function disappears. The most common situation is that of returning a reference to an object that was created in the stack. Doing so will make the reference point to an invalid memory location, and will cause the program to crash as soon as the reference is used. Fortunately, most compilers seem to detect this situation and will issue a warning.

Even if you are not yet sold on the idea of references, it is almost impossible to avoid them altogether. You will see references popping up in copy constructors and in binary operators, so you should at least be familiar with their usage. Hopefully, the rest of this section will convince you to use them in your own code, also.

```
// Copy constructor
Matrix4x4::Matrix4x4 (const Matrix4x4 & matrix);

// Binary operator
const & Matrix4x4 Matrix4x4::operator*(
                      const Matrix4x4 & matrix);
```

Advantages of References

If references are just like pointers with some different syntax, why use them? Why not stick to pointers? There are several reasons, even though as far as the compiler is concerned, they are pretty much just pointers. The reasons all have to do with making life easier for us, the programmers.

The first advantage of references is their syntax. Even the most experienced C programmer has to admit that it is a lot cleaner to use references than pointers, without asterisks and arrows all over the place. Which of these two lines of code do you find more readable?

```
// Using pointers
position = *(pEntity->GetPosition());

// Using references
position = entity.GetPosition();
```

The next advantage of references is that they can never be NULL like a pointer. They always have to be pointing to an object, or at least to something the compiler was tricked into thinking it was an object. In any case, it is usually a lot more difficult to pass an invalid reference than it is to pass a NULL or initialized pointer.

Just because a reference was pointing to a valid object at some point does not mean that the object will still be valid by the time it is accessed. The same problem occurs with pointers. This is called the "dangling pointer" problem, in which we keep a pointer to a place in memory that is freed, but the pointer is unchanged, and buggy code can attempt to dereference the pointer. However, recall that references have to be initialized when they are first created and can never change values. Thus, it is usually harder to keep a reference around, pointing to some object in memory, after the object is destroyed. Most references go in the stack and disappear when they fall out of scope, so the problem is alleviated to some extent.

Another advantage of references is that there is never any doubt as to whether or not the object pointed to by the reference should be freed by the code that is using the reference. This can only be done through a pointer, not a reference. So if we are working with a reference, it is safe to assume that somebody else will free it.

All of these advantages can be summarized by saying that using references is a slightly higher-level way of manipulating objects. It allows us to forget about the details of memory management and object ownership, so we can simply concentrate on the logic of the problem we are trying to solve. After all, we have to remember why we are writing a program in the first place. It is not to show our technical prowess in dealing with low-level details or to use all the latest features of C++. It is to create a great game. The more we can focus on the game and the less we have to worry about memory leaks and other implementation details, the faster we will finish, and the more robust the game will be.

Some people will argue that one of the drawbacks of using references instead of pointers is that it is unclear whether objects are passed by reference or value just by looking at the calling code. It can be argued that it is not particularly useful for the calling code to know whether objects are passed by value or by reference. The important point is whether or not they can be modified by the function, and that will depend on whether the reference (or the pointer) is a `const` or not. In either case, examining the function declaration will reveal all that information. With today's code-browsing tools, which are often integrated into the development environment, looking up that information takes nothing more than a mouse click.

Another slightly more sensible, often repeated piece of advice is to use `const` references for objects that will not be modified by the function, and use pointers for those that will. The argument, again, is that there is no need to look at the function declaration to know more about what the function's intentions are with respect to its parameters. While it might be true to a certain extent, there are still times when we will need to pass a pointer to a function even though the object will not be modified. Besides, not everybody is going to follow this convention, which means that we need to check the function declaration in any case.

When to Use References

Are pointers obsolete then? Should we use references all the time? Not at all.

A good rule of thumb is to use references whenever possible. They are the cleaner, least error-prone interface. However, there are some situations where pointers are still necessary.

If an object needs to be created or deleted dynamically, then we have to use a pointer to that object. Usually, the owner of a dynamically created object will keep a pointer to it. If anybody else needs to use that object, they can use a reference to make it clear that they are not responsible for freeing that object. If at some point the ownership of the object needs to be transferred, it should be done through a pointer instead of a reference.

Sometimes we need to change the object to which we are pointing. In that case, unless we change the structure of the program, a pointer is the only way to go, since a reference can never point to a different object.

At other times we actually rely on the fact that a pointer can be NULL, either by returning a NULL pointer from a function as a sign that the function failed, or as an optional parameter to a function. References cannot point to nothing (NULL), so they will not serve that purpose. It is questionable whether or not a good program design relies on pointers sometimes being NULL. A better solution might be to refactor the program to indicate failed functions in a different way, and use references instead.

Finally, the last reason for using a pointer over a reference is pointer arithmetic. With pointer arithmetic, we can iterate through a section of memory, interpreting its contents based on the type of pointer we are using. This is an extremely low-level way of working, has a high risk of introducing bugs, and could be a maintenance nightmare. When possible, avoid it at all costs. But if you have to introduce pointer arithmetic at times, then you just have to. There might come an occasion, deep in your inner loops, when the extra overhead of iterating through a loop in a type-safe manner becomes unacceptable, and your profiler has clearly shown that a significant amount of time is wasted there. Then, and only then, would a technique like pointer arithmetic be justified. Until then, avoid it at all costs.

Some studies have shown that a very large percentage of bugs in C++ are caused by memory leaks. The more we can think of objects in a higher level through references instead of pointers, the more reliable and robust our programs will be.

CASTING

A conversion is the process of changing some data into a different type of data. In this case, the vague term "data" refers to anything from built-in types to user-created objects. The compiler has a set of rules to determine when a conversion is possible and should take place. For example, just assigning a float to an int will trigger a conversion.

```
int a = 200;
float b = a;     // Conversion from int to float

char txt[] = "Hello";
float c = txt;     // No conversion possible
```

Casting is a directive we add to the source code to force the compiler to apply a particular conversion. It is done by adding the type we wish to cast to in parentheses before the variable that is to be cast.

```
int n = 150;

// n is an integer, which divided by an integer results
// in another integer. f1 == 1.0
float f1 = n / 100;

// n is cast to a float, and when divided by an integer,
// the result is a float. f2 == 1.5
float f2 = (float)n / 100;     // cast to a float
```

The Need for Casting

Casting is an often-despised practice by most programmers. In truth, there are usually better, cleaner ways of accomplishing the same purpose. Every time we cast an object into a different type, we are foregoing C++ strong-typed language benefits. We are telling the compiler, "forget what you know about the type of this object and assume it is a different type instead." Since people make mistakes a lot more often than computers, it is a good idea to minimize the use of casting.

Sometimes, however, casting is the way to go. One reason for casting is to interface with a different section of the code. The interface expects a particular type, but we want to feed it data of a different type that is already in the correct format. A type cast will do the job just fine in that case. This is most common in C libraries, since they do not use inheritance or polymorphism.

Imagine a generic function that takes some data and a flag indicating how to interpret that data. Incidentally, this is a pretty terrible function, and the same could be accomplished in a much safer way using some C++ features, but it serves as an example of why casting is sometimes necessary.

```
void SerializeWrite (DataType type, void * pData);

char txt[] = "This is a string";
::SerializeWrite (SerializeString, (void *)txt);

float fPitch;
::SerializeWrite (SerializeFloat, (void *)&fPitch);

const Matrix4x4 & rot = camera.GetRotation();
::SerializeWrite (SerializeMatrix4x4, (void *)&rot);
```

Another reason for casting arises from the polymorphic use of objects. Imagine we have an extensive inheritance tree, and most of the code deals with objects through a pointer of the type of a common parent class. Sometimes it is necessary for the code to find out exactly what type of object it is dealing with and call a specific function in that object. This is often a sign of poor design, but it will happen. Assuming there is no RTTI information enabled, the program will have to find out the type of the object by calling some function and then casting it to the appropriate type.

```
void GameEntity::OnCollision (GameEntity & entity)
{
    if (entity.IsType(GameEntity::PROJECTILE)) {
        GameProjectile & projectile = (GameProjectile &)entity;
        projectile.BlowUp();
    }
    // ...
}
```

C++ Style Casting

It seems that we can cast anything we want to our hearts' content with the C-style casts. Why do we need a new type of casts from C++? The new casts offer finer control over the casting process, allowing us to control different types of casting.

There are four types of cast operators in C++, depending on what we are casting: `static_cast`, `const_cast`, `reinterpret_cast`, and `dynamic_cast`.

The C++ cast operators also have a slightly different syntax than the traditional cast. They are a little more verbose than the old cast, and they tend to stand out from the source code. But do not be put off by the extra typing; it is also more readily apparent what the code is doing than with the C-style casts. The new casts follow the format:

```
static_cast<type>(expression)
```

The following code uses the C++-style cast:

```
// C++-style cast
float f2 = static_cast<float>(n) / 100;    // cast to a float
```

The other advantage of C++ casts is that they are more explicit in what they do. A programmer can glance at the code and immediately determine the purpose of a cast. Yes, they require more typing, but they are worth it.

static_cast

The operator `static_cast` is a restricted version of its C counterpart. It will tell the compiler to attempt to convert between two different data types. Like the C cast, it will convert between built-in data types, even when there is some potential loss of precision. However, unlike the C cast, `static_cast` will only convert between related pointer types. It is possible to cast pointers up and down the inheritance hierarchy, but not to a type outside of the hierarchy.

```
class A
{
};

class B : public A
{
};

// Unrelated to A and B
class C
```

```
{
};

A * a = new A;

// OK, B is a child of A
B * b = static_cast<B*>(a);

// Compile error. C is unrelated to A
C * c = static_cast<C*>(a);

// The old C cast would work just fine (but what would
// the program do?)
C * c = (C*)(a);
```

The only other difference is that static_cast cannot involve a change in constness. As with the C cast, if it is not possible to convert one type into another, the conversion will fail.

const_cast

The operator const_cast cannot cast between different types. Instead, it just changes the constness of the expression it is applied to. It can make something const that was not const before, or it can cast the constness away. Usually, there is no need to change something from non-const to const. That conversion happens automatically, since it is a less restrictive change. Going the other way, from const to non-const, can only be done through a cast. Having to use const_cast is a sign that something does not fit correctly in the program design. It is like filing a square peg to make it fit in a round hole. Hopefully, most instances of const_cast are due to calling older C-style functions with const expressions. If you find yourself using const_cast when calling your own program, immediately stop and rethink your design.

reinterpret_cast

The operator reinterpret_cast has the same power as the C-style cast. It can convert from any built-in data type to any other, and from any pointer type to another pointer type. It can even convert between built-in data types and pointers without any regard to type safety or constness. The results of reinterpret_cast are totally implementation-dependent and rely on the particular memory layout of each of the objects being cast. Use `reinterpret_cast` extremely sparingly, and only when absolutely necessary and when the other types of casts are not enough.

dynamic_cast

In our discussion on multiple inheritance in Chapter 2, `dynamic_cast` was briefly covered. All the other cast operators are evaluated at compile time by the compiler, and the cast is either successful, or it results in a compile error. In either case, there is no runtime cost involved. But `dynamic_cast` is quite different. It can only be applied to pointers or references, no built-in data types, but the key difference is that at runtime it checks whether the conversion is possible. It does not just check whether two pointers are part of the same inheritance tree, like `static_cast`; it checks the actual type of the objects referred to by those pointers, evaluates whether the conversion is possible. If so, it returns a new pointer, even accounting for any offsets necessary to deal with multiple inheritance. In the case that it is not possible to convert between the two types, the cast fails and it returns a `NULL` pointer. Clearly, to be able to do that, runtime type information must be enabled in the compiler. If you prefer not to have RTTI enabled, you must find alternatives to `dynamic_cast`. We will explore these alternatives in Chapter 12.

CONCLUSION

In this chapter we covered three new concepts introduced in C++:

- The keyword `const` allows us to mark a variable as read-only. Any attempts to modify it will cause a compile-time error. This variable can be a simple data type, or it can be an object of a complex class type. Flagging a member function as `const` indicates that the function will not modify the state of the object, so we are allowed to call `const` member functions on `const` objects. And `const` is particularly useful as a tool for passing objects to and from functions in combination with pointers or references.
- References are alternate names for an object. They behave in very similar ways to pointers, but with some clear differences. In general, references allow us to deal with objects in a higher level, rather than passing memory locations around as pointers.
- The new casting operators introduced by C++ allow us to be much more specific with respect to what we are casting and how we are

doing it, and they provide some compiler checking. In addition, `dynamic_cast` introduces some new functionality for casting with multiple inheritance.

SUGGESTED READING

Here are sources of several good opinions and guidelines on the use of `const`:

Meyers, Scott, *Effective C++*, 2nd ed., Addison-Wesley, 1997.
Murray, Robert B., *C++ Strategies and Tactics*, Addison-Wesley, 1993.
Stroustrup, Bjarne, *The C++ Programming Language*, 3rd ed., Addison-Wesley, 1997.

More readings on C++-style casting:

Meyers, Scott, *More Effective C++*, Addison-Wesley, 1995.

TEMPLATES

IN THIS CHAPTER

- The Search for Generic Code

- Templates

- Drawbacks

- When to Use Templates

- Template Specialization (Advanced)

ometimes we find ourselves writing almost the same code over and over. Perhaps the code is not something that can be put in a function and called repeatedly, because it requires different classes and data types, not just different data. *Templates* are a new concept in C++ that addresses this issue. With templates, we are able to write generic code that does not depend on specific data types, and to later reuse that code in different parts of our program with different classes.

THE SEARCH FOR GENERIC CODE

Before we dive into a detailed explanation of templates, let us take the time to understand the need for generic code, to see the real need for templates, and to look at a common use of templates through an example.

We will take a very simple situation that will arise all the time in game programming and that you have already tackled in past projects—lists. Lists are used everywhere in games: the game entities in the world, the scene nodes to be rendered, the meshes in a model, the actions to be performed in the future by an AI, or even the names of all the players in the game. Chances are, a full game will need many dozens of different types of lists.

How do we go about implementing those lists? There are many different ways. Let us examine some of the possibilities.

First Solution: List Built into the Class

The most straightforward approach is to just build the list into the class itself. After all, it is not all that difficult; just add a next pointer (and a previous pointer if it is a doubly linked list), throw in a few quick functions to insert and delete elements, are we are done.

```
class GameEntity
{
public:
    // All GameEntity functions here
    GameEntity * GetNext();
    void RemoveFromList();
    void InsertAfter(GameEntity * pEntity);
private:
    // GameEntity data
    GameEntity * m_pNext;
};
```

Is it really that simple? Not quite. Like many bad designs, it will work, but when it is put to the test on a large project, it will sink under its own weight. The first thing we need to realize is that even if we are very good programmers, we are bound to make mistakes. Almost the same code needs to be written for every class that needs to be part of a list. It is too easy to accidentally forget to set a pointer to NULL or to check the special case when we are removing an element from the end of the list. Failure to do any of these things (or many other small things) correctly will most likely cause the program to crash.

Even if we manage to write the code correctly the first time through, what if we need to make a change? We have written custom linked-list code in several different classes. Now we realize that we want to change our implementation to use end guards or maybe use a doubly linked list. Imagine having to go through all the classes making those changes. Even if you end up not causing any bugs (unlikely), doing such a tedious and boring job is guaranteed to drive you out of your mind.

Just in case you were not already convinced of the problems with this approach, here are a few more. The different lists in the project are likely to have different interfaces. After all, other programmers probably wrote a few more lists from scratch, and they probably had different ideas on how the lists' interfaces should be. Maybe you used GetNext() in your list, but they used Next() or something even more exotic. What if you want to know how many elements are in a list? Maybe you have a GetNumEle-ments() function that returns a number in constant time, but their implementation has a function called Count() that iterates through all the elements in the list, counting the number of elements. This would be quite a shock if you had expected it to be a trivial function. The point is, you do not have a standard interface to iterate through lists, and you never quite know which functions to call and how they are implemented underneath.

As a consequence, you also cannot have common functions that work on any linked list. With a standard linked list, it would be possible to have a set of functions to sort the elements in a list, move sections of a list around, or look for duplicate elements. With separate implementations, each list would only have the functions it absolutely needs, and new functions would have to be written as the need arises for each type of list—which leads to even more code duplication and general waste of time.

Second Solution: Using Macros

We can solve most of the issues described in the previous section with the use of preprocessor macros. We can create a set of macros that will make adding linked-list functionality to our classes a snap. We would simply create two macros, and then to use them, all we have to do is add LIST_DECL(MyClassName) to the header file and LIST_IMPL(MyClassName) to the .cpp file.

```
// In GameEntity.h
class GameEntity
{
public:
    // All GameEntity functions here
    LIST_DECL(GameEntity);
private:
    // GameEntity data
};

// In GameEntity.cpp
LIST_IMPL(GameEntity);
```

Now all the lists in our program will use a unified interface, so we know what to expect when we are manipulating the code. Also, if we ever need to make changes to the list implementation, we can just change the macro, and all our classes will immediately get the latest list implementation.

Unfortunately, this solution introduces a few more problems of its own. Preprocessor macros are notorious for being difficult to develop, maintain, and especially debug. Their code is expanded in place by the preprocessor, so when the compiler comes along and attempts to compile that section of code, it does not look any different than any code we wrote by hand. Any compiler errors will be flagged as happening in the line that contains the macro, with no information of where exactly in the macro they happened. This can make debugging long macros very tiresome.

If that were the only drawback of this approach, we might be able to overlook a bit of discomfort when debugging macros for the ideal solution. There are still two fundamental problems with this approach that run deeper than any macro can fix.

The first problem is that we still cannot write a function that will act on any type of list. We have managed to standardize our list interface across all the classes, but there is still no type-safe way of dealing with all the different class types that implement a list. We will address this problem with the next solution (inheritance).

The second problem is one that we are not going to fix right away, so it is more of a heads up on what is coming. So far, we have successfully added the list functionality to our classes. Now, it is very easy to keep all the game entities in a list. But what if the same entity needs to be in more than one list at a time? For example, the `Player` class might want to keep a list of entities in the field of view so it can then pick the best one to target. Do we need to add a second list to every entity? What if we want them to be in more than two lists at once? Or in a tree? Clearly, we cannot add all those possible data structures to the class itself. Instead, we can make the list a separate class and completely remove the list implementation from our classes. We will see that in more detail in the fourth solution.

Third Solution: Inheritance

Instead of using a macro to add list functionality to any class, we can create a base class that is a list element. It contains all the normal list data, like `next` and `previous` pointers, and the appropriate functions, like `Insert()` and `Delete()`.

Any class that wants to have list functionality only has to inherit from this newly created list element class, and it will automatically get all the benefits of the list. Even if the class already inherits from a parent class, we can use multiple inheritance and also inherit from the list class (see Figure 4.1).

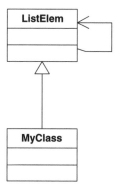

FIGURE 4.1   Any class that wants to be part of a list can inherit from ListElem.

Things get trickier if the parent class, in turn, also inherits from the list class; then we get the dreaded diamond of death. Even though in this case things will work as expected (your new class will be able to be in several lists at once), you will still need to deal with ambiguity and having to specify what parent list you are accessing. This is the first blow against this approach (refer to Chapter 3 for more details on the problems of multiple inheritance).

Unlike the solution involving macros, debugging is trivial using this approach. All the list code is just regular code, so it is possible to see it in the debugger and step into it, just like you would with any other code.

Another advantage of this approach is that we can treat list elements polymorphically. That is, since they all inherit from a base class `ListElem`, we can write functions that work on pointers and references of type `ListElem`, and that will work for any of our lists.

This approach is almost perfect. It has the problem of multiple inheritance creeping in, but it would be possible to live with that. The major problem it does not solve is the separation of the list functionality from the class itself. As we mentioned earlier, this approach does not support having an object in multiple lists, or in a list and a tree, or some other data structure. For that, we need to separate the list from the elements container in the list.

Fourth Solution: Container List of Void Pointers

In our quest to find the perfect solution for a linked-list implementation, we will now try to totally separate the list from its contents. We treat a list as a container for the elements we choose to add to it.

The problem is, we want to have lists of many different types of classes. We could write one list for every type of class we want to add to it, but then we would have gone full circle and ended up back at a variant of the first solution. We already saw why the first solution was not a good idea.

If all the different types of classes that needed to use lists inherited from a common parent class, we could make it so the list contained pointers to that class. In a real project, though, that is not likely to be the case. Even if we have a root class for game entities, chances are that meshes, AI commands, or players do not inherit from it. We might also want to have a list of integers, strings, or floats, and those certainly do not inherit from any common base class.

A simple solution is to just make the list deal with `void` pointers. Whatever gets added to the list gets cast into a `void` pointer, and whenever it is retrieved from the list, we cast it back to its real class. The list code does not need to manipulate its elements in any way other than to copy them around, so it does not matter what the real type of the data we added is, as long as it is only as large as a `void` pointer, which is 32 bit for most current platforms (see Figure 4.2).

Class diagram

Object diagram

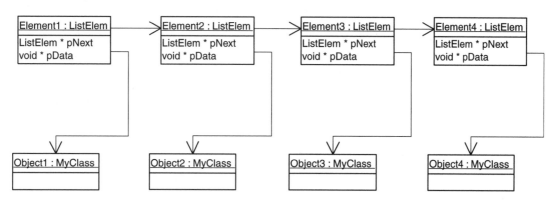

FIGURE 4.2 A list of void pointers can be used with any class.

What we are giving up is type safety. It is now up to us (up to the code) to remember what type the elements in a list are. If we make a mistake, the compiler will not catch it, and we will cast an element to the wrong type. If we are lucky, this will result in a runtime crash; if luck is not on our side, it will result in bogus data and strange program behavior. Tracking down these kinds of bugs can be extremely difficult, so this is a fairly important drawback.

One advantage of structuring a list this way is that we can now deal with a list class, not just with list elements. It makes much more sense to have global operations and queries done on the list itself, such as getting the total number of elements or clearing the list.

There is one more downside to this solution—not a major problem, but an annoyance nonetheless. We have totally separated the list nodes from the data they contain. That means that creating a new object and adding it to the list will result in two memory allocations: one of the object, and one for the list node that points to it. When the list data was built into the object itself, as in the first solution, only one memory allocation was required. In platforms with slow memory allocation or that have problems with memory fragmentation, the difference could be significant (see Chapter 7 for more information and strategies for memory allocation).

To find a better solution, we need to look at C++ templates. The next few sections will cover templates in detail and then revisit this particular problem, and come up with a solution based on templates.

TEMPLATES

Templates allow us to write a piece of code without being tied to a particular class or data type. Code written in this way is said to be "generic." Whenever we want to use it, we instantiate the template to work with a specific class. There are two types of templates: class templates and function templates, depending on what type of code is being templatized.

Class Templates

Let us start with a simple example that might not be worth implementing with templates, but it illustrates the concept very nicely. We need a rectangle class in our game or tools. There are many uses for it: window coordinates, the size of some GUI (Graphical User Interface) component, viewport position and size, and so forth. A straightforward implementation looks something like this:

```
class Rect {
public:
    Rect(int px1, int py1, int px2, int py2) {
        x1 = px1; y1 = py1; x2 = px2; y2 = py2; }
    int GetWidth() { return x2-x1; }
    int GetHeight() { return y2-y1; }

    int x1;
    int y1;
    int x2;
    int y2;
};
```

It is not the best class design, and it probably needs a few extra functions to make it useful, but it will do for now.

So far, the rectangle class has served us very well, but at some point later in the project we find ourselves needing to use a rectangle in a different coordinate system whose coordinates vary between 0.0 and 1.0. We cannot reuse our existing class because it uses integers and not floats, which is what we need to represent the new coordinates. We could copy and paste the code, and make a new class called `RectFloat` by replacing all appearances of variables of type `int` with ones of type `float`.

By now, we should realize that anything that requires copying and pasting is usually a sign of trouble, so let's avoid it. Instead, we can use templates and make it so the rectangle class does not explicitly use integers or floats until it is instantiated.

```
template<class T>
class Rect {
public:
    Rect(T px1, T py1, T px2, T py2) {
        x1 = px1; y1 = py1; x2 = px2; y2 = py2; }
    T GetWidth() { return x2-x1; }
    T GetHeight() { return y2-y1; }

    T x1;
    T y1;
    T x2;
    T y2;
};
```

As you can see, any occurrences of the type `int` have been replaced with a `T` instead. `T` is the class type the template depends on. To create a rectangle that uses integers, we use the following code:

```
Rect<int> myIntRectangle (1,10,2,20);
```

When the compiler encounters that definition, it goes through the original template, replaces all instances of `T` with `int`, and compiles the new class on the fly. Similarly, the following code does the same thing with floats.

```
Rect<float> anotherRectangle;
```

We could create rectangles of imaginary numbers or just about anything else if we had a class to represent them. The only restriction in this case is that we must be able to subtract objects of the class we use, since both the `GetWidth()` and `GetHeight()` functions rely on that functionality.

If we tried to instantiate a template with a class that did not support subtraction, we would get a compile-time error that would be caught right away.

One important thing to notice is that all the template code needs to be visible to the compiler when it instantiates the template with a particular class. That means that we must put all the template code in the header file; otherwise it will not be visible and it will not be compiled (which will result in a link-time error). As we will see later, this has some unfortunate consequences with dependencies and compile time.

The C++ standard actually has a provision to avoid having to put the full implementation of the template in a header file. It allows the implementation of a template to reside in a .cpp file, but use the keyword export to make that implementation 'visible' to the compiler. Such a scheme would allow us to avoid any extra dependencies when using templates. Unfortunately, virtually no commercial C++ compilers have currently implemented this feature. Hopefully, in a few years we will see some support for this feature. For now, our only option is to clump all the implementation in the header file and live with the consequences.

Function Templates

Once you understand the concept of a class template, function templates are easy. They are very similar to class templates, but they work on a function instead of a class. The main difference is that we do not need to explicitly instantiate a function template. Instead, it gets created automatically, based on the type of the parameters passed to it.

Here is another very simple example. This function swaps the two values of two objects, but it is not tied to any particular class type:

```
template<class T>
void swap(T & a, T & b) {
    T tmp(a);
    a = b;
    b = tmp;
}
```

This function will work for integers, floats, strings, or any class with a copy constructor and assignment operator. The function is instantiated based on the type of the parameters passed to it.

```
int a = 5;
int b = 10;
```

```
swap(a, b);     // Integer version is instantiated

float fa = 3.1416;
float fb = 1.0;
swap(fa, fb);  // Float version is instantiated
```

Notice how both parameters to the swap function are of the same type. What happens if we pass two parameters of different types? We cannot. It would result in a compile-time error. Even if one of the objects has an implicit conversion to the correct data type, it would still result in an error.

```
// The following is illegal. Compile error.
swap(a, fb);
```

List Example Revisited: Template Solution

Armed with our new knowledge about templates, let us tackle the list example from earlier in this chapter again. This time we will use C++ templates to come up with a much more refined solution that addresses most of the problems. As a reminder, the objective we are trying to accomplish is to write a list class with the following characteristics:

- The class can be used on a wide variety of different classes.
- All the list code is in one location, not copied for every class type that becomes part of a list.
- All lists have a standard interface.
- The list code itself is separated from the class code.

By now you should see how templates allow us to do all those things with extreme ease. We will create a list class that is templated on the type of its elements. We will also create two different classes: one for the list object itself and one for the list nodes, which contains the data elements and the list pointers.

```
template<class T>
class ListNode {
public:
    ListNode(T);
    T & GetData();
    ListNode * GetNext();
private:
    T m_data;
};
```

```
template<class T>
class List {
public:
    ListNode<T> * GetHead();
    void PushBack(T);
    //...

private:
    ListNode<T> * m_pHead;
};
```

We use this list just like any other templated class.

```
List<int> listOfIntegers;
List<string> listOfStrings;
```

Now we can effortlessly create lists to hold just about any type of object or data type we want, without tying those classes to the list itself. The template solution for this particular problem is by far the best of all of them.

It needs to be mentioned here that you will hopefully never have to write such a common data structure by yourself. The C++ Standard Template Library (STL) has a large variety of data structures and algorithms that you can use freely in your programs. One of the many data structures included is a list, and you would use it in the same way as the list we just created:

```
std::list<int> myListOfIntegers;
```

We will have a detailed look at the STL in Chapters 8 and 9.

DRAWBACKS

Templates are quite far from being perfect. But they are the best solution for many problems we have right now. Knowing their drawbacks and tradeoffs is just as important as being familiar with their syntax.

Complexity

The biggest problem with using templates is complexity. Compare again the code in the previous section, where we solved the list implementation with templates, to the straight list from the first solution. Which one is easier to read? Which one do you feel more capable of modifying and updating in the future?

To make things worse, even if you get past all the little brackets and references to a generic class T and other templates, templated code is notoriously difficult to debug. Granted, it is not as bad as preprocessor macros, but it comes close. A lot of debuggers will get very confused when you attempt to step into a section of templated code, and some will produce some rather incomprehensible error messages at the tiniest typing mistake.

Dependencies

In addition, there are a few more issues with templates. As we mentioned earlier, all the code belonging to a template needs to reside in a header file so it is 'visible' to the compiler when it is time to instantiate the template. The unfortunate side effect is that it increases coupling between different classes in the program. Any class that includes a template will automatically include all the header files needed by the implementation of that template. Apart from the negative architectural ramifications of extra coupling, it will be noticeable in an everyday kind of way by longer compile times when only a small change was made. On a large project that makes heavy use of templates, this becomes a significant problem, since waiting minutes for a compile to finish between minor changes is unacceptable.

Templates will also cause our compile times to go up independently of the tighter coupling between classes. When a template is instantiated, the compiler creates a new class and compiles it on the fly. Fortunately, this extra time is not a very large factor and will go mostly unnoticed for most projects.

Code Bloat

The other problem that template detractors will often bring up is that of code bloat. Whenever we create a list of a new class, the compiler has to create a whole new list class on the fly. This means that all the functions will be duplicated, as well as all the static member variables. The same thing will happen if we use templated functions, and new function code will be generated for every type of parameter we pass to the function. On the whole, it is not as big an issue as it might seem. The typical size of code is very small compared to the amount of data today's games move around. You should only start worrying about code bloat when you start creating combinations of templates of templates. Then you might cause a combinatorial explosion of templates, and the amount of extra code generated by the compiler will start to become noticeable in the overall size of the project.

Assuming code bloat becomes a significant issue in your project, you could attempt to move some of the common code out of the template into a normal function that is called from the templated code. This way, the function will not be repeated once for every instantiation of a template. Unfortunately, this is often not possible or significant enough. Unless we have huge templated functions, it is not easy to pull out any significant amount of common code.

Compiler Support

Finally, one thing you need to be very aware of if you decide to use templates is their level of support in your compiler and platform. Templates were finalized and added to the C++ standard only quite lately. Even though they had been around for quite a while, they existed only as proposed solution and did not have a firm standard. This shows in the lackluster template support in most compilers. Fortunately, most compilers have basic template support, but many fail in the more advanced features, such as partial template specialization. This is even more important if you are planning on using third-party libraries with heavy template usage.

WHEN TO USE TEMPLATES

The best bit of advice related to template usage is the same as for inheritance: use them with caution. Be very aware of the level of expertise of your current (and future) team members, and use templates accordingly. There are few things more difficult and frustrating than untangling a badly designed mess of templates in a large project while a deadline is breathing down your neck. You would have wished for a much simpler implementation at that point.

Remember that there is no point in using templates for the sake of using 'advanced' C++ features. It is a tool, and it is there to make your life easier and save time. If you save a few hours now, only to cause you many lost days down the line, using templates does not look like a good deal.

That being said, there will be times when you want to apply a set of code to a variety of totally unrelated classes, and you want those classes to continue being totally independent of each other. C++ templates might be a good solution at that point, which is very similar to the list example presented earlier this chapter.

One of the best candidates for template use are container classes, data structures that contain objects of many different classes. Fortunately, a lot of those have already been written for us in the STL. See Chapter 8 for more details on the STL. In the meanwhile, there will be some specific containers that the STL does not have available, such as a good tree container, some special priority queue, or something very dependent on your situation. Templates might be a good solution in that case.

You might also want to look at the Boost library. It is a set of C++ libraries that, for the most part, make heavy use of templates and are intended to extend and complement the STL. If what you need is not in the STL, check out Boost. Only then decide to write it on your own if you still have not found what you need.

One good suggestion is to try to write any template code in a style similar to the STL. The Boost library is a good example of this. It will allow for a much easier integration with the rest of the code, it will make life easier on other programmers already familiar with STL, and it might even allow for some interaction with STL algorithms, iterators, or containers. Other potential candidates for templatization are manager/factory classes (classes that take care of creating and keeping track of objects), resource loading code, singletons, and serialization of objects.

TEMPLATE SPECIALIZATION (ADVANCED)

By default, all new classes created from a template will be exactly the same, but they will apply to different class types. The problem with writing totally generic code is that we have very little idea of what data types it will work on. With large objects, we definitely want to avoid copying them as much as possible, so adding a few extra pointers to avoid any copies seems like a good trade-off. On the other hand, a very small object, or even a pointer itself, can be copied around very easily; keeping several pointers around to manage a single 32-bit object seems like overkill.

Template specialization allows us to add some customization to a template for a particular class or set of classes. That way, we can provide optimizations for specific classes that we plan on using frequently, such as pointers or strings. Optimizations can be both in the form of a more efficient implementation or one that takes less memory, depending on what our needs are.

Full Template Specialization

The first type of specialization is *full template specialization*. It allows us to provide a custom version of a template for a specific class.

Let's revisit the simple template from earlier in this chapter. It provides a list implementation for any data type, we have fleshed out its implementation to be very efficient, and then we used it everywhere in our game. Toward the end of the project, we realize that we have many lists of very small elements; in particular, we are using lists of game entity handles all over the place.

A game entity handle is a tiny class that just holds an integer and has no virtual functions or any type of inheritance, so an object of that class is just 32 bits. Having a whole list node allocated for every entity handle is very wasteful. Not only does a list node have two other pointers, which triples the size of the data we care about, but since it is allocated dynamically, it might have some extra overhead from the memory system, which wastes even more memory. (For more details on memory allocations and possible solutions to this problem using a pool system, refer to Chapter 7, Memory Allocation.)

For now, let us improve this situation by using template specialization. We can write a custom version of the list template that stores its elements in a contiguous block of memory. Inserting and deleting elements from the middle of the list will be somewhat more costly, but since the size of the game entities is so small, it is a small price to pay for cutting down memory usage by a factor of three.

The following code would not replace the previous template, but it would complement it. It also must appear after the declaration of the general template, not before. Any functions the specialized template implements will override the default ones from the general template.

```
template<>
class List<GameEntityHandle> {
public:
    ListNode< GameEntityHandle > * GetHead();
    void PushBack();

private:
    GameEntityHandle * m_pData;
};
```

Of course, along with the template declaration, we would also provide an implementation for those functions that take care of managing a list of game entity elements on a contiguous block of memory. In this case, we also need to provide a specialization for the list node `ListNode<GameEntityHandle>` so it can work in conjunction with the specialized version of the list.

Partial Template Specialization

What if we realized that the lists we were using were not of one class type, but of many different types that had elements in common? For example (and this is a very likely situation if we are using object-oriented design and polymorphism), what if most of our lists contain pointers to different types of objects? Pointers are small, probably the same size as the a game entity object, so they would also benefit from a specialized list implementation. For this situation, we would use the second type of specialization, which is *partial template specialization*. The following code uses partial template specialization to create a template for a list of pointers of any type:

```
template<class T>
class List<T *> {
public:
    ListNode<T *> * GetHead();
    void PushBack();

private:
    T * m_pData;
};
```

Whenever we instantiate a new type of list, the specific template will be chosen based on the classes we are using to instantiate the template.

```
// Normal templated list is used
List<Matrix4x4> matrixList;

// Fully-specialized list, because it stores GameEntityHandles
List<GameEntityHandle> handleList;

// Partially-specialized list, because it stores pointers
List<Matrix4x4 *> matrixPtrList;
```

CONCLUSION

In this chapter, we introduced the concept of templates. Templates allow us to write code that does not depend on specific data types, and the compiler takes care of instantiating them at compile time as they are needed in our programs. Templates come in two flavors: class templates, which apply to whole classes, and function templates, which apply to individual functions. The major advantages of templates are:

- Code is not duplicated in different places.
- We have type safety.
- We are not forced to inherit from a common base class.

However, templates are not without drawbacks:

- Code becomes more complex and difficult to maintain and debug.
- Extra dependencies are included, and compile times are increased.
- Code size might increase.
- Compiler support is not totally available.

Knowing the tradeoffs of templates and when to use them is a very important aspect of development. Finally, we covered the concept of template specialization, which allows us to customize parts of a template for a specific class or set of classes. We can use this feature to write more optimized versions of a template for specific data types.

SUGGESTED READING

The sources below are some gentle introductions to templates and discussions on their use:

Murray, Robert B., *C++ Strategies and Tactics*, Addison-Wesley, 1993.
Stroustrup, Bjarne, *The C++ Programming Language*, 3rd ed., Addison-Wesley, 1997.

More in-depth coverage of templates can be found in:

Vandevoorde, David, and Nicolai M. Josuttis, *C++ Templates: The Complete Guide*, Addison-Wesley, 2003.

The following has some very advanced and mind-stretching uses of templates:

Alexandrescu, Andrei, *Modern C++ Design*, Addison-Wesley, 2001.

EXCEPTION HANDLING

IN THIS CHAPTER

C++ introduces a new technique for dealing with errors: exception handling. Exception handling allows us to write robust, simple code that deals correctly with any errors or unexpected situations. This chapter will cover the reasons to use exceptions, how to use exceptions effectively in our programs, and the tradeoffs involved in their use, especially with respect to how they affect performance. We will finish by making some specific recommendations on the use of exceptions in game programming.

DEALING WITH ERRORS

From the very beginning of the history of computers, programmers have had to deal with errors. There has never been an ideal solution, and typically we either spend too much time and effort worrying about errors, or we ignore them altogether. This section shows what the alternatives are dealing with errors and introduces the concept of C++ exceptions.

Ignore Them!

The first strategy when dealing with errors is to ignore them. It may sound ridiculous, but that is how most programs deal with errors—or at least with the great majority of them. Sure, we all check whether opening a file was successful or not, but who checks the return value from printf? (Yes, it does return an error code, I just looked it up.)

A lot of programs will be able to get by fine this way. As long as nothing unexpected happens, everything will go well. However, as soon as things take a turn for the worse, the program is likely to crash. What if there is not enough memory? What if the desktop display is set to 8-bit color depth? What if there is no more disk space, or if the user pulls the CD-ROM out while the game is loading?

Ignoring errors might be a fine way of handling them in quick and dirty tools, or maybe even for internal development tools (depending on the internal standards of quality that your company expects). But this is clearly not the way we want to handle things in the programs we sell to users, so we need to look for alternate solutions.

Error Codes

We could use the time-honored approach of returning error codes from functions. Every function that could fail returns an error code, or at least a

Boolean, indicating whether the function was successful or not. The calling code checks that `return` value and handles any failed calls correctly.

In theory, this approach works just fine. In practice, it falls short when applied to a full project. First of all, it leads to really ugly code that becomes difficult to maintain. A function that could have been a really simple two-statement function now becomes an ugly, 30-line mess of tangled `if-then-else` statements. It is not just that it is ugly (which it is), but most importantly, it is now difficult to discern what the function is really doing. The error-handling code obfuscates the real purpose of the function.

The following code loads a mesh from a data stream. The top function does not do any form of error checking; the second one does. Which function is more readable?

```
void Mesh::Load(Stream stream)
{
    ParseHeader(stream);
    ParseFlags(stream);
    ParseVertices(stream);
    ParseFaces(stream);
}

int Mesh::Load(Stream stream)
{
    int errCode = OK;
    errCode = ParseHeader(stream);
    if (errCode != OK) {
        FreeHeader();
        return errCode;
    }
    errCode = ParseFlags(stream);
    if (errCode != OK) {
        FreeHeader();
        return errCode;
    }
    errCode = ParseVertices(stream);
    if (errCode != OK) {
        FreeHeader();
        FreeVertices();
        return errCode;
    }
    errCode = ParseFaces(stream);
    if (errCode != OK) {
        FreeHeader();
```

```
                    FreeVertces();
                    FreeFaces();
                    return errCode;
          }
        return errCode;
    }
```

The source code speaks for itself. But we are not letting error codes get off the hook that easily. There are still some major problems with every function returning error codes. Checking error codes is not only ugly and cumbersome, it is also wasteful. If every function we call has if statements surrounding it, the overall effect could be felt in the game as a marked decrease in performance.

Then there are the logistical problems of where the error codes are kept. Are they one huge file that everybody includes, or does each subsystem have its own set of codes? How can they be converted from the numerical code to a human-readable string? There has to be a better way.

Blow up (with Asserts)

One legitimate way of handling errors is to throw up our hands and surrender—except that instead of letting the computer crash by itself, we will stop it by using the assert function (or a customized assert function like the one that will be described in Chapter 16). At least by stopping the program, we can report more information, such as the file name and line number of the error, and maybe a descriptive message. It is better than nothing, but it still leaves much to be desired.

Setjmp and Longjmp

Hardcore C programmers will probably be familiar with the functions setjmp and longjmp; setjmp allows us to set a place in the code (along with the stack state) to be called in the future, and longjmp restores the program to that particular location and stack state. We could supposedly handle errors by calling longjmp every time there is some sort of error. Unfortunately, apart from being very inflexible, this approach does not mesh well with C++. The longjmp function unwinds the stack, but it does not destroy the objects that were in the stack. So the destructor of the objects in the stack would never be called, which probably means memory leaks or resources that were not freed. If we are planning on exiting the program right away, this is probably not a big deal, but if we intend to recover from the error and continue, it is an unacceptable solution that will cause the program to run out of resources and eventually crash.

C++ Exceptions

Now we come to C++ *exceptions*. So far, all the proposed error-handling mechanisms had major drawbacks. Before we see the exact syntax of C++ exceptions, let's look at how they are used in a general way, and why we might prefer to use them over the previous error-handling methods.

How Exceptions Work

Exceptions work as follows: whenever a program comes up against something unexpected, it can throw an exception. That will cause the execution of the program to jump to the nearest exception-handling block. If there is no exception-handling block in the function where the exception was thrown, the program will unwind the stack (correctly destroying all the objects there) and go to the parent function looking for an exception-handling block. It will continue going up through the function call stack until an exception-handling block is found, or the top is reached—at which point the default exception-handling code will be triggered and the execution of the program will be stopped.

In a exception-handling block we can do anything we want. We can report the error, try to fix the problem, or even ignore it. We can also do different things, depending on what caused the exception (e.g., we probably want to treat a corrupt file differently than a division by zero). Once the exception-handling block has been executed, program execution resumes as normal from this point on, not from where the exception was thrown.

Advantages

The first advantage of exception handling is that it does not result in messy code. A loading function that uses exception handling could look just like the previous version, which had no error checking at all. Clean code is easier to understand and easier to maintain; it is more than just aesthetically nicer.

Exceptions are flexible. We can handle different types of errors in different ways. Sometimes we will want to recover; at other times, we will want to terminate the program, just like `assert` did.

Exceptions also make it a lot easier to pass information about the nature of the error to layers of code higher up. Usually, if something goes wrong deep in the bowels of the file IO code, we want to report that error all the way up the chain of caller functions so we can display an error message to the user in our GUI. In order to do that with return codes, every single function along the way needs to be prepared to return failure codes that are passed from below. With exception handling, the error will automatically propagate up to the nearest `try-catch` block, and the exception object can contain much more meaningful information than just one error code.

There was one situation we did not even mention when talking about return codes: constructors. A constructor returns no values, so it makes life very difficult if our own error-reporting mechanism is based on returning error codes. We could set some variable on the object marking it as failed, but then the calling code would have to check it before it did anything with the object. Alternatively, we could avoid doing anything that could fail inside a constructor, but that would limit its usefulness. A very common idiom is *resource acquisition on initialization*, which relies on objects fully initializing themselves when they are created, instead of having a separate step. That allows us to always treat objects as correctly initialized, instead of having to constantly check.

Incidentally, destructors are in the same situation, but since the object is being destroyed, it usually does not matter as much whether or not something failed. Nobody should be able to touch the object after it is destroyed, anyway. Still, we might want to at least report that something went wrong while the object was being destroyed.

You can probably imagine where all this is leading: exceptions let us report errors that occur inside a constructor. We will see exactly how this is accomplished in a moment.

Finally, and this is a relatively minor point, exceptions avoid the need for a large error code table that needs to be maintained project-wide. There is also no need to convert between error codes and human-readable error messages. Often, exceptions themselves contain the error-description strings, which will make debugging much easier.

USING EXCEPTIONS

In the previous section, we were treated to a nice preview of what we will get when using exceptions. Yes, they also have their drawbacks, but we will see those later. For now, let's see how to use exceptions in our own programs.

Overview

The syntax to use exceptions in C++ is very easy. Whenever the code needs to throw an exception, it uses the keyword throw. Control is passed to the nearest exception-handling block, which is indicated by the keyword catch. The catch block must be found immediately after a try block, which surrounds the code that might throw an exception. Here is a very simple code snippet that throws an exception and handles it:

```
void f() {
    printf ("Start function f.\n");
    throw 1;
    printf ("End function f.\n");
}

main() {
    printf ("Start main.\n");
    try {
        printf ("About to call f.\n");
        f();
        printf ("After calling f.\n");
    }
    catch (...) {
        printf ("Handling exception.\n");
    }
    printf ("Ending main.\n");
}
```

The output from this program will be:

```
Start main.
About to call f.
Start function f.
Handling exception.
Ending main.
```

Notice that as soon as the exception is thrown, the rest of function f is skipped, as well as the rest of the code inside the try block. Execution resumes inside the catch block and then continues as normal.

Throwing Exceptions

As we saw in the previous section, the throw keyword takes an identifier that it uses as the exception to throw. It turns out that C++ is extremely flexible, and it lets us throw an object of any type as an exception.

In the previous example, we just did throw 1 because we did not really care what type of exception we were throwing; the important part was just to throw an exception. It turns out that most of the time we will want to be more explicit about our exceptions. If we have different parts of the code throwing exceptions for different reasons, how are we going to know what the cause of the exception was when we catch it?

To solve that problem, we can create our own exception objects that will contain all the information we need. We will throw them whenever we have an exception, and they will be passed to the catch statement. Here is a simple exception class:

```
class MyException {
public:
    MyException(const char * pTxt) : pReason(pTxt){};
    const char * pReason;
};
```

To use it, we just throw an exception with an object of that type. The following code attempts to read vertex data from a stream, and throws an exception if it cannot read enough data because the file is too short:

```
void Mesh::ParseVertices(Stream stream) {
    for (int i=0; i<m_numVerts; ++i) {
        VertexData data;
        int nRead = stream.Read(data, sizeof(VertexData));
        if (nRead < sizeof(VertexData)
            throw MyException("File too short");
        Vertex vertex(data);
        m_verts.push_back(vertex);
    }
}
```

We will see in a moment how the object we created is passed to the catch statement. This can then be used to do different things, based on its contents.

If our program has many different reasons for throwing exceptions, we might want to create different types of exceptions for different categories. For example, we could have a category of exceptions related to file

IO, another one for graphics hardware, another one for math functions, and so on. This is particularly true because we might want to handle exceptions of one type differently than exceptions of another type. For example, graphics hardware-related exceptions are probably going to be a lot more serious than file-related exceptions.

To accomplish this, we can create a hierarchy of exception classes. By arranging them in a hierarchy, no only do we get to share some common implementation, but we can also take advantage of the hierarchy organization when we process the exceptions in the catch statement. A possible exception hierarchy is shown in Figure 5.1.

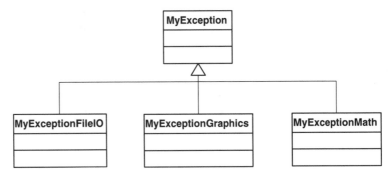

FIGURE 5.1   An exception hierarchy.

It turns out that C++ already has a set of standard exceptions organized in a hierarchy for different general types. Some of the broad types are logic_error and runtime_error, while some of the more specific exception types are out_of_range, bad_alloc, or overflow_error. Some of the functions in the standard C++ library throw these types of exceptions, so you might want to be prepared to deal with them correctly.

Catching Exceptions

So far, we have only seen one form of catching exceptions—using the catch (...) statement. This statement means that we want to catch all exceptions, regardless of what type they really are.

Catching One Type

Normally, it is far more useful to catch specific types of exceptions. We can do this by using a slightly different form of catch that takes a specific exception type as a parameter. The following code demonstrates how to catch a file IO exception in our mesh-loading code:

```
void Mesh::Load(const char * filename) {
    try {
        Stream stream(filename);
        Load(stream);
    }
    catch (MyExceptionFileIO & e) {
        // Do something with the exception here
    }
}
```

Since we suspected that creating a new stream from a file name or loading the mesh from the stream could cause an exception, we surrounded that code with a `try` statement and followed it with a `catch` statement. If an exception of the type `ExceptionFileIO` is thrown in that code inside the `try` block, our handler will catch it and deal with it.

Catching Multiple Types

What if there is an exception, but it is of a different type? Our handler will not deal with it, so the exception will continue propagating up the function call chain until it finds an adequate handler or reaches the top of the chain. At that point, it will call the predefined `terminate` function, which will stop the execution of the program.

We would prefer to handle other types of exceptions in this function instead of allowing the program to crash. We can add multiple `catch` blocks, each accepting a different type of exception, almost as if it were a `switch` statement. Let's improve the example above to deal with possible math exceptions:

```
void Mesh::Load(const char * filename) {
    try {
        Stream stream(filename);
        Load(stream);
    }
    catch (MyExceptionFileIO & e) {
        // Do something with the exception here
    }
    catch (MyExceptionMath & e) {
        // Deal with it here.
    }
}
```

This has the potential to become really cumbersome if we have to write one `catch` statement for every type of exception we want to handle. We could easily have dozens of different exceptions, making the writing of error-handling code very cumbersome, which was one of the things we were trying to avoid in the first place.

Remember how we organized our exceptions in a hierarchical manner? Now we can really take advantage of that organization. A `catch` statement will handle exceptions of the type indicated in its parameter or any type derived from it. This means that if we do not need to be more explicit, we can write a handler for exceptions of the type `MyException`, and it will handle all its derived types as well.

Going back to the previous example, it turns out we were not so much concerned with catching the math exceptions, but we just wanted to make sure there were no exceptions getting out of the `Load` function. We can accomplish this in a much better way by using the base class of our exception hierarchy.

```
void Mesh::Load(const char * filename) {
    try {
        Stream stream(filename);
        Load(stream);
    }
    catch (MyExceptionFileIO & e) {
        // Do something with the exception here
    }
    catch (MyException & e) {
        // An exception that was not file IO-related was thrown.
        // Deal with it here.
    }
}
```

The order in which the `catch` statements appear is important. They will be processed from top to bottom, and as soon as one is found that can be used for the current exception, the rest will be ignored.

If we wanted to make our `Load` function totally bomb-proof and make sure that absolutely no exceptions get out, we could also attempt to catch all other types of exceptions, even the ones that are not derived from our exception base class, by adding another `catch` statement at the end.

```
void Mesh::Load(const char * filename) {
    try {
        Stream stream(filename);
```

```
                Load(stream);
        }
        catch (MyExceptionFileIO & e) {
                // Do something with the exception here
        }
        catch (MyException & e) {
                // An exception that was not file IO related
                // was thrown. Deal with it here.           }
        catch (...) {
                // A different exception was thrown.
        }
}
```

Rethrowing an Exception

So far, when we catch an exception, we have assumed we handled it correctly and that program execution can continue as usual. It is also possible that we caught an exception, tried to solve the problem, and were not able to; so we would like other parts of the program to deal with it. Or maybe we caught an exception, looked at it in more detail, and decided it was not something we wanted to deal with.

Whenever an exception handler decides it does not want to fully handle an exception, it can *rethrow* it. To do that, it just needs to use the keyword `throw`, without any parameters, from within the `catch` block, and it will automatically throw the same exception to let the next `try-catch` block deal with it.

For example, the following code will only process exceptions that are caused by corrupt data. All other exceptions, including all other file IO exceptions, will be handled by other parts of the program.

```
void Mesh::Load(Stream stream)
{
    try {
        ParseHeader(stream);
        ParseFlags(stream);
        ParseVertices(stream);
        ParseFaces(stream);
    }
    catch (MyExceptionFileIO & e) {
        if (e.IsDataCorrupt()) {
            // Handle corrupt data here
        }
        else {
            throw;     // Throw the same exception again so it
```

```
                                        // can be handled somewhere else
                    }
                }
            }
```

EXCEPTION-SAFE CODE

Using exceptions in our programs is more than knowing how to call `throw` or how to set up a `try-catch` block. To use exceptions effectively, we need to write code that will work correctly in the face of exceptions, without leaking memory or stranding resources.

Resource Acquisition

Resources, in the context of C++, refers to anything that the code acquires, but then has to explicitly release so it can be used by the rest of the system. They can be in the form of memory, file handles, or what we traditionally call resources in game development, such as textures, geometry, sounds, and so forth.

The Problem

The problem this section addresses is: once a resource has been acquired, if there is an error, how can we release that resource? This is not a new problem. We have to struggle with it no matter what type of error-handling system we are using. Using exceptions just makes it much more noticeable, because there are no easy hacks around it.

The following function illustrates the problem in the simplest way. The function is supposed to create a new texture from a file. It opens the file, gets the texture's dimensions, allocates the texture, and reads the data into it. So far, it does no error checking at all.

```
Texture * CreateTexture(const char * filename) {
    FILE * fin = fopen(filename, "rb");
    TextureHeader info;
    ReadTextureHeader(fin, info);
    Texture * pTexture = new Texture(info.width, info.height,
                                     info.colorDepth);
    ReadTextureData(fin, pTexture);
    fclose(fin);
}
```

We will try several approaches on this function in this section, so let's have a closer look at it. How many resources are acquired in this function? We do not know exactly what the functions ReadTextureHeader and ReadTextureData do, but assuming they do not acquire any resources of their own, the CreateTexture function gets two resources. One is the file handle, and the other is the texture object that was created in the middle of the function. Of these, only the file handle is released. The texture is supposed to be passed on to the function that called CreateTexture.

Return Codes

How would the previous function look if we used return codes for error handling? It would look something like this:

```
Texture * CreateTexture(const char * filename) {
    FILE * fin = fopen(filename, "rb");
    if (fin == NULL)
        return NULL;

    TextureHeader info;
    if (!ReadTextureHeader(fin, info)) {
        fclose(fin);
        return NULL;
    }
    Texture * pTexture = new Texture(info.width, info.height,
                                     info.colorDepth);
    if (pTexture == NULL) {
        fclose(fin);
        return NULL;
    }
    if (!ReadTextureData(fin, pTexture)) {
        delete pTexture;
        fclose(fin);
        return NULL;
    }

    fclose(fin);
    return pTexture;
}
```

As you can see, there is duplicate code all over the place, and adding new steps to the function makes it very error-prone. If we are able to get past our reluctance to use goto statements, we could make the code a little cleaner:

```
Texture * CreateTexture(const char * filename) {
    bool bSuccess = false;
    Texture * pTexture = NULL;
    TextureHeader info;
    FILE * fin = fopen(filename, "rb");
    if (fin == NULL)
        goto cleanup;
    if (!ReadTextureHeader(fin, info))
        goto cleanup;
    pTexture = new Texture(info.width, info.height,
                            info.colorDepth);
    if (pTexture == NULL)
        goto cleanup;
    if (!ReadTextureData(fin, pTexture))
        goto cleanup;
    bSuccess = true;

cleanup:
    if (!bSuccess) {
        delete pTexture;
        pTexture = NULL;
    }
    fclose(fin);
    return pTexture;
}
```

This is a little better, but only slightly. At least the use of goto is limited to skipping to the end of the function, so it is still reasonable readable.

Exceptions

When we use exceptions, we get the goto jump for free if there is an error, and the code is not cluttered with error checks.

```
Texture * CreateTexture(const char * filename) {
    FILE * fin = NULL;
    Texture * pTexture = NULL;
    try {
        fin = fopen(filename, "rb");
        TextureHeader info;
        ReadTextureHeader(fin, info);
```

```
                    pTexture = new Texture(info.width, info.height,
                                           info.colorDepth);
                    ReadTextureData(fin, pTexture);
            }
            catch(...) {
                delete pTexture;
                pTexture = NULL;
            }
            fclose(fin);
            return pTexture;
    }
```

This is certainly the cleanest of all the options so far. Still, it would be great if there were a simpler way. Also, what if we wanted to actually let the exception go up to the calling function? Then the only reason to set up the `try-catch` block would be to release the resources we acquired, and we would have to rethrow the exception again.

Resource Acquisition Is Initialization

A much cleaner approach is to use the 'resource acquisition is initialization' idea. When an exception is thrown and the current function is exited, all the objects created during the function are destroyed. In this case, the object `info` of type `TextureHeader` is destroyed correctly because it was in the stack, but the variables `fin` and `pTexture` are just pointers, so they do not really have a destructor. What we would really like is for their destructors to release the resources they are holding.

For the case of the file handle, we could create a simple class that wraps the file handling. Whenever the object is constructed, it opens the file, and whenever it is destroyed, it closes it. Now we just need to create an object of that type on the stack, and the file resource will be released as soon as it falls out of scope.

For the other resource, the texture pointer, we have an easier solution that we can apply to all pointers—the `auto_ptr` class. The `auto_ptr` class, which is part of the standard C++ library, is very similar to the class we used with a file handle, but it applies to pointers instead of files. Whenever the `auto_ptr` object is destroyed, the pointer it holds is deleted. Apart from that, it can be dereferenced and used just like a regular pointer. This is how our example would look using the new classes to release resources automatically:

```
auto_ptr<Texture> CreateTexture(const char * filename) {
    FilePtr fin (filename, "rb");
```

```
        TextureHeader info;
        ReadTextureHeader(fin, info);
        auto_ptr<Texture> pTexture = new Texture(info.width,
                                                 info.height,
                                               info.colorDepth);

        ReadTextureData(fin, pTexture);
        return pTexture;
    }
```

This is much better. Notice how now we do not do any exception handling in this function, and instead let the calling function deal with it, though all the resources have been released correctly.

There are other alternatives to auto_ptr, some of which might be more appropriate to your specific situation, depending on whether you want shared ownership, reference counting, or a variety of other options. The Boost library offers several different smart pointers that could be used instead of auto_ptr.

Also, it is worth noting that we could have used the same technique in the case where we were handling errors through return codes. Doing that would definitely improve the clarity of the code, allow us to return right away, and know that all the resources would be correctly released.

Finally, if all that wrapping of resources in objects that automatically release them seems like overkill, well it might very well be true. If exceptions are truly exceptional and are hardly ever expected to happen, maybe in your specific circumstances it is fine to leak a bit of memory here and there. Just make sure not to abuse it.

Constructors

Constructors have always been different. As we mentioned earlier, constructors do not have a return value, so it becomes impossible to return error codes that indicate something has failed.

Exceptions work well with constructors because they do not rely on any return codes. However, they present some unique challenges. Consider the following code:

```
    class Bitmap {
    public:
        Bitmap(int width, int height) {
            m_pData=new(width*height);
            // ...
        }
```

```
        ~Bitmap() { delete m_pData; }
    private:
        byte * m_pData;
    };
```

It is a very straightforward class. Whenever an object is constructed, it allocates enough memory to store a bitmap of the specified size; whenever it is destroyed, the memory is released. So far, the code looks good.

What happens if an exception is thrown in the constructor after the memory in m_pData is allocated? The stack will unwind, and the execution will be transferred to the nearest try-catch block, just like it did before. But what will happen to the memory we just allocated? It will be leaked; it is a resource we did not release.

The reason is that the destructor for the object will not be called. After all, since the constructor failed by throwing an exception, it makes no sense to call the destructor. However, the objects that were created so far in the constructor will be destroyed. Unfortunately we were using a dumb (i.e., not 'smart,' or 'normal') pointer; so even though the pointer is destroyed, the memory it points to is still allocated.

A way to write the same constructor in an exception-safe manner would be to use auto_ptr again so that the memory will be freed as soon as the auto_ptr object is destroyed. As a side benefit, we do not need to free the memory in the destructor; it will happen automatically for us.

```
    class Bitmap {
    public:
        Bitmap(int width, int height) :
            m_pData(new(width*height)) {
            // ...
        }
    private:
        auto_ptr<byte> m_pData;
    };
```

Destructors

Destructors are not as problematic as constructors, as far as exceptions go. After all, we are destroying an object, so it is not like anybody is going to try to access it after we are done with it.

The only rule that we need to keep in mind is that a destructor is not allowed to throw an exception if the destructor was called in response to another exception; that is, an exception was thrown somewhere, and as part of the stack unwinding, the object's destructor was called. If the destructor were to throw an exception at that point, what should the system do? Ignore the older one and deal with this one? Queue them? Instead, C++ disallows that situation, and if it ever does happen, the function `terminate` will be called, stopping the execution of the program.

If you are worried about that situation, you can always wrap calls that potentially throw exceptions in your destructors in a `try-catch` block that catches all exceptions and either ignores them or deals with them in some fashion.

COST ANALYSIS

The specifics of the implementation of exceptions are left totally up to the compiler writers, so there is no way to talk in absolutes about the performance cost of exception handling. On the other hand, it is a very important aspect of the implementation, especially for game programming. As with some other topics, take the information in this section as a general rule of what you might expect, but measure what the results are in your platform, or look at a disassembled version of the code involved in your exception-handling setup.

First of all, we need to differentiate between two totally different situations: the situation in which no exceptions are thrown, and the second situation in which an exception is thrown.

When an exception is thrown, all sorts of things happen: the program searches for the nearest exception-handling block, it unwinds the stack, destroying the objects there in the process, and transfers execution to the `catch` statement. Is that operation slow? Yes. Do we care? Absolutely not.

Exceptions should be exactly that—exceptional. Exceptions are not used to indicate whether a unit gets killed or not, they are used to let us know we just ran out of memory, or maybe that the DVD was removed. Those are truly exceptional circumstances that should either never happen or happen very rarely. We really do not care if the process of throwing and catching an exception is slow. Chances are we are going to temporarily stop the game and tell the user about some problem, so we can certainly afford to spend 100 ms unwinding the stack.

What we really care about is whether performance is affected when no exceptions are thrown. Another interesting question is whether the use of exception handling requires more memory. It turns out those two questions are tied together.

There are two main ways of implementing exception handling. The first and simplest way requires very little extra memory, but it imposes a slight performance overhead every time a `try-catch` statement is reached. The second way has virtually no performance overhead, but it might require a significant amount of memory to efficiently deal with exceptions. The worst part is, you have no control over which implementation is used, other than changing compilers. So if that is a concern to you, refer to the compiler's documentation to find out which implementation will be used.

The other important aspect of implementation to consider is the frequency of `try-catch` statements and what the alternatives are. If `try-catch` statements appear infrequently in the code, or only appear in situations where performance is not as crucial, such as during resource loading, then any performance overhead might go totally unnoticed. On the other hand, if they are executed several thousands of times per frame, they might add up to a more noticeable performance hit.

Also, when evaluating the performance of exception handling, we need to think about what the alternatives are. We cannot compare it to code that does no error checking at all. If you can live without error checking, then don't waste your time with exception handling. Most commercial tools and games require some level of robustness, so we are forced to deal with errors in some way. A small overhead for setting up the stack unwinding might seem very reasonable when compared to a function with dozens of nested `if` statements.

On the other hand, if your compiler implements the version of exception handling that trades memory for speed, the drawback might be more than you can afford, especially in some game consoles with very limited system memory. Run some quick experiments before you commit to either using or ignoring exceptions.

WHEN TO USE EXCEPTIONS

By this point, we know how to use exception handling, what changes it demands in our code, and how much it costs us. The question is when should we use exceptions? Or even, should we use exceptions at all?

First, it is important to reiterate a previous point, exceptions should be exceptional. Never lose sight of that. Avoid the temptation to use the new 'toy' for everyday uses. A good rule to follow is to only use exceptions where errors could happen but are never expected. When exceptions occur, they might require the user's attention. Some good examples of situations where using exception handling is a good idea are a data file being corrupt, hardware failing to operate correctly, defective media, or even a sudden disconnection from the network. We should have some way to deal with those situations, but they will hopefully never happen during normal usage.

What that means is that exception handling is no substitute for returning error codes from functions. There are many circumstances where return codes are the best solution. For example, if we attempt to open a file with a previous position of the game saved, it is quite likely that the file name was misspelled. Attempting to open the file and returning an error code if it does not exist is a perfectly valid approach. Sometimes you might also want to try to perform an operation and then check whether it was successful or not. Clearly, a failure in that case is not an unexpected result, so error codes would be a much better, simpler solution.

Both approaches can coexist peacefully, each applied to circumstances where it is the best solution. It is important to carefully document which error-handling method different parts of the program use. We do not want other programmers putting try-catch blocks around functions we wrote that return error codes.

So far, the argument seems to be to use exceptions sparingly for things like development tools, but is it a good idea to use exceptions inside our game? What if it is a console game? The answer is probably yes in both cases. As long as exceptions are used rarely and indicate truly exceptional situations, they can save a lot of ugly code, busy typing, and a lot of squinting through if statements when debugging the code.

CONCLUSION

Before our introduction to exceptions, we saw what the alternatives were for handling errors in our programs: ignore them, return error codes, or use the C-centric setjmp and longjmp functions. All of these alternatives had major drawbacks.

Exceptions can be used to report errors in a very clean way. They do not require that we fill our code with if statements, and they are also foolproof, since they cannot be easily ignored (unlike return codes). Unfortunately, writing exception-safe code is not a trivial matter, especially in the case of constructors.

We then saw how different exception-handling implementations can have very different performance and memory requirements. However, if exceptions are used sparingly for situations where errors are possible but not expected, the overhead they introduce should be negligible to the point where it is worth considering using them in the game code itself.

SUGGESTED READING

There is a fair amount of literature out there dealing with exceptions. These are some great references, which include some very sound advice on appropriate situations to use exception handling as well as some discussions on writing exception-safe code.

Stroustrup, Bjarne, *The C++ Programming Language*, 3rd ed., Addison-Wesley, 1997.

Murray, Robert B., *C++ Strategies and Tactics*, Addison-Wesley, 1993.

Dattatri, Kayshav, *C++ Effective Object-Oriented Software Construction*, Prentice Hall, 2000.

Sutter, Herb, *Exceptional C++*, Addison-Wesley, 2000.

The Boost library has several types of smart pointers that can be used effectively with exception handling.

C++ Boost Smart Pointer Library, *http://www.boost.org/libs/smart_ptr/index.htm*.

PERFORMANCE AND MEMORY

All the right ingredients are there: compelling gameplay, breathtaking visuals, and an outstanding soundtrack. Now the game will stand or fall based on how well it runs. If it is a clunker running at five frames per second, it will be a beautiful clunker, but will not be very popular. If the game bogs down after 10 minutes of play because of memory leaks, a lot of angry customers are going to be returning your game.

Internal development tools are not exempt from efficiency requirements, either. If loading the level editor takes a minute, or if scrolling through the tree of entities in the world is sluggish and unresponsive, the productivity of the designers and the final product quality will definitely suffer.

C++ is a very complex programming language. There are two sides to that: with that complexity we can accomplish things other languages could only dream of, but on the flip side, it has a fairly steep (and long) learning curve, and a large potential for programming errors. With great power comes great responsibility.

Part II deals with the nuts and bolts of C++: how to avoid common performance pitfalls and what things to do to speed up the program, how to deal with memory management efficiently, and how to use high-level data structures and algorithms easily and effectively.

PERFORMANCE

S ome people claim that C++ is just too complicated. You might even be starting to fall into that category after having read the previous chapters. There is no denying that C++ is a very complex language. But fortunately, the glass is not just half empty, it is also half full.

C++ is complicated, but along with that complexity comes the potential for high performance. Compare it to other languages like Java. They are considered to be easier and less complex, but they usually give less control over the final performance of our programs. For game programming, control is particularly important. Other languages might offer similar performance, but they are usually not available for target platforms other than PCs.

In this chapter, we will see some of the most common performance pitfalls and how to use C++ effectively to avoid them. Specifically, we will see the different types of function calls and the overhead involved with each of them, and how to minimize their impact in our programs. We will also go in detail about some of the hidden costs of C++, things that happen behind your back without being explicit in the source code, such as generation of temporaries or the cost of constructors and destructors.

Understanding what is happening behind the scenes and keeping a few rules in mind makes it possible to tame the complexity of C++ and walk away with all the performance benefits that it provides.

PERFORMANCE AND OPTIMIZATIONS

Performance is not everything. This might seem surprising in a chapter dedicated exclusively to performance, but it is true. At some point, we have all become focused on a tiny section of a program, trying to make it faster by pulling every trick in the book. It can be an exhilarating experience to wring out all the performance the hardware can provide, and then some. At times this might be necessary, but most often than not, it is wasted effort. Figure 6.1 illustrates the profile of a typical PC game that makes good use of an accelerated graphics card.

There are several interesting things in that profile. First of all, a large amount of the time is spent in the graphics card. All the C++ optimizations in the world are not going to make the graphics card any faster. Instead, we will need to look into other ways of making the graphics part of the game more efficient, such as rearranging the vertex data, reducing the number of state changes, or using better shaders.

On the CPU side, there are some interesting patterns: 90% of the code execution time is spent on about 10–12 different functions. If we heavily optimize a function outside those top functions and make it twice

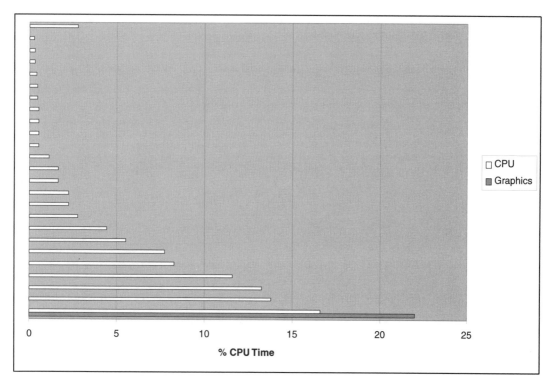

FIGURE 6.1   Typical PC game performance profile.

as fast, we will not even notice the frame rate increase. It would be completely wasted effort.

What is worse, even if we optimize one of those top 10 functions, we might not get any improvement, because the CPU might just spend more time waiting for the graphics card to be done. In the future, as we see more specialized hardware for different tasks, maximizing parallelism will become even more important. This situation is already true for most game consoles, since they have several specialized chips in addition to the main CPU.

As if this picture were not grim enough, let's consider some of the dangers of optimization with an imaginary story that is not far from reality. Programmer Pete decides it is time to speed up the AI pathfinding function, so he spends a whole day pulling every trick in the book to speed things up and sweats over every cycle. At the end of the day, Pete times his improvements and notices he has gotten a 20% performance boost in the pathfinding functions. Very proud of himself, he does the programmer victory dance, pats himself on the back, checks the code in, and goes home for a well-deserved rest.

The next morning, Programmer Pete runs the full build of the game and notices that it is not appreciably faster. When he looks at the frame rate, he sees that it is indeed running faster: about 2% faster. This is not surprising, since the AI pathfinding was 10% of the CPU usage; so the overall improvement was not as dramatic as he might have hoped, but any small improvement is desirable, so Pete moves on to something else.

A week later, Programmer Pete is asked to add pathfinding for flying units. What he had so far was only for land-based units. This should be no problem, he thinks. He pulls out the optimized code he worked so hard on last week and realizes that it is impossible to cleanly add flying units. It is so optimized that is completely inflexible. No only that, but Pete is afraid to even touch it, since it is very hard to understand what exactly is going on. Making any changes could break all the pathfinding, and the project has a milestone just a few days away!

The story probably ends with Programmer Pete undoing all of his clever optimizations, putting the old code back, and adding the flying unit support. That is the happy ending. The alternate ending is that Pete is stubborn and hacks in flying-unit support, spends three days doing it, and then it never works right and crashes half the time, leading to the missed milestone and eventual cancellation of the project. The moral of the story is that optimizing at the wrong moment, or thinking too much about optimizations from the very beginning, will cause more problems than it will solve.

Nobody denies that performance is important, though. As a matter of fact, it is much more important in games than in most other types of software development. It just needs to be dealt with carefully and at the right time. Performance should be addressed in two distinct phases: during program development and at the end of development.

During Program Development

During program development, the primary aim is to avoid doing something grossly inefficient. We should not be too concerned about exact cycle counts, hand-tuned assembly language, or cache interactions. We are only trying to avoid doing something that will unnecessarily slow everything down. This chapter addresses many issues that come up during the development phase. A good example of something to watch out for during this phase is copying objects when it is not necessary.

It is not always a clear-cut decision to decide what to optimize and what to leave for later. A lot of that will depend on experience, team expertise, and our own abilities. A good rule of thumb is that if you are in doubt as to whether or not to incorporate a particular optimization now, then leave it out.

Also during this phase, it is important to keep rough algorithmic performance in mind. Do not be too concerned whether or not a search is optimal, but at the same time, avoid searching a large list for the same element a hundred times during a frame. Instead, cache that result and reuse it whenever you need it. Or, if you know your game is going to have many units and objects in the world at once, avoid traversing the whole list of game objects to search for elements; use a spatial database for fast spatial queries instead.

At the End of Development

The end phase does not just refer to when we are getting the game ready to ship. It can be at the end of the development of a particular subsystem (e.g., the graphics renderer), or when we have decided that enough is enough, and we are not going to tweak the pathfinding algorithms anymore.

At this point we can pull some of the more esoteric optimizations. We will be trading readability and maintainability for faster performance. If we want to reuse this code in a future project, we should think long and hard about what we do to it. If it is very well encapsulated, maybe optimizing it heavily would be fine. Otherwise, we should go easy and carefully document all the optimizations in the code itself for future reference. There is nothing more frustrating that digging up some code you wrote a while ago that is so cleverly optimized that it runs blazingly fast, but you have no idea what it does.

Keep in mind that optimizations at this phase usually are not going to result in major performance improvements. The big gains come from decisions we made in the previous phase, during development: choice of algorithms, avoiding unnecessary computations, and so forth. Optimizing the code itself will get us a few percentages of improvement here and there for the overall program performance—maybe even a total boost of 10% to 15% increase in performance; but do not expect much more than that.

That said, what is the point of this chapter, then? This is not a chapter about bit-twiddling or replacing C++ with assembly code. It is also not about choosing the best algorithms to solve the problem at hand or about avoiding doing duplicate or unnecessary work. It is about avoiding potentially expensive operations in everyday C++ usage, things to keep in mind both when you are designing a piece of code and when you are implementing it.

FUNCTION TYPES

Function calls are something we have used in many programming languages before, and we have come to expect a certain overhead for each function call. There are two reasons to bring it up here:

- In addition to normal function calls, C++ introduces class member function calls, class static function calls, and virtual function calls. Knowing what the costs are of each of them will help improve the performance of the program.
- C++ encourages a more object-oriented approach, which typically involves more function calls than a procedural program. So function call overhead might be more noticeable than in a straight C program.

In C++, function calls will fall into one of four categories: *global functions, class static functions, nonvirtual member functions*, and *virtual member functions*. There are also two distinct cases of virtual members from a performance perspective: virtual functions under single inheritance and virtual functions under multiple inheritance.

Global Functions

These are the same types of function calls we encountered in C. For example:

```
int nHitPoints = GetHitPoints (gameUnit);
```

This type of function resolves to a call to a specific memory location that is computed at link time. So the only overhead comes from the actual jump to a different memory location, and its effects on the code cache and CPU pipeline. In most modern platforms, the cost is fairly negligible. It is possible to set up situations where the overhead of global function calls starts becoming noticeable, but these situations are fairly unlikely to happen during real development, especially with some judicious inlining (which will be the topic of the next section, so hang in there). Since global functions are the simplest and fastest type of function, we will use them as our baseline to analyze and compare the other types of function calls.

Usually, a good rule to follow is to forget about performance overhead and make a new function call anytime it makes sense to do so. Getting in the habit of using functions liberally has many benefits that totally outweigh any minor performance drawbacks. Using functions in this way:

- Encourages a solution to be implemented in smaller substeps
- Produces more-readable code, because each function has only one objective, which can be quickly understood just by reading the function name
- Results in more maintainable code, since it is possible to replace or fix just one of the many functions that went into solving a larger problem
- Encourages reuse, since many problems might require some of the same substeps in their solutions

The main drawback of using a large number of functions is that it might be difficult to follow the flow of the execution of the program, particularly if calls happen across multiple files. Having a good tool, such as an IDE (Integrated Development Environment) or source code browser to navigate the code, can be very helpful in those situations. If at some point the performance of the function calls becomes noticeable in some particularly sensitive section of code, it is always very easy to merge several functions together and eliminate most of the performance overhead.

Class Static Functions

Class static functions are similar to global functions, except that their scope is limited to a particular class. They are different than member functions because they are not associated with objects of that class, just the class itself.

Class static function calls are treated by the compiler in the same way as global function calls. They just have a slightly different appearance in the code, because their scope parameter indicates what class they belong to.

```
// Class static function
int numUnits = GameUnit::GetNumUnits();
```

The exact same comments apply as for normal static functions with respect to performance and use. The only thing that class static functions provide is a way to organize a group of related functions under one class, which helps us, the programmers, understand the code better.

Nonvirtual Member Functions

Member functions are functions associated with a particular objects. Here, we will only talk about member functions that are not marked as virtual.

```
GameUnit gameUnit;
int nHitPoints = gameUnit.GetHitPoints();
```

This type of function call is very similar to the previous two types. As before, the address of the function to call is determined at link time, because the type of the object it is called from is also known at compile time (but that will change in the case of virtual functions).

The only difference is that member functions refer to a particular object. This is implemented under the hood by having a hidden `this` parameter that points to the object being called. Internally, the function call shown above would be converted to something like this:

```
GameUnit gameUnit;
int nHitPoints = __GameUnitClass__GetHitPoints( &gameUnit );
```

The extra underscores (_) are just a way for the compiler to rename member functions in order to know what class they belong under. This is referred to as "name mangling" and is usually much less attractive than the example above.

What is the extra performance cost when compared to a global function call? The cost is only the extra parameter passing. Most of the time this will mean there is no difference at all, so feel free to use member functions to your heart's content. We will look in more detail at the performance of parameter passing in later in this chapter.

Virtual Functions Under Single Inheritance

Virtual member functions have the potential to be most expensive. (For a detailed explanation of how virtual functions are implemented, both in the case of single and multiple inheritance, refer to Chapters 1 and 2.) Normally, virtual function calls are used when we are using polymorphism on objects they are called on. To continue with the previous example with the `GameUnit` class, we now have a reference of the type `GameUnit`, but it can point to a derived class. `RunAI()` is a virtual member function declared in the `GameUnit` class itself.

```
GameUnit * pGameUnit = new SomeGameUnit;
pGameUnit->RunAI();
```

In this case, calling `RunAI()` will trigger the virtual mechanism, and will incur some extra overhead of dereferencing the vtable (see Chapter 1). The equivalent code shows how the compiler interprets the above call:

```
GameUnit * pGameUnit = new SomeGameUnit;
(pGameUnit->vptr[3])(pGameUnit);
```

In this particular case, `RunAI()` is the third virtual function in the vtable, so the compiler invokes it by accessing the vtable and calling the function in the first slot by doing `this->vptr[3]()`. Notice how an extra parameter gets passed in, pointing to the object the function is acting on, just like with nonvirtual member functions.

The cost of this extra dereferencing varies from platform to platform. Until it becomes an issue by being called thousands of time per frame, it is probably not worth losing much sleep over. As we saw in Chapter 1, if you truly need the functionality of a virtual function, that is about as fast as it is going to get.

Actually, this is not precisely true. Any type of virtual function mechanism is going to require the use of an indirection before making the function call, but what can make the difference is where that indirection happens. Using C++ inheritance, the indirection happens by indexing into the vtable for the class of the object we are making that call on. There is only one vtable per class, and it can be stored anywhere in memory, even far from the object itself. That means that the vtable access could cause a data cache miss, especially if we are calling virtual functions for many different classes, and we are in a platform with a small data cache. This problem is compounded if the platform we are working on has slow memory access whenever there is a cache miss, as is the case with some of the game consoles. In a situation like this, it might be slightly faster to have a custom method where each object stores its own table of function pointers. It is one of those classic memory-space trade-offs, but it can make a difference in some very specific circumstances.

A particularly frustrating aspect of the performance hit, which is caused by vtable cache misses, is that it is extremely difficult to narrow down. The overall slowness will show up in unexpected places in a profiler, and apparently simple loops will seem to take much longer than they should. Making a few changes will simply move the performance hot spots around. If you run into a similar situation and are making extensive use of virtual function calls, you might want to look into this possibility.

Something that you might be wondering is what is the effect of hierarchy size on virtual function call performance. Does a very deep hierarchy mean worse performance? In the case of single inheritance, fortunately the answer is no. Each class has its own vtable; it does not matter how it was derived.

Finally, there is one situation under which virtual function calls will not cost any more than a normal static function call. That will happen whenever a virtual function is invoked directly on the object, not through a pointer or a reference. C++ only supports the concept of polymorphism on references, not objects themselves; so if we make a call to a member function of an object, the compiler will be able to resolve the final address during compilation, bypassing all the virtual function mechanisms at runtime.

In the following example, even though RunAI is a virtual function, it will be invoked just like any nonvirtual member function because it is applied on the object directly.

```
GameUnit gameUnit;
gameUnit.RunAI();
```

On the other hand, the following code shows the same function being called through a pointer to the object. Since the compiler has no way of knowing the true type of the object at runtime, the function call will go through the virtual function lookup.

```
GameUnit * pGameUnit;
pGameUnit->RunAI();
```

Virtual Functions Under Multiple Inheritance

In Chapter 2, we saw how multiple inheritance was implemented—specifically, how the vtable of a class that used multiple inheritance was created by appending the vtables of its parent classes. When it comes time for a virtual function call, the compiler needs to index into the vtable, just like in the case of single inheritance. What is unique about multiple inheritance is that depending on the parent from which we inherited that virtual function, the vtable pointer might need to be offset to point to the correct section. That offsetting will incur a relatively minor performance cost.

Everything else is the same as for single inheritance, even the cache misses due to the vtable lookup. Even though the vtable is composited from its parents' vtables, it is still in one contiguous location in memory.

A class that makes extensive use of multiple inheritance, especially toward the bottom of a large hierarchy tree, could have a very large vtable, since it might inherit a large number of functions from all of its parents. This makes the data cache misses when calling many different virtual functions in the same object somewhat worse, because the vtable is so large that it might result in more cache misses and slower overall performance.

INLINING

Function inlining is a technique that can greatly reduce function over-head in some specific cases. To use it effectively, we must learn how it works and under what situations it is beneficial.

The Need for Inlining

Consider the following code:

```
class GameUnit {
public:
    bool IsActive() const;
    // ....
private:
    bool m_bActive;
};

bool GameUnit::IsActive() const {
    return m_bActive;
}


// .....

if ( gameUnit.IsActive() ) {
    // ....
}
```

To evaluate the `if` statement, we must first make a function call to `GameUnit::IsActive()`, with all the regular costs involved in a member function call. As we saw in the previous section, those costs are fairly small, but the function itself is trivial, so it feels like a waste to have to do all that work for so little payoff. Besides, if we need to call that function several thousand times per frame, all of a sudden that extra overhead starts adding up and eating into the frame rate.

We could make m_bActive a public variable and access it directly. That will certainly avoid any extra performance costs. Unfortunately, that solution will cause more trouble in the long run than it is worth. Some compelling reasons not to have public member variables are the difficulty involved in changing the class implementation when other parts of the code are accessing variables directly, the difficulty of keeping track of how and when certain variables are accessed, and the impossibility of restricting certain variables to read-only access.

Another, even larger practical problem with that approach is what to do when the function does something other than return a member variable. What if the IsActive() function from our example was defined this way:

```
bool IsActive() const { return m_bAlive && m_bRunning };
```

Then things start getting ugly. If we get rid of the function and let other parts of the code access the variables directly, it means we have to expose both m_bAlive and m_bRunning. Whenever any part of the code wants to check whether a game unit is active or not, it has to check both variables. What if later on we decide that IsActive() should be like this instead:

```
bool IsActive() const { return (m_bAlive && m_bRunning) ||
                               m_bSelected };
```

Imagine the nightmare to update all your code everywhere. We should look at other alternatives.

Inline

Instead, we can use *inline* functions. Inlining will have the exact same performance results as accessing the variables directly, with none of the drawbacks. All we have to do is flag a function with the keyword inline, and the compiler will take care of removing the function call and embedding its contents directly into the calling code. Inlining the previous example would look like this:

```
class GameUnit {
public:
    bool IsActive() const;
    // ....
private:
    bool m_bActive;
};

inline bool GameUnit::IsActive() const {
    return m_bActive;
}



// .....

if ( gameUnit.IsActive() ) {
    // ....
}
```

The function call still looks the same, but internally the compiler will substitute the function call with the body of the function itself, like this:

```
if ( gameUnit.m_bActive ) {
    // ....
}
```

All of the costs associated with function calls totally disappear. For small, frequently called function calls, inlining them can be a huge performance boost. This is particularly true of functions whose performance cost is so small that it is comparable to the function call overhead itself.

Using inlining is very straightforward, but there are a few ways it can trip you up. The first way is that for a function to be inlined, it has to be defined in the header file. This is because the compiler only 'sees' the header files we have told it to include for the file it is compiling. If it is going to substitute the body of the function in the calling code, it has to have access to it, and it is not smart enough to open the .cpp file by itself.

There are two ways to declare a function inline and provide its definition in the header file. The definition can be provided right after the declaration:

```
class GameUnit {
 inline bool IsActive() const { return m_bActive };
 // ....
};
```

or the definition can be provided after the function declaration, like we saw in our example. This tends to look neater and is better for functions longer than a single line of code.

```
class GameUnit {
 bool IsActive() const;
 // ....
};

inline bool GameUnit::IsActive() const {
 return m_bActive;
}
```

Be aware that some compilers will refuse to inline functions unless the inline keyword appears both in the declaration and definition of the function. If you are dealing with one of those compilers, you might want to get in the habit of putting the inline keyword in both locations.

The second potential trip-up is that there is no guarantee a function will be actually inlined. The `inline` keyword is nothing more than a hint for the compiler. In the end, the compiler will decide whether to inline it or not. Usually, the simpler the function, the more likely it will be inlined. As soon as the function becomes longer, makes calls to other functions, or has complex loops or operations, chances are the compiler will refuse to inline it. You cannot even rely on the inlining behavior being consistent across different platforms, since different compilers have different rules about inlining.

It would be nice to get a warning or an error if a function marked as inline does not get inlined. Unfortunately, we have no such luck. Most compilers will silently ignore the `inline` keyword if they cannot comply with it. The ways you can tell if an inline worked is by noticing the improved performance or by looking at the disassembly of the generated code. This is not the most convenient way, but it might be worth the effort to verify that some particularly crucial section of the code is indeed being inlined.

When to Use Inline

So, why not use inlining all the time? Ironically, that could easily degrade the game's performance instead of improving it. As if that were not bad enough, there are other reasons why indiscriminate inlining can be problematic. Let's start with performance—since, after all, that is what this chapter is about.

At first, the idea of inlining every function sounds good. After all, it means we can get rid of all the function call overhead. The first problem is that the size of the executable would skyrocket out of control, because every part of the code that calls a function would duplicate that function's code. Apart from consuming more memory, it will result in very poor use of the code cache, resulting in constant cache thrashing and significantly lowering the program's performance.

The other main reason why indiscriminate inlining is a bad idea has to do with the location of the function definition. We saw earlier that for a function to be inlined, its definition has to be present in the header file. That means that include statements that could otherwise be in the .cpp file have to be moved to the .h file, which results in longer compile times. This might not be a big deal for one, two, or a few files. But if done on a consistent basis across a project with thousands of source files, it can exponentially increase compile times (see Chapter 15, Dealing with Large Projects, for more information).

Then what is the best way to use inline? Avoid inlining while you are developing code; then, when that code is mostly complete, profile the program and see if any small functions appear toward the top of the most-called functions. Those will be great candidates to inline, and you should see immediate performance improvements as a result.

There will be times when we know right from the beginning that a function should be inlined. For example, some of the functions in a Point class, where the operations are almost trivial and the performance is critical, might be perfect targets for inlining. Go ahead and inline those functions right away; just do not get in the habit of inlining everything.

Die-hard C programmers will often ask: "What the difference is between inline functions and macros?" After all, the preprocessor will always expand a macro, unlike an inline function, which is left to the mercy of the compiler. The main advantage of inlining is that it will still provide the same amount of type checking as a normal function, while a macro has no type checking whatsoever. That is quite important for catching potential errors right away at compile time. Inline functions are also easier to debug and step into in the debugger; they also mesh a lot better with classes, since they can be part of a class and access all its private and protected members, while a macro has no intrinsic knowledge about classes at all.

There might come a time when we are sure that inlining a function would result in a net performance gain, yet the compiler steadfastly refuses to inline it. In that case, we can fall back on the use of a simple macro with the contents of the function we were trying to inline. It might not be pretty, but at least the macro is not going to refuse to do its job.

MORE FUNCTION OVERHEAD

The overhead introduced by functions does not end with the actual function call. The parameters we pass to them and their return values can greatly affect the performance of a function.

Function Parameters

The most important thing to remember when dealing with function parameters is to never pass an expensive object by value. Doing so will cause a temporary copy of the object to be created, which is potentially a very expensive operation. (We will deal with temporaries later on in this chapter.) Unless we are really confident about the small size of an object, we should always pass objects by reference.

The following function takes a matrix and updates the bounding volumes for that node. This code will work just fine, but it will be slower than it should be:

```
// Slow version of the function
void SceneNode::UpdateBV (Matrix mat) {
    m_BV.Rotate (mat);
    // ...
}
```

Instead, we could rewrite it to take a reference, and we will get the same functionality, but much better performance:

```
// Much faster version of the same function
void SceneNode::UpdateBV ( const Matrix & mat ) {
    m_BV.Rotate (mat);
    // ...
}
```

Notice that not only did we change the matrix to a reference, but we made it into a const reference. The reason for this is because the function is not supposed to change the matrix object passed to it. Specifying the reference to be constant enforces that restriction at compile time, so any attempts to modify it will result in a compile error. We saw that in detail in Chapter 3.

Very small objects or basic data types do not need to be passed by reference. It can depend on the platform, but with most current hardware, a reference or a pointer is 32 bits. There is usually no reason to pass anything of that size or smaller by reference, unless it has particularly expensive constructors or destructors.

Assuming that all the parameters are basic data types or that we are passing any larger objects by reference, is there a penalty for passing many parameters to a function? The answer is usually yes, but the penalty is fairly small, and the specifics depend on the platform and compiler.

Usually, compilers will try to put as many parameters as possible into CPU registers so they can be accessed directly in the called function. Some CPUs have a large number of registers, so this is usually not a limiting factor. However, in other architectures, like PCs, it is only possible to fit so many parameters before we run out of unused registers, so the rest are put in the stack. Doing so means copying them to the stack memory location, and retrieving them from the called function when they are needed. This is by no means a large overhead (as long as the objects are passed by reference), and the stack is in the data cache, since it is used so frequently, so this is usually not something that will cause performance to degrade significantly.

However, the most important lesson to be learned from parameter passing does not involve performance; rather, it involves people. A computer does not care how many parameters we pass to a function. As we saw, the computer will simply put them in the stack when they do not fit in registers. People are not as fortunate, and there are only so many things we can juggle in our minds at once. As a rule of thumb, if you ever find yourself writing a function that takes more than five to seven parameters, you should really consider if there is another, better way of writing it. You will be glad you did it when that part of the program needs to be changed or debugged in a few months. Chances are, we can encapsulate some data into a new class or structure and make the program a lot clearer. It will even be a tiny bit faster. For once, clarity and performance are not at odds with each other, so there is no reason not to do it.

Return Values

Returning a basic data type, like an integer or a float, is usually 'free.' Again, this depends on the platform, compiler, and calling convention, but typically, the `return` value will be copied to a register and checked by the calling code.

References and pointers will usually be treated the same way. So as long as we need to return objects that already exist somewhere in the code, references to existing objects are one of the most efficient ways to go. Just remember never to return a reference or pointer to an object that was created in the stack, because it will not be there when the function returns. Fortunately, most compilers are able to detect this at compile time and issue a warning. The following code makes good use of returning references (especially if the function is marked as inline):

```
const Matrix & SceneNode::GetMatrix () const {
    return m_matrix;
}
```

But what about when we need to return an object that does not exist already? Then we have three options:

- Return a copy of the object.
- Create an object outside the function, pass it as a non-const reference, and fill it inside the function.
- Dynamically allocate the object inside the called function and return a pointer to it.

The third option will always be very efficient as far as `return` values are concerned, but it has several major drawbacks. The main problem is that it will dynamically allocate an object. That in itself is not a bad thing, but it can be a serious drawback in a performance-intensive function. Also, if done very frequently, it can seriously affect the memory heap, leading to fragmentation and loss of performance. There are ways to avoid this situation, as we will see in detail in Chapter 7, Memory Allocation.

Another major problem is that the third option, as it stands, is not a very safe solution. It requires the function to dynamically allocate the object and return a pointer to it to the caller, and it is then up to the caller to deal with the object correctly (e.g., free it, store it, etc.). This can become a serious maintenance headache later on.

The cleanest and simplest option is the first one. Unfortunately the second option can be much more efficient. If both solutions were just as fast, returning a copy of the object would make things more consistent. That way we could always return all the objects directly from a function, independently of their size. As it is we have to do different things, depending on the internal implementation of the class we are calling, which is less than ideal from a software engineering point of view, but sometimes we have to make small concessions to get big performance gains.

This is how the `GetMatrix()` function would look if we did not have a matrix already in the `SceneNode` object and needed to return it from the function:

```
void SceneNode::GetMatrix (Matrix & matrix) const {
    // This object has a rotation object, but not a matrix, so
    // we need to fill the one that gets passed in.
    m_rotation.ToMatrix (matrix);
}
```

If it returned a copy of the matrix, we might incur an extra copy and a performance penalty:

```
// This code is potentially much slower
Matrix SceneNode::GetMatrix () const {
    return m_rotation.GetMatrix();
}
```

This second version is cleaner looking and more consistent with returning objects by reference, but it is potentially slower because of what the compiler does with it. A well-optimizing compiler will internally convert the second version into something that looks like the first version. So we still get the cleanest syntax, but also the best performance. That optimization is called *return value optimization* (RVO). Check your compiler's documentation to find out whether or not it supports RVO. RVO is a fairly common optimization these days, so chances are it will be supported.

There are two types of `return` value optimizations: named and unnamed. The easiest one for compilers to implement is the unnamed one, which we saw in the previous example. The `return` value is just a temporary (i.e., an unnamed variable), and the compiler creates and assigns it directly into the object that gets the `return` value from the function.

Named return value optimization is a bit trickier for the compiler to support. It works just like the unnamed return value optimization, but with an actual named variable, not just a temporary. For this optimization to work, all `return` paths of the function must return the same value. The following is a function where the compiler could apply named return value optimization:

```
Matrix SceneNode::GetTransformedMatrix () const {
    Matrix mat = m_matrix;
    if (m_pParent != NULL) {
        mat.Concatenate(m_pParent->GetMatrix());
    }
```

```
        return mat;
    }
```

As usual when dealing with optimizations, you should also take into consideration how efficient the function needs to be. If we are talking about returning a `Point3d` object (which would be just three floats), and the function is hardly ever called, then returning a copy of the object is a perfectly good approach. If the function gets called in an inner loop many times per frame, unless we know for a fact that our compiler will perform the return value optimization, then it is worth the extra inconvenience of passing in a non-`const` reference to be filled in by the function in order to save a few precious CPU cycles.

Empty Functions

At first it might seem an odd thing to talk about the performance of completely empty, useless functions. Why would anybody write such functions? Surprisingly, they are not as uncommon as we might expect.

Sometimes development teams have a set of templates that create the code for a new class from scratch. In that template, a function might be declared and implemented with an empty body for convenience and in order to save some typing later on. At other times, a macro is used to give a class certain behavior, and it too might contain empty functions.

Will the compiler get rid of them? As usual, it depends. Sometimes the compiler will get rid of them, but that is often not the case. Typically, unless the empty function is inlined, the compiler will have no way to know it is empty and will leave it untouched. Any calls to that function will go through all the motions of putting the parameters in registers and the stack, dereferencing the vtable if it is a virtual function, calling its address, and returning. All of that for nothing.

The obvious advice is, do not do it. There is usually no good reason to have empty functions. If we are creating a skeleton class for some people to fill later, we should consider using pure virtual functions. That way we set up the interface, and by flagging the functions as pure virtual, we force the programmers who flesh out the class to create an implementation for those particular functions.

Another common mistake is to provide almost empty functions in a class hierarchy, whose only function is to call the equivalent parent class function (which in turn is empty, except for a call to its parent's class, all the way to the root). The mechanics of virtual functions will already do that for us by calling the closest implemented function from a parent class if that function has not been overridden. They will also do it much more efficiently, avoiding a whole chain of calls every time a virtual function is called. Not only that, but adding those functions everywhere makes it much more difficult to change the interface of that function at a later time, since it involves going into every single class file and changing the source code there.

AVOIDING COPIES

Do not copy objects unless you have to. This may sound obvious, but it crops up surprisingly often. Things are not helped by the fact that C++ tends to copy objects behind your back as soon as you are not paying close attention.

Unlike in C, the consequences for copying an object can be quite unexpected. Creating a new object from an existing one will call its copy constructor, which will often call the copy constructors for the objects it contains, and so on down the line. All of a sudden, copying that object does not seem like such a great idea.

Arguments

The first thing to do to address this problem is to use `const` references when passing objects to and from functions whenever we can. That way, the syntax is the same as for passing an object by value, but we avoid any performance hits for extra copies. For example, we want to avoid declaring a function like this:

```
bool SetActiveCamera (Camera camera);
```

Instead, we want to declare it like this:

```
bool SetActiveCamera (const Camera & camera);
```

The `const` part is not necessary in order to avoid the extra copy; it is simply there to indicate that the camera object we passed in should not be modified by the `SetActiveCamera` function.

Temporaries

The next thing to do is to watch out for temporaries. Temporaries are objects created by the compiler without any explicit instructions in the code to do so. These can be hard to catch unless you are familiar with the rules for creating temporaries. Also, because the creation of temporaries can happen extremely often, it has the potential to dramatically affect the overall game performance.

We have already seen a place where a temporary is generated under the hood—the passing of arguments by value. Nowhere in the code there is an explicit copy of the object being made, yet one will be created silently.

A fairly common and hard-to-catch type of temporary is the one caused by type mismatch. Consider the following piece of code:

```
void SetRotation (const Rotation & rot);

float fDegrees = 90.0f;
SetRotation (fDegrees); // Rotate unit 90 degrees
```

Everything looks fine, and it compiles and works as expected. But what is happening under the hood? After all, the SetRotation function does not take a float as a parameter. Looking closely at the Rotation class, we notice some of its constructors:

```
class Rotation {
public:
    Rotation ();
    Rotation (float fHeading, float fPitch = 0.0f,
            float fRoll = 0.0f);
    // ....
};
```

Things start becoming clearer. The compiler is trying to be helpful. Since it detected that we are passing a float to a function that takes a Rotation reference, and it knows that it is possible to create a Rotation object from a float, it went ahead and did that for us. That is a perfect example of a hidden temporary.

This is one of those features that is rarely helpful in game development. Maybe in a few specific cases it will come in handy and save a bit of typing, but most of the time it just gets in the way. Chances are the caller of that function did not want to pay the associated cost with creating an extra Rotation object. Maybe if the code had been more explicit about the costs, the programmer could have chosen a different, cheaper function instead.

Being Explicit

Fortunately, C++ provides a feature to disable those type conversions. We can flag certain constructors as `explicit`. If we did that with the `Rotation` class, it would look like this:

```
class Rotation {
public:
    Rotation ();
    explicit Rotation (float fHeading, float fPitch = 0.0f,
                       float fRoll = 0.0f);
    // ....
};
```

That means that the previous code calling `SetRotation` with a `float` will result in a compile-time error. If we still want to go ahead and construct a `Rotation` object, we can do it explicitly like this:

```
float fDegrees = 90.0f;
SetRotation (Rotation(fDegrees)); // Rotate unit 90 degrees
```

The resulting code is going to be exactly like the first version, but this time the temporary is explicit in the code. Anybody reading over this section of code will be aware of the object that is being constructed and passed along.

Disallowing Copies

In game development, we will usually have many classes that are not intended to be copied. This is different than other types of software development where the flexibility provided by copying objects outweighs the possible performance implications. For these types of objects, we would like to be warned right away if anybody tries to copy them, even if it is the compiler through the creation of a temporary object. A very useful technique for these classes is to provide a private declaration for a copy constructor and an assignment operator, but not provide a definition. That results in perfectly legal C++ code that will compile and run correctly. However, as soon as anybody tries to copy an object of that type, it will result in a compile (or link) error. That way, the code that attempted the copy can be changed right away.

For example, if we have a geometry mesh that we do not want easily copied around because requires some expensive object creation (probably a smart decision), the code would look like this:

```
class GeomMesh {
public:
    // ....
private:
    // Private copy constructor and assignment op to avoid
    // copies
    GeomMesh ( const GeomMesh & mesh );
    GeomMesh & operator= ( const GeomMesh & mesh );
};
```

This is an invaluable technique for catching potential performance drains early on. The beautiful thing about it is that having those functions declared does not incur any extra cost, so it is a perfectly safe solution. It is so useful that you might want to consider putting it in all your classes by default. If later you need to create a class with a real copy constructor and assignment operator, make them public and provide the appropriate implementation, or comment them out all together and use the default C++ copy constructor and assignment operator.

Allowing Copies

Sometimes we need to copy objects around. There's nothing wrong with that as long as we're aware of the performance implications. The smaller and 'simpler' the object it is, the safer it is to copy it around. A simpler object is one that contains fewer nonbasic data types than another object. Still, we might be concerned with the potential for unwanted temporaries that happen without us knowing it if we just create a normal copy constructor and assignment operator.

A good alternative that still provides us the ability to copy an object is to create copy functions by hand. Usually, we want to have two separate functions: Clone, which just makes a new instance of the same object, and Copy, which copies the contents.

```
class GeomMesh {
public:
    // ....
```

```
        GeomMesh & Clone () const;
        void Copy ( const GeomMesh & mesh );
private:
        // Private copy constructor and assignment op to avoid
        // copies
        GeomMesh ( const GeomMesh & mesh );
        GeomMesh & operator= ( const GeomMesh & mesh );
};

GeomMesh & GeomMesh::Clone () const {
        GeomMesh * pMesh = new GeomMesh();
        pMesh->Copy (*this);
        return *pMesh;
}

void GeomMesh::Copy (const GeomMesh & mesh) {
        // Do the actual copying here
}


// To use it we just call Clone
GeomMesh * pNewMesh = pMesh->Clone();
```

Finally, keep in mind that there will be times when leaving the default copy constructor and assignment operator, or writing your own is going to be perfectly fine. Plain structures are perfect candidates for this architecture, as well as very simple, basic classes, like vectors or points.

Operator Overloading

Operator overloading is one of those C++ features that people tend to either love or hate. There are good reasons for both, but this is not the point of this section. The point is to highlight one of the potential dangers of a specific type of operator overloading.

The type of operator overloading that has some potential performance implications is the one that returns an object of the type it had worked on, usually binary operators. For example, operator+() is one of those operators. Consider the following code:

```
Vector3d velocity = oldVelocity + frameIncrement;
Vector3d propulsion = ComputePropulsion();
Vector3d finalVelocity = velocity + propulsion;
```

Vector3d clearly has the `operator+()` function overloaded to add two 3D vectors. The code looks clean and straightforward. Unfortunately, there is a hidden temporary in the last line. So `operator+()` is probably implemented like this:

```
const Vector3d operator+ (const Vector3d & v1,
                          const Vector3d & v2) {
    return Vector3d (v1.x+v2.x, v1.y+v2.y, v1.z+v2.z);
}
```

Notice that the `return` type of the operator is not a reference or a pointer, but an object itself. That means that the compiler will first create a temporary object, load it with the result of the function, and then copy it into the variable `finalVelocity`.

In this case it might not be a big deal. After all, the `Vector3d` class is probably fairly lightweight, and copying it a few times is not going to slow things down much. That may be true, but the class might be copied more often than we think. What if that code were executed to update the particles in a particle effect system? Then it would probably get executed many thousands of times per frame, which might begin to make a difference. Also, `operator+()` might be defined for other heavier classes, like a matrix, rotation, or a game object.

The good news is that there is a way around it that still allows us to use operator overloading, yet does not incur in any extra performance overhead. The solution is to replace binary operators of the form `operator+()` with unary operators of the form `operator+=()`. The latter type of operator acts directly on the object that it was invoked on, so there is no extra copying of temporaries. The definition of operator `+=()` is:

```
Vector3d & Vector3d::operator+= (const Vector3d & v) {
    x += v.x; y += v.y; z += v.z;
    return *this;
}
```

Notice how we are not copying any objects; we are just returning a reference to the object the function acted upon (by dereferencing the `this` pointer). The code that uses it would then look like this:

```
Vector3d velocity = oldVelocity + frameIncrement;
Vector3d propulsion = ComputePropulsion();
Vector3d finalVelocity = velocity;
finalVelocity += propulsion;
```

or, even better:

```
Vector3d velocity = oldVelocity + frameIncrement;
velocity += ComputePropulsion();
```

It is possible for the compiler to optimize out some of the temporaries generated when using binary operators; it is a very similar process to the return value optimization. In that case, the performance of binary and unary operators might be similar. If you prefer to use binary operators, check to verify what optimizations the compiler is doing so you do not get a surprise later on in the project.

CONSTRUCTORS AND DESTRUCTORS

Constructors and their counterparts, destructors, are extremely useful features of C++. They take care of initializing or destroying objects automatically, which greatly simplifies the code and reduces potential for bugs.

However, like all automatic procedures, sometimes they might do things you do not want, you do not expect, or that you simply do not remember. As with many other C++ features, having a good understanding of what is going on underneath will help you avoid major performance hits.

As a quick review, consider the classes with the inheritance chain shown in Figure 6.2.

This is a simplified version of the sequence of calls when an object of type C gets created:

- The new function gets called to allocate memory for the object.
- The constructor for A gets called.
- The constructor for B gets called.
- The constructor for C gets called.

In addition to each constructor being called, if class A, B, or C contain any objects, then their constructors and all their parents' constructors will also be called. The destruction sequence is similar, but in reverse:

- The destructor for C gets called.
- The destructor for B gets called.
- The destructor for A gets called.
- Memory gets freed by calling the delete function.

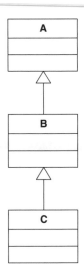

FIGURE 6.2   Simple class hierarchy with single inheritance.

Again, any objects contained in those classes will be destroyed in turn. What this means is that constructors and destructors have the potential to be very expensive by triggering a long chain of function calls. It is up to us to be aware of the cost associated with each object and avoid creating them many times in performance-critical sections.

However, C++ was created with performance in mind, and one of the overriding design goals of the language is that we should only pay for the things we want to use. For example, notice that member variables in an object are not automatically initialized to some default value when the object is created; it is up to us to set them to some appropriate value if we care. Sometimes that is an annoyance, but it is the price we pay for performance. This allows the compiler to avoid generating a constructor (or destructor) altogether if there is no need for one.

There will only be a constructor or destructor call if we explicitly create one, or if the object contains other objects that have a constructor or destructor themselves. Also, if a class belongs to some inheritance chain, and the class itself does not have a constructor, that constructor call is skipped completely during the object creation, and the constructor for its child is called instead. The same principle applies for destructors.

However, constructors and destructors are extremely useful. Avoid unnecessary ones in performance-critical classes, but do not get rid of them when you need them. If they were doing useful work that needed to be done, we would probably not get any performance improvement by using an initialization function for the same task.

One simple approach to reduce the call overhead of constructors and destructors is to inline them. Constructors and destructors are like any other function in many aspects, and inlining them works beautifully. Be aware, though, that only very simple ones will be inlined, and if they are part of an inheritance chain, most compilers will have a really hard time trying to inline them. Also, in the case of destructors, any class that has a destructor and is part of an inheritance chain should have a virtual destructor in order to make inlining of the destructor very difficult or even impossible.

Another technique to reduce the overhead of constructors is to use initialization lists. One of the typical functions of a constructor is to set member variables to some default values, or perhaps to the values that were passed as parameters to the constructor. This is the way it would be done in any normal function:

```
// Inefficient SceneNode's default constructor
SceneNode::SceneNode () {
    m_strName = "Scene node";
    m_position = g_worldOrigin;
    m_rotMatrix.SetUnit();
}
```

This will clearly work, but it is also inefficient in the case of a constructor. A better way of doing it would be to use *initialization lists*. This is a feature only available in the constructor; it allows us to call the constructor for each member object with specific parameters. Doing so avoids wasting a call to the default constructor for an object and then changing its state again.

In the example above, the variable m_strName is of the type string. Before the first line of that constructor is executed, m_strName is initialized to an empty string, maybe even causing some dynamic memory allocations. Then as soon as the first line of the constructor is executed, it is replaced with a different string. Clearly, whatever was done as part of the string's default constructor was wasted time. The same thing applies to the point m_position and the matrix m_rotMatrix. A more efficient way of writing the above constructor is as follows:

```
// Better SceneNode's default constructor
SceneNode::SceneNode () :
    m_strName("Scene node"),
```

```
        m_position(g_worldOrigin),
        m_rotMatrix(Matrix::Unit)
    {}
```

In this case, all the initialization happens only once as the objects are constructed and initialized. Notice that the code assumes that this particular matrix class has a constructor that will generate a unit matrix (probably not a bad idea). This is not always going to be the case, though; sometimes there is work that needs to be done in the constructor that cannot be done as part of the initialization list because it cannot be performed as a constructor call for the object being initialized. In that case, the best thing is to leave the object completely uninitialized in the initialization list and then initialize it in the constructor body.

In the example above, imagine that the Matrix class cannot be set to a unit Matrix through its constructor. Then, the next best thing to do is to prevent it from doing any work in its constructor, and then set it to a unit Matrix by hand.

```
// SceneNode's default constructor
SceneNode::SceneNode ( void ) :
    m_strName("Scene node"),
    m_position(g_worldOrigin)
{
    m_rotMatrix.SetUnit();
}
```

By not calling any specific constructor on the Matrix object, the default constructor is called automatically. Hopefully, the default constructor for that Matrix class does nothing, and leaves all the values uninitialized. Having default constructors that avoid doing expensive initializations can sometimes be very useful for high-performance classes that get created frequently.

Finally, even when the constructor cannot be made any faster, it might still be possible to make the overall program faster. Do not call the constructor unless you absolutely have to. This may sound simple, but for programmers coming from many years of C, it can take some getting used to. All it requires is to delay the declaration of the object until it is actually needed. Consider the following code:

```
void GameAI::UpdateState () {
    AIState nextState;

    if ( IsIdle() ) {
```

```
                nextState = GetNextAIState();
                // ...
            }
            else {
                ExecuteCurrentState();
            }
        }
```

Unless `AIState` is a trivial object, its default constructor and its destructor will get executed every time the function is called. Considering that this function is probably called once per frame for every game AI in the world, the cost quickly becomes very noticeable. To make things worse, most of the time the AIs will probably not be idle, so the `nextState` local variable is not used the majority of the time. To avoid paying for its costs when we are not using it, we just need to defer the declaration of the variable until we need it:

```
        void GameAI::UpdateState ( void ) {
            if ( IsIdle() ) {
             AIState nextState = GetNextAIState();
             // ...
            }
            else {
             ExecuteCurrentState();
            }
        }
```

Even if `AIState` were just a structure without any constructors, it would still be better to declare it right before it is used. `AIState` might change over time and become an expensive object. Since there is no drawback to delaying its declaration as much as possible, we might as well do it right from the beginning. Additionally, not only is the new version of the code faster, but it is easier to read, since the type of the variable is declared near where it is used. You might want to consider getting in the habit of declaring all of your local variables that way, even simple data types like `int` or `float`.

DATA CACHES AND MEMORY ALIGNMENT (ADVANCED)

Memory alignment can play a crucial role in most modern hardware architectures. CPU speeds keep getting faster and faster, but memory speeds are not increasing at the same rate. This means that the gap between what a CPU can theoretically do and what it does when paired up with slower memory is increasing. This pattern is not likely to change any time soon, so it is a problem we will have to keep dealing with in the foreseeable future.

Ideally, we would like our CPU to be always running at maximum capacity, without being slowed down by memory at all. That is what *memory caches* do. A memory cache is a small but very fast memory, much faster than the main memory for the system, where recently used data and code is stored. This works because most programs do not access data and code uniformly. The rough rule of thumb is that a program spends 90% of its time in 10% of the code; this is called the *principle of locality*.

Some architectures will even have more that one cache level, each of them of increasing size and lower speed. This is called a memory hierarchy, and it helps keep the CPU running as fast as possible under most normal usage.

Caches are often divided into data caches and code caches. Here we will concentrate only on data caches, since those are the ones we have more control over and are the ones that can net us some significant performance gains.

Caches, by definition, are small, so they cannot hold all the data that the CPU needs to use during program execution. The ideal case is when the CPU needs to use some data that is already in the cache. Then the data can be read right away, and the CPU does not have to wait long. On the other hand, whenever some data is needed that is not in the cache, a *cache miss* occurs, and the CPU has to wait for several cycles while the data is fetched from the slower main memory. The faster the CPU and the slower the main memory, the more cycles it will have to wait, causing all the programs to halt until the data is retrieved. This is a situation we want to avoid as much as possible.

As an example, consider the following situation: a three-gigahertz CPU is humming along at full speed. Whenever it fetches some data from the fastest cache, it is just one CPU cycle. All of a sudden, it needs a piece of data that is not in any of the caches, so it has to wait for a full main memory access.

With some of the fastest memory available today, it takes six memory cycles to fetch a cache line from main memory. However, even with memory buses running at 512 MHz, the CPU will still have to wait about 36 CPU cycles. Using faster processors or slower memory will make things even worse. So, code that looks like just an innocent access to a variable can cause a major stall and be 36 times slower than another part of the code that looks exactly the same, but which is able to find its data in the cache. Fortunately, we can adapt our program to be as cache-friendly as possible and minimize the number of cache misses.

Memory Access Patterns

The first technique we can apply is to change our access pattern to the program's data. Take for example the updating of all game entities for one frame. Normally, we want to give each entity the opportunity to update its state and run any logic it needs to.

A very cache-unfriendly way of doing it would be to randomly traverse all the entities once we figure out which ones need to execute. Then, as a second step, execute all those entities, and finally do another pass over all the entities again. In this scenario, the first step consisted of traversing all entities. Since we have a few thousand game entities, there is no way they can fit in the lowest-level cache; so it is normal that every time we come to a new entity, we cause a cache miss. There is nothing we can do about that. However, what makes this approach very inefficient is that we then make a second and a third pass over the entities. This means that we are going to incur a second and third cache miss for every entity again.

A much better approach would be to do everything we need to do to each entity in one pass. That way we cause a cache miss, we do all the updating and anything else on that entity, and we move on to the next one. The difference in performance between the two approaches can be a huge one.

Be careful with this technique, however. It is one of those optimization techniques that requires a major organizational change. This is not a matter of rewriting a small loop in assembly; this could potentially require that we rethink our algorithms and change the sequence of events inside our game loop. We might also sacrifice some encapsulation and clarity for performance, but that is a common tradeoff for a lot of optimizations.

The best approach is to avoid doing multiple passes over large sets of data when one pass suffices from the very beginning, but not to obsess about memory access patterns until later on in the project. It is much more important to get the code working correctly, and to have it clear and easy to change, than to have some very efficient, but incorrect and flaky code. Later in the project, if some loop shows up as being particularly slow, and you suspect multiple cache misses, it is probably worth looking into restructuring how the code accesses memory in order to improve performance.

Object Size

One thing we did not mention when talking about memory caches is the granularity of the data in a cache. Caches are typically organized in *cache lines*, which are the smallest units of memory that can be cached in and out independently. They will clearly vary from architecture to architecture, so you should find out what they are for your target platform. In the case of most PCs, a cache line is 32 bytes.

What this means is that if we ever need to fetch a single byte that is not in the cache, we are also going to get the corresponding 32 bytes for that cache line for free. This has some important implications for our code.

First of all, for objects that we expect to have hundreds or thousands of, and which need to be processed extremely efficiently, we would like to keep their sizes at 32 bytes, or if they have to be larger, a multiple of 32 bytes. That way, accessing any part of the object will only use up one or two cache lines.

A perfect example of an object that fits this description are particles in a particle system. We are expected to deal with thousands of particles, and we need to touch and update every single one of them in every frame. If we manage to squeeze a particle into 32 bytes, we might obtain much better performance than if it were 100 bytes.

Member Variable Location

Not only size is important, but the location of the most accessed elements is also important. A data cache knows nothing of C++ objects; it only knows about the addresses of the memory we have requested and cache line sizes. That means that even if our particle objects were 100 bytes, as long as we only update their first 32 bytes, we should only cause one cache hit per particle. So in cases like that, it is definitely worthwhile to rearrange the member variables of a class so that the most commonly used ones are at the top.

Also, remember that an object that has virtual functions will have a vtable, which is usually a pointer at the very beginning of the object. If we make any virtual function calls, we will have to access the vtable pointer, which will bring the first 32 bytes of the object into the cache. That is one of the reasons why we want to put the frequently accessed variables at the top and not in some other place in the object.

Member variables are ordered in memory in the exact same order they are specified in the class declaration, so to move a particular variable toward the top, just declare it before the other member variables.

Memory Alignment

If a cache line is 32 bytes, as we have been assuming so far, it will not pull in just any 32 bytes from memory. Those 32 bytes will have to be aligned on a 32-byte boundary address. This means that the beginning of each cache line will always map to an address that is a multiple of 32 bytes. As an example, if we request the contents at memory location 0xC00024, the cache line will be filled with the data from 0xC00020 to 0xC0003F.

Again, this has very important implications for how we lay out our objects. Imagine the following disastrous situation. We have 1,000 particle objects that need to be updated this frame, and each object is 32 bytes. This sounds like an ideal situation for our data cache. Every time we access an object, we should just have one cache miss, since it fits nicely in one cache line.

Here is the big problem: the particle objects have been allocated in memory carelessly, so they are not guaranteed to start in a 32-byte boundary. What does that mean for us from a performance point of view?

If a 32-byte object is not aligned on a 32-byte boundary, to access all its variables will cause two cache misses, and it will take up two full cache lines. So even though the object size has not changed, because of its alignment in memory, it will become twice as expensive.

Sometimes compilers will try to align things correctly for us, but we might have to turn on specific compiler options about memory alignment. Otherwise, dynamic memory allocations might only be four-byte aligned, with potentially terrible performance consequences. Memory alignment of dynamic memory allocations is something we also need to be aware of if we end up using our own memory allocation strategy, as will be described in Chapter 7.

When objects are allocated in the stack, we have even less control over their alignment. They will usually be added to the top of the stack without any consideration as to whether they start at a 32-byte boundary or not. Dynamic allocation is a better alternative for objects for which we want to guarantee certain alignment.

Memory alignment also influences the ideal size of an object. An object that is 40 bytes in size (which sounds like a nice, round number) could cause a total disaster if we create an array of them. Unless the compiler intercedes and pads the objects for us, the beginning of each object will not be at a 32-byte boundary, causing more cache misses than necessary. In a situation like this, we might want to pad our own objects to become a multiple of 32 bytes, so that whenever they are allocated in contiguous memory, they are all aligned on a 32-byte boundary.

Memory alignment is a crucial aspect of high-performance programming. Every time we look into data cache optimizations, we should verify that the alignment of our objects is optimal.

CONCLUSION

In this chapter, we have seen what some of the most common C++ performance issues are and have presented ways to incur those performance hits only when we absolutely need to, or even to bypass them completely. First we saw all the different types of function calls that C++ offers, what the performance implications of each type were, and when each should be utilized. Then we saw how to minimize the overhead of small functions by using the inlining optimization. Other aspects of function overhead, such as parameter passing and `return` values, were also examined.

We then saw how there are some situations under which C++ will silently create temporary objects that might be cost us some performance without us ever being aware of it. We also examined the role of constructors and destructors, and their potential performance implications. Finally, we covered an important topic for high-performance games: the effects of the data cache, and what we can do in our program to be as cache-friendly as possible.

SUGGESTED READING

There is a large amount of material written about C++ performance. These books cover some aspects of C++ performance in detail, such as when temporaries are generated, the constructor call sequence, and the effects of different function calls.

Meyers, Scott, *More Effective C++*, Addison-Wesley, 1995.

Meyers, Scott, *Effective C++*, 2nd ed., Addison-Wesley, 1997.

Bulka, Dov, and David Mayhew, *Efficient C++*, Addison-Wesley, 2000.

Pedriana, Paul, "High Performance Game Programming in C++," *Conference Proceedings*, 1998 Game Developers Conference.

Isensee, Pete, *C++ Optimization Strategies and Techniques*, http://www.tantalon.com/pete/cppopt/main.htm.

Here are some specific references on return value optimization:

Meyers, Scott, *More Effective C++*, Addison-Wesley, 1995.

Lippman, Stanley B., and Josee Lajoie, *C++ Primer*, 3rd ed., Addison-Wesley, 1998.

Lippman, Stanley B., *Inside the C++ Object Model*, Addison-Wesley, 1996.

The following is a great, in-depth book about computer architecture, with a superb section on data caches and memory hierarchies.

Hennessy, John L., and David A. Patterson, *Computer Architecture: A Quantitative Approach*, 2nd ed., Morgan Kaufmann, 1996.

CHAPTER

7

MEMORY ALLOCATION

IN THIS CHAPTER

- The Stack
- The Heap
- Static Allocation
- Dynamic Allocation
- Custom Memory Manager
- Memory Pools
- In Case of Emergency...

ost C++ programs need to create new objects and allocate new memory during program execution. Applications have the choice of stack-based allocation or heap-based allocation. Each type of allocation has its own characteristics of how objects can be allocated, and what their lifetimes are.

As normal application developers, that is all we need to know. As developers of high-performance applications such as games or high-load servers, we need to pay much more attention to this problem. This chapter deals with the performance problems associated with heap allocation and suggests some possible solutions and tricks that are often used in games to alleviate those problems.

We will see how, by giving up on some flexibility, we can restrict ourselves to static allocations and bypass all the associated problems with dynamic allocation. We will also see how to make effective use of full dynamic memory allocation at runtime, and still be able to keep a good idea of what memory is allocated. Finally, we will see how memory pools can help us use dynamic memory allocation with minimal runtime cost, and avoid most of the inherent problems of the heap.

THE STACK

When programs need to create new objects during program execution, if these objects are only going to be used temporarily in a limited scope, sometimes it is enough to create them on the *stack*. The arguments passed to a function, or the variables declared local within a function, are all created on the stack.

The stack is a pretty nice place. Things are always added at the bottom (or top if your particular implementation grows upward), and they are always removed in the opposite order they were added. Since the stack has a limited size, trying to push too many objects onto it will result in a stack overflow exception or some other error. Fortunately, we have control over the size of the stack when we compile our program, and we can always increase it if stack use is heavy and we run out of room. The memory address to return to from the current function is also stored in the stack, so if some of the memory there were to get corrupted or overwritten, our program would be left stranded, not knowing how to go back. Other than that, there really are not many things that can go wrong with the stack.

Figure 7.1 shows an image of the stack before any allocations (a) and after a lot of allocations and deallocations (b).

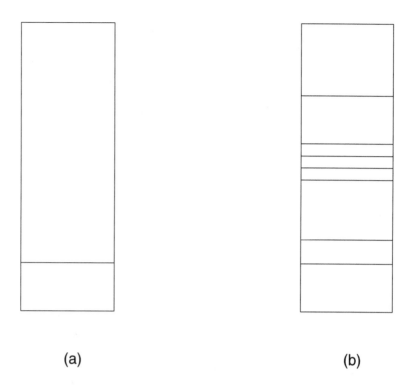

(a)   (b)

FIGURE 7.1   Image of the stack (a) before any allocations and (b) after a lot of allocations and deallocations.

Unfortunately, the stack often does not meet our needs. When we need to create a new object, but its use is not temporary or limited in scope, we need to allocate it in a different way. This is done in the heap. Memory is allocated in the heap through the use of `new` or `alloc`, and removed from it through their respective calls, `delete` and `free`.

THE HEAP

In the same way that the stack is a very orderly place, the *heap* can be an extremely chaotic one. It is the Wild West of memory allocations. There are no rules, and you can probably get away with just about anything. The heap is the source of many recurring problems: memory leaks, dangling pointers, memory fragmentation, and so forth. Figure 7.2 shows an image of the heap before and after a lot of allocations and deallocations occur. Notice how, unlike the stack, the free space has became very fragmented.

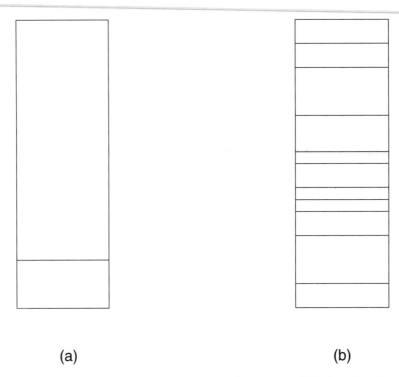

(a)   (b)

FIGURE 7.2   Image of the heap (a) before any allocations and (b) after a lot of allocations and deallocations.

Allocation Performance

The main performance problem of heap allocation boils down to the time it takes from the moment the memory has been requested to the time when the correct amount of memory is returned. The exact amount of time it takes is completely platform dependent, and it can even vary wildly from request to request.

Before you are ready to dismiss this problem as not much of an issue, consider the following example. Our game is humming along at a nice, solid 60 frames per second. That means that, at most, we are spending 16.7 ms per frame, including input handling, AI, physics update, collision detection, network update, and graphics rendering. Imagine that in some frames we are requesting up to 500 memory allocations. For all those allocations to take under one ms (six percent of our frame time), they would each need to be completed in an average of 0.002 ms. This is quite speedy; so clearly, allocations must happen blazingly quickly, or else we cannot use them in our games.

Even if your game is not locked in to a particular frame rate, you cannot afford to have a frame take a long time to display while some memory allocation is going on, because minimum frame rates are often more important than average or peak frame rates as far as the user's experience is concerned.

The time taken by a single memory allocation request is typically highly variable. Most memory system implementation will usually do some searching through tables and lists of memory blocks, and sometimes do some additional types of work, such as compacting when a request comes in. Often, single requests can take a few milliseconds by themselves—clearly not an acceptable situation for performance-sensitive games. If we run out of physical RAM in a system with *virtual memory*, then the cost of allocation will skyrocket up to hundreds of milliseconds or more while the virtual memory system is swapping out memory to the hard drive.

Dynamic memory allocation is not likely to get much better with faster CPUs, either. As hardware improves, CPUs increase in speed, but chances are we will have more memory available, making heap management even more difficult, so this will continue to be a problem in the foreseeable future.

Memory Fragmentation

Another, more subtle problem is *memory fragmentation*. Because of the nature of the heap, memory sections are allocated and freed in an apparently random order, certainly not in the nice first-in, last-out order of the stack. That allocation pattern will lead to memory fragmentation.

Before any memory allocation takes place, the heap is a pristine place with just one big block of contiguous free memory. No matter what allocation size we request (as long as it is under the memory total), it will be almost trivial to allocate. As more memory is allocated and freed, things start looking a bit uglier. Blocks of memory of wildly differing sizes are allocated and freed in almost random order. After a while, the large, contiguous memory block has been shredded to pieces, and while there might be a large percentage of free memory, it is all scattered in small pieces.

Eventually, we might request an allocation for a single block of memory, and the allocation will fail, not because there is not enough free memory, but because there is no single block large enough to hold it. Because of the nature of memory fragmentation, there is no easy way to predict when this will happen, so it could cause one of those really hard-to-track-down bugs that are almost impossible to reproduce when you need to.

A *virtual addressing* system will greatly help reduce this problem. Virtual addressing is an extra level of indirection offered by the operating system or the memory allocation libraries, usually relying on hardware features to make its performance cost almost free. The way it works is by using a virtual address instead of the physical address of the memory for a particular memory location. Physical memory is divided into equally sized blocks (four kilobytes, for example), and each block can be given a different virtual address. That virtual address goes through a table that translates it into the corresponding physical address. All of this is done transparently to the user of the memory allocation functions. The key point is that, under such a scheme, two separate memory blocks in completely different parts of the physical memory could be made to map to two contiguous blocks in the virtual address (see Figure 7.3). Thus, one of the major problems with memory fragmentation has almost disappeared, since we can always piece together a larger memory block from several scattered ones.

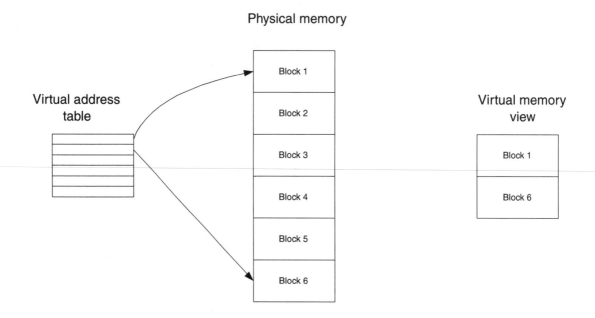

FIGURE 7.3   Virtual addressing mapping two disjointed physical memory blocks into one consecutive virtual address block.

As with any indirection system, virtual memory addressing will introduce a bit of overhead. This overhead usually does not amount to much, but as memory gets more fragmented, the algorithm to find and collect unused blocks will have to do more work, leading to some of the extreme performance problems mentioned in the previous section. All in all, the advantages of having virtual addressing more than make up for the small performance overhead they introduce. Besides, as we will see later in this chapter, we can always take more control over memory allocation where it matters, bypassing all expensive allocation operations caused by virtual addressing.

Both the PC and the Xbox have virtual addressing as part of their standard OS and libraries. In the PC, it is taken a step further, and when memory is tight, some of the least recently used memory blocks are saved to the hard drive to make room for new allocations. This is called a *virtual memory* system. Needless to say, that is usually not an acceptable situation for games, because it causes major slowdowns in the game while memory is being read from or written to the disk.

It is possible to build such an addressing scheme in a platform that does not support it natively, but it is a fairly involved task and will not be as fast without hardware support. The allocation and translation part is relatively straightforward; it is the fact that every pointer and every memory address needs to be translated that becomes the issue. Such a change will be very pervasive across all the source code. Because there is no way to automatically translate pointers every time they are about to be used, we would either need to call some sort of `Translate()` function directly, or we would need a special pointer class that does it automatically. Neither of these solutions is particularly encouraging. The problem will be even worse when we use some third-party source code or library, since it will not be using our pointer translation scheme.

Other Problems

In addition to the above problems, the heap is a source of other nonperformance-related problems that will plague projects from the start. They are mentioned here because some of the techniques we will employ later on to tame the heap will also solve, or at least help with, these problems.

Two of the most common heap problems are *dangling pointers* and its flip side, *memory leaks*. Dangling pointers are pointers that use to refer to a valid memory location, but that location has since changed, and the pointer remains the same. This can happen when multiple pointers are pointing to the same place in memory, and that location is freed without updating them all. If an attempt is made to dereference that pointer, two things can happen:

- If we are lucky, an access violation exception will be raised and the program will either catch it or it will crash. This will happen if the location pointer to the dangling pointer is either still unallocated or was allocated by a different process. The best thing about this option is that it will be caught right away, and it will be relatively easy to track down and fix.
- If we are not lucky, the memory location pointed to by that pointer will be reallocated at a later time by the program for a different use. Trying to read from it will return meaningless data—and even worse, trying to write to it will overwrite and trash an apparently unrelated part of our own game. This is called a *memory overrun*, and it is considered one of the hardest bugs to track down.

Virtual addressing improves this problem a bit, because the range of virtual addresses is usually much larger than the range of physical addresses; so the likelihood of the virtual address pointed to by the dangling pointer being reused is quite small. Most of the time, under a virtual addressing mode, accessing a dangling pointer will result in an immediate exception.

Memory leaks are exactly the opposite: they are memory chunks that the program allocated and then 'forgot' about, without giving them back to the system. The consequences of this are fairly obvious. Memory consumption will continue to increase as the program executes, fragmentation will increase, and eventually memory can run out or force the system to page memory out to disk if a virtual memory system is implemented (with the consequent slowdown that it causes). We have all seen games that start slowing down after half an hour of play and eventually crawl to a halt, forcing us to exit and restart to be able to continue playing at normal speed. That is a typical telltale sign of rampant memory leaks.

One thing that we sometimes want to do, especially when tracking down one of these problems, is to get an accurate report on the status of the memory. We usually want to see the differences in the heap between two points in the execution of the program, or we simply want to see a map of all the allocated memory.

Sometimes we just want more information about a memory block: what section of the code created it, when was it created, how large is that block, and so forth. Finally, a very useful feature is to be able to do a dump of memory, not to display the raw allocations, but to give a higher-level overview: how much memory is allocated in textures, how much in geometry, or how much in pathfinding data. These types of reports can be invaluable for tuning the memory consumption of game levels, which is much more important on consoles than on the PC, as well as tracking down memory-related bugs.

STATIC ALLOCATION

One of the oldest solutions to all dynamic memory allocation problems is to avoid them altogether. A program could be designed so it never uses `new` and `delete` (or `malloc` and `free`), and relies exclusively on statically allocated objects or objects created on the stack. These are some examples of static allocation:

```
// Create a fixed number of AI path nodes
#define MAX_PATHNODES   4096
AIPathNode s_PathNodes[MAX_PATHNODES];

// Create a fixed-size buffer for geometry
// 8 MB
#define GEOMSIZE        (8*1024*1024)
byte * s_GeomBuffer[GEOMSIZE];
```

This approach has some definite advantages. Clearly, dynamic allocation performance is not an issue, since it never happens. Also, since everything is statically allocated by the compiler and nothing changes during the execution of the game, neither memory fragmentation nor the potential to run out of memory is an issue.

Another advantage of static initialization is that it is very straightforward to keep track of where memory goes and how much each type of data takes. We explicitly decide how large each array and buffer will be at compile time, and we know they will never grow, so just glancing at the source code is enough to know the memory distribution. In the example above, it is clear we are reserving eight megabytes for geometry, and 4,096 times the size of a path node of pathfinding memory.

So far, all the advantages listed address the main problems we set out to solve in this chapter. Does that mean that static allocation is the answer we were looking for? It might be, under some very specific circumstances, but it probably is not.

The first major drawback of static allocation of memory is wasted memory. We are forced ahead to time to decide how much memory will be dedicated to each aspect of the game, and that memory is allocated all at once. That means that for a game with a lot of things happening on the screen and changing over time, we are wasting large amounts of memory. Think of all the explosions, particle effects, enemies, network messages, projectiles in the air, temporary search paths, and so forth. All of these things would have to be created ahead of time; while with dynamic memory allocation, only the ones that we currently need would be allocated, and we would allocate more only as we require them. It is unlikely we would ever need as much memory at once as with static allocation.

It is important to note that it is not enough to decide ahead of time how many objects of a whole hierarchy branch we want allocated. We must decide exactly how many we need of each individual class type. For example, if we have a game object hierarchy from which other, more concrete object types derive (e.g., enemies, players, projectiles, triggers, etc.), it is not enough to say that we will have 500 game objects. Instead, we need to decide exactly how many enemies we need, how many projectiles, and so on. The more detailed the class hierarchy, the more difficult it becomes—and the more wasteful of memory it becomes. On the other hand, having a complex inheritance hierarchy is probably not the best of designs, so it is not such a bad thing that static allocation discourages this approach.

One apparent advantage of static allocation is that it seems to reduce the chances of dangling pointers, since the memory referred to by a pointer will never be freed. It is very possible, though, to have the contents of that memory become invalid (e.g., after a projectile explodes and its object is marked invalid), at which point the pointer will still be valid, but it will access meaningless data. That is an even more difficult bug to track down than a dangling pointer to an invalid memory location, because using the dangling pointer would most likely result in an immediate access violation exception with dynamic memory allocation. But under this scheme, the program will silently continue to run with bad data and possibly crash at a later point.

Finally, one of the disadvantages of static allocation is that objects need to be prepared to be statically initialized, with all its consequences. When dealing with dynamic allocation of objects, it is a good practice to make sure the object gets fully initialized when it is first constructed, and that it gets correctly shut down when it is destroyed. With static allocation, objects will be constructed ahead of time, but will not be initialized until some time later. That means we need to add extra logic to all our objects to correctly initialize and shut down multiple times without ever being freed.

In addition, we need to be extremely careful with any initialization done in the constructor. We plan to create static arrays of those objects, and, as you may recall, static initialization is a sticky issue with C++. In short, you have very little control over what order things become initialized. So we cannot rely on our pathfinding data being ready when the enemy objects are initialized or the effects system being ready when the special effects objects are created. As a matter of fact, in a situation like this, it is probably best to leave all initializations until later and not do anything at all in the constructor, other than set default values and mark the object as uninitialized.

When to Use Static Allocation

The question is still open: when is static allocation preferable to dynamic allocation? The answer is, it depends on the circumstances.

A good piece of advice would be to only use static initialization when there is no other easy way around it. If the platform you are using has extreme penalties for any type of dynamic memory allocation, then it would be a good idea to only use static allocation. Also, if your game is a mostly static world with the player running around, then it might be advantageous to statically allocate everything you will need. However, games are moving in the direction of increasing interactivity, not less, which makes static allocation more difficult. Players nowadays expect to interact with any part of their environment—to pick up things, to destroy things, to move things, to create new things. Dynamic memory allocation is a better fit to that type of environment.

How about mixing the two approaches? Objects that will not change during the course of the game (if there are any) will be created statically, and everything else will be created dynamically. The combination is not as attractive as it seems. In a way, it seems to introduce the worst problems from each world instead of the other way around. By having some objects created dynamically, we will have to deal with all the performance and fragmentation problems that come along with it. But also, by allocating some objects statically, we will need to make sure our objects have a separate initialization and shutdown pass, mixing two fairly incompatible architectures and programming mentalities. Then, unless the free process is automated, there is the danger of forgetting whether an object was statically or dynamically allocated, and releasing it the wrong way, causing even more havoc.

Instead of mixing the two allocation styles, one of the best approaches is to adopt dynamic memory allocation exclusively, follow the advice in the rest of this chapter, and use pools extensively for performance-sensitive allocations. We will see all about memory pools later in this chapter. That approach should provide us with all the advantages with very few of the disadvantages.

Dynamic Allocation

When static allocation is not enough, we need to turn to the flexibility offered by dynamic allocation. As usual, understanding exactly what goes on during dynamic memory allocation is the key to finding efficient solutions that allow us to use dynamic memory allocation at runtime with very few drawbacks.

Call Chain

Before we start customizing the memory system, we need to understand what exactly happens as a result of a memory allocation request.

1. Everything starts with an innocent-looking object creation in the code.

```
SpecialEffect * pEffect = new SpecialEffect();
```

2. The compiler internally substitutes that call with two separate calls: one to allocate the correct amount of memory, and one to call the constructor of the SpecialEffect class.

```
SpecialEffect * pEffect = __new (sizeof(SpecialEffect));
pEffect->SpecialEffect();
```

3. The global operator new must then allocate the amount of requested memory. In most of the standard implementations, the global operator new simply calls the malloc function.

```
void * operator new (unsigned int nSize) {
    return malloc(nSize);
}
```

The call sequence does not end there; malloc is not an atomic operation. Instead, it will call platform-specific memory-allocation functions to allocate the correct amount from the heap. Often, this can result in several more calls and expensive algorithms that search for the appropriate free block to use.

Global operator delete follows a similar sequence, but it calls the destructor and free instead of the constructor and malloc. Fortunately, the amount of work needed to return memory to the heap is usually much less than the work done allocating it, so we will not look at it in detail.

Global Operators New and Delete

With that in mind, we can now override the global operators `new` and `delete` to suit our purposes better. We will not change the allocation policy yet, so we will continue calling `malloc` and `free`. However, we will add some extra logic to allow us to keep track of what system the allocated memory belongs to. Later on, we will add more parameters to give us finer control over memory allocation.

To specify our memory allocation preferences, we will create a heap class. For now, this heap does not correspond to a fixed amount of memory, or even to a set of contiguous memory. It is just a way for us to logically group some memory allocations together. To start, all the heap class needs is a name.

```
class Heap {
public:
    Heap (const char * name);
    const char * GetName() const;
private:
    char m_name[NAMELENGTH];
};
```

Now we are ready to provide our first version of the global `new` and `delete` operators.

```
void * operator new (size_t size, Heap * pHeap);
void operator delete (void * pMem);
```

In addition, we will need one version of `operator new` that does not take a heap parameter. That way, all the code that does not explicitly pass a heap will still work correctly. Because there is only one `operator delete`, it always needs to correctly free the memory allocated by any of the different `operator new` functions. In effect, that means that if we create any `operator new`, then we need to override all of them and the `operator delete`.

```
void * operator new (size_t size) {
    return operator new (size,
            HeapFactory::GetDefaultHeap() );
}
```

Before we look at how `operator new` will be implemented, let's see how it will be used. To call our special version of `operator new`, we need to explicitly pass a heap reference as a parameter to the `new` call.

```
GameEntity * pEntity = new (pGameEntityHeap) GameEntity();
```

Admittedly, it does not look like the cleanest and most unobtrusive plan, but this will improve. Bear with it for the moment and hold on to the promise that it will get better soon. Our implementation of `operator new` is going to start very simply. For now, all we want is to keep the association between the heap it was allocated from and the allocated memory itself. Notice that the `delete` operator only takes a parameter as a pointer; so, somehow, we need to be able to go from a pointer to its information.

For now we will allocate a little bit more memory than was requested, enough to fit a header for each memory allocation with the information we need. For simplicity, this header will just contain a pointer to the correct heap.

```
struct AllocHeader {
    Heap * pHeap;
    int    nSize;
};
```

The functions `operator new` and `operator delete` look something like this now:

```
void * operator new (size_t size, Heap * pHeap) {
    size_t nRequestedBytes = size + sizeof(AllocHeader);
    char * pMem = (char *)malloc(nRequestedBytes);
    AllocHeader * pHeader = (AllocHeader *)pMem;
    pHeader->pHeap = pHeap;
    pHeader->nSize = size;

    pHeap->AddAllocation (size);

    void * pStartMemBlock = pMem + sizeof(AllocHeader);
    return pStartMemBlock;
}

void operator delete (void * pMem) {
    AllocHeader * pHeader = (AllocHeader *)
                ((char *)pMem - sizeof(AllocHeader));
    pHeader->pHeap->RemoveAllocation (pHeader->nSize);
    free(pHeader);
}
```

These two functions are doing the bare minimum to get the job done. There are a lot of things that they should do to be a robust memory manager, but we will add those later. For now, these are a good starting point. Some of the features they are lacking are error checking, ability to detect memory overruns, and correct memory alignment.

Even with those limitations, they are already quite useful. At any point in time, we could traverse all the heaps and print their names, number of allocations per heap, amount of memory allocated in each heap, peak memory usage, and so forth. We also have enough information to detect memory leaks during the execution of the program. We will see that implemented later on.

So far we have been purposefully ignoring the close relatives of operator new and operator delete: operator new[] and operator delete[]. Their job is to allocate and free memory for a whole array of objects. For the moment, we can just treat them like their nonarray counterparts and call operator new and operator delete from them.

Even though this system starts being useful, it is still quite cumbersome to have to explicitly pass the heap to every allocation we care about. Overriding the class-specific new and delete operators will automate this task, and finally make it useful enough to use in our game and tools.

Class-Specific Operators New and Delete

So far we have ignored another step in the dynamic allocation call chain: the class-specific operator new and operator delete. When a class overrides those operators, the call to new will call them instead of calling the global operator new. These functions can do any bookkeeping and then allocate the memory themselves, or call the global operator new or malloc directly.

We can use the class-specific operator new to automate some of the complexities of our memory management scheme. Since we usually would like to put all objects from a certain class in a particular heap, we can have the class operator new deal with calling the global operator new with the extra parameters.

```
void * GameObject::operator new (size_t size) {
    return ::operator new(size, s_pHeap);
}
```

Now every time an object of the class GameObject is created with new, it will automatically be added to the correct heap. That starts to make things easier. What exactly do we need to add to each class to support that? We need to add an operator `new`, an operator `delete`, and a heap static member variable to each class.

```cpp
// GameObject.h
class GameObject {
public:
    // All the normal declarations...

    static void * operator new(size_t size);
    static void operator delete(void * p, size_t size);

private:
    static Heap * s_pHeap;
};

// GameObject.cpp
Heap * GameObject::s_pHeap = NULL;

void * GameObject::operator new(size_t size) {
    if (s_pHeap==NULL) {
        s_pHeap = HeapFactory::CreateHeap("Game object");
    }
    return ::operator new(size, s_pHeap);
}

void GameObject::operator delete(void * p, size_t size) {
    ::operator delete(p);
}
```

By the fifth time we add those same functions to a class, we realize that there has to be an easier way instead of doing all that error-prone typing. And there is. We can easily provide the same functionality with two macros, or even with templates if you really must. Here we will show the simpler macro version. The class above would now look like this:

```cpp
// GameObject.h
class GameObject {
    // Body of the declaration
private:
    DECLARE_HEAP;
};

// GameObject.cpp
DEFINE_HEAP(GameObject, "Game objects");
```

One important observation: any derived classes from a class that has custom `new` and `delete` operators will use their parents' operators unless they have their own. In our case, if a class `GameObjectTrigger` inherited from `GameObject`, it will also automatically use `GameObject`'s heap.

Now it is finally very simple to hook up new classes to our memory management system, and it would probably be worthwhile to apply this technique to all the most important classes in our game. An object could also do *raw memory allocation* from the heap during execution. A raw memory allocation is caused by allocating a certain amount of bytes straight from memory, not allocating new objects. If this is the case, the allocation can be redirected to point to that object class' heap to keep better tabs on memory usage.

```
char * pScratchSpace;
pScratchSpace = new (s_pLocalHeap) char[1024];
```

At this point, we have the basis for a simple, but fully functional memory management system. We can keep track of how much memory is used by each class or each major class type at any time during the game execution. We also have access to some other useful statistics, such as peak memory consumption. With a few more features, it will be ready for use in a commercial game.

CUSTOM MEMORY MANAGER

ON THE CD

The time has come to put all the concepts from the past two sections together and build a fully functional memory manager. The source code is on the CD-ROM, located in the \Chapter 07. MemoryMgr\ folder (the Visual Studio workspace for the project is MemoryMgr.dsw), and you can refer to it for the details. In this section, we will cover some interesting features that were left out of the descriptions in the past two sections, as well as add a few new useful features and describe how they are implemented.

Error Checking

In order to make the memory manager truly something that can be used in commercial software, we need to consider the possibility of error and misuse. The memory manager described in the past two sections had no provision for errors. If we accidentally passed the wrong pointer to delete, it would still try to interpret it as a valid memory pointer and try to delete it anyway.

The first thing we want to do is make sure that the memory we are about to free was allocated through our memory manager. The way operator new and delete are implemented, this should always be the case; there is the possibility of another library allocating the memory, or perhaps some part of the code is calling malloc directly. In addition, this check will catch any stray pointers that are referring to other parts of memory, as well as problems with memory corruption, where allocated memory was later overwritten by something else.

To accomplish all that, we will add a unique signature to our allocation header:

```
struct AllocHeader {
    int nSignature;
    int    nSize;
    Heap * pHeap;
};
```

Of course, there is no 'unique' number we can add, nor even any combination of numbers. There is always the possibility that somebody will allocate memory with that exact same number, but the possibility of this occurring at exactly the place we are looking at is pretty slim. Depending on our comfort level, we can add more than one integer at the cost of higher overhead, but one will be enough for this example and for most purposes.

What should that unique number be? Anything that is not a common occurrence. For example, using the number zero is not a good idea; it happens too much in real programs. Same thing with 0xFFFFFFFF, common assembly opcodes, or addresses to virtual memory. Just typing any random hexadecimal number will usually be good enough. Purely for its amusement value, one of the old favorites is 0xDEADCODE. Our implementation for operator delete and new looks like this:

```
void * operator new (size_t size, Heap * pHeap) {
    size_t nRequestedBytes = size + sizeof(AllocHeader);
    char * pMem = (char *)malloc (nRequestedBytes);
    AllocHeader * pHeader = (AllocHeader *)pMem;
    pHeader->nSignature = MEMSYSTEM_SIGNATURE;
    pHeader->pHeap = pHeap;
    pHeader->nSize = size;

    pHeap->AddAllocation (size);
```

```
    void * pStartMemBlock = pMem + sizeof(AllocHeader);
    return pStartMemBlock;
}

void operator delete (void * pMem) {
    AllocHeader * pHeader =
            (AllocHeader *)((char *)pMem -
                                sizeof(AllocHeader));
    assert (pHeader->nSignature == MEMSYSTEM_SIGNATURE);
    pHeader->pHeap->RemoveAllocation(pHeader->nSize);
    free (pHeader);
}
```

One common mistake when dealing with dynamically allocated memory, especially in the form of an array, is to write past the end of the allocated block. To check for this situation, we can add a guard number at the end of the allocated memory. Just a simple magic number will do for now. Additionally, we will also save the size of the allocated memory block to double check against it when we attempt to free the memory.

```
    void * operator new (size_t size, Heap * pHeap) {
        size_t nRequestedBytes = size +
                sizeof(AllocHeader) + sizeof(int);
        char * pMem = (char *)malloc (nRequestedBytes);
        AllocHeader * pHeader = (AllocHeader *)pMem;
        pHeader->nSignature = MEMSYSTEM_SIGNATURE;
        pHeader->pHeap = pHeap;
        pHeader->nSize = size;

        void * pStartMemBlock = pMem + sizeof(AllocHeader);
        int * pEndMarker = (int*)(pStartMemBlock + size);
        *pEndMarker = MEMSYSTEM_ENDMARKER;

        pHeap->AddAllocation (size);

        return pStartMemBlock;
    }

    void operator delete ( void * pMemBlock ) {
        AllocHeader * pHeader =
                (AllocHeader *)((char *)pMemBlock -
                                    sizeof(AllocHeader));
        assert (pHeader->nSignature == MEMSYSTEM_SIGNATURE);
        int * pEndMarker = (int*)(pMemBlock + size);
```

```
        assert (*pEndMarker == MEMSYSTEM_ENDMARKER);

        pHeader->pHeap->RemoveAllocation(pHeader->nSize);
        free (pHeader);
    }
```

Finally, as another safeguard, a good strategy is to fill the memory we are about to free with a fairly distinctive bit pattern. That way, if we accidentally overwrite any part of memory, we will immediately see that it was caused by attempting to free a pointer. As an added advantage, if that pattern is also the opcode for an instruction indicating a halt of program execution, our program will automatically stop if it ever tries to run in a section that was supposed to have been freed.

By now, we have added a fair amount of overhead: memory overhead with our expanding allocation header and end marker, as well as performance overhead with the operations we do while allocating or freeing the memory. Since the original purpose of creating our memory manager was to get better performance out of it, we do not seem to be heading in the right direction. Fortunately, most of what we are doing here will only be enabled for debug builds. As we will see in a later section, most of the overhead we are introducing will not appear in retail builds.

Walking the Heap

Sometimes it is necessary to iterate through all the allocations in one heap in order to check for consistency, to gather more information, to defragment a heap, or simply to print a detailed heap status for debugging purposes. The point is, walking the heap is not something we can do with what we have so far. In order to do this, we need to add some extra information to our allocation header.

```
struct AllocHeader {
    int         nSignature;
    int         nSize;
    Heap *      pHeap;
    AllocHeader * pNext;
    AllocHeader * pPrev;
};
```

We have added the pNext and pPrev fields, which point to the next and previous allocations done in this heap. Under different circumstances, it would have been better to use an STL list, but this is such a low-level system that it is preferable to do it this way to avoid any extra memory allocations.

Operators `new` and `delete` will take care of correctly updating the list pointer for each allocation and each free call. Since we are maintaining a doubly linked list, the performance overhead for maintaining the list is trivial. Now it is finally possible to start with the first allocation of the heap and walk through all of the allocations in order.

Bookmarks and Leaks

One of the pleasures of having your own custom memory manager is the fact that you can do anything with it that you need to. Tracking down memory leaks comes up very often, so let's modify our memory manager to support this task.

The concept of finding out memory leaks is simple. At one point in time, we take a bookmark of the memory status; later on we take another bookmark, and report all memory allocations that were present the second time but not the first time. Surprisingly, the implementation will be almost trivial.

All we have to do is keep an allocation count. Every time we have a new allocation, we increase the allocation counter and mark that allocation with its corresponding number. In this example, let's assume that we will never have more than 2^{32} allocations. If that is a problem, we need to keep 64 bits for the allocation count, or devise a scheme to wrap around. In either case, it is reasonably easy to implement. Our allocation header now looks like this:

```
struct AllocHeader {
    int          nSignature;
    int          nAllocNum;
    int          nSize;
    Heap *         pHeap;
    AllocHeader * pNext;
    AllocHeader * pPrev;
};
```

and operator `new` is just like before, except that it fills in the `nAllocNum` field. Next, we create a trivial function, `GetMemoryBookmark`. All it does is return our current allocation number.

```
int GetMemoryBookmark () {
    return s_nNextAllocNum;
}
```

Finally, the function that will do a bit more work is `ReportMemoryLeaks`. It takes two memory bookmarks as parameters and reports all memory allocations that are still active that happened between those two bookmarks. It is implemented simply by traversing all allocations in all heaps, looking for allocations that have a number between the two bookmarks. Yes, it is potentially very slow to traverse all allocations in all heaps, but this is a luxury we can permit ourselves this time, since this function is used purely for debugging, and we do not really care how fast it executes. The memory leak reporting function is shown next in pseudo-code form.

```
void ReportMemoryLeaks (int nBookmark1, int nBookmark2) {
    for (each heap) {
        for (each allocation) {
            if (pAllocation->nAllocNum >= nBookmark1 &&
                pAllocation->nAllocNum < nBookmark2) {
                // Print info about pAllocation
                // Print its alloc number, heap, size...
            }
        }
    }
}
```

Hierarchical Heaps

One aspect of heaps that we left out earlier is their hierarchical arrangement. This might seem like a cosmetic change, but it will come in very useful during the development of a large program.

Heaps tend to proliferate. What starts out as a heap for all graphics memory quickly becomes 15 different heaps: one for vertex information, another one for index lists, another one for shaders, another one for textures, materials, meshes, and so forth. Before we realize it, our game is using hundreds of heaps, and trying to find relevant information becomes a slow, tiresome process. Besides, sometimes we just want the big picture, and the art lead will ask "How much memory is our graphics data taking as a whole?"

Here is where hierarchical heaps come in. There is nothing inherently different about them. They are just regular heaps, like we have seen so far, but they are arranged in a tree shape. Every heap has a parent and potentially many children. The only difference is that each heap will keep statistics on both itself and itself combined with all its children.

For example, earlier we might have had the memory heap report shown in Table 7.1.

Table 7.1   Nonhierarchical Memory Heap Report

HEAP	MEMORY	PEAK	INST
Vertices	15346	16782	1895
Index lists	958	1022	1895
Textures	22029	22029	230
Materials	203	203	321

With a hierarchical heap, we instead have the report shown in Table 7.2.

Table 7.2   Hierarchical Memory Heap Report

	LOCAL			TOTAL		
Heap	Memory	Peak	Inst	Memory	Peak	Inst
Renderer	0	0	0	38536	40036	4341
Geometry	0	0	0	16304	17804	3790
Vertices	15346	16782	1895	15346	16782	1895
Index lists	958	1022	1895	958	1022	1895
Materials	0	0	0	22232	22232	551
Material objects	203	203	321	203	203	321
Textures	22029	22029	230	22029	22029	230

From an implementation point of view, the only difference is that we need a way to indicate where in the hierarchy a heap will be created, and we need to keep track of its parent and children. There is nothing complicated in that, and it is mostly a lot of pointer handling, so refer to the source code on the CD-ROM for the details (\Chapter 07. MemoryMgr\MemoryMgr.dsw).

ON THE CD

Other Types of Allocations

Unfortunately, overriding global `new` and `delete` is not the end of the story. That will take care of all `new` and `delete` calls, both global and overridden ones, but there are other types of dynamic memory allocation.

Direct calls to `malloc` will not be intercepted by our memory manager. Neither will calls to platform-specific memory allocation functions (such as `VirtualAlloc` or `HeapAlloc` under Win32). In situations like these, there is no other solution than to try to fix the problem by hand.

One possibility is to create a custom version of `malloc` that takes a heap pointer and calls it instead of `malloc`. That will work fine as long as we have access to the source code and it is not being called in many places.

Another alternative, especially if we do not have access to the original source code that is making those memory allocation calls, is to keep track of the allocations by hand. Before calling a function that we know will perform some memory allocations out of our control, we get the total memory status, make the call, then find out how much memory was allocated; we then assign that amount to a particular heap.

```
int nMem1 = GetFreePhysicalMemory(); //Platform-specific call
// Made-up function that will use platform-specific
// memory allocation functions.
DirectXAllocateBuffers();
int nMem2 = GetFreePhysicalMemory();
pDirectXHeap->AddAllocation( nMem2-nMem1 );
```

This will only work as long as there are not many of those calls, and as long as it is always very clear when memory is allocated and freed. If those function calls try to cache some of the allocated memory, then it will be impossible to keep track of it reliably.

Some of the better-designed APIs have hooks for the memory allocation functions. They will allow you to provide an object (or a series of function pointers if they are not very C++ inclined) that will be called every time the API needs to do any sort of heap memory allocation. In a situation like that, we can create an object that calls our version of `operator new` and `delete` with a specific heap to allocate memory, and all the memory allocated by the API will be tracked in our heaps.

Memory System Overhead

We have added a lot of very useful features to our custom memory manager that will really help us keep tabs on memory usage and improve performance. But, there is a problem, we have added several bytes to each allocation to keep track of our information. It might seem like a few bytes will not matter, but this is wrong. Here is our allocation header so far:

```
struct AllocHeader {
    int        nSignature;
    int        nAllocNum;
    int        nSize;
```

```
Heap *         pHeap;
AllocHeader * pNext;
AllocHeader * pPrev;
};
```

Assuming four bytes per int and pointer, that is 24 bytes right there. As we will see later, we might want to round that up to 32 bytes in some platforms in order to improve the memory alignment of the allocation that will be returned. In addition, there is an additional four-byte end marker for each allocation block, so that adds up to a grand total of 36 bytes.

This would be a perfectly acceptable overhead if there were only a few dynamic memory allocations and if they were mostly large blocks of allocated memory. But if that were the case, then this entire chapter would be unnecessary, since dynamic memory allocation performance and memory fragmentation would not be an issue. As we saw at the beginning of this chapter, C++ encourages a lot of small and frequent heap allocations, so our overhead will very quickly become significant. This situation is made even worse on consoles with limited amounts of memory.

A C++ game designed to fit in 64 MB of memory can easily have 50,000 or more heap allocations in memory at once. At 36 bytes per allocation, that is 1.7 MB of overhead introduced by our system. On a 64-MB platform, this is probably not an acceptable solution.

In debug mode, things are even worse. If our implementation of the global operator new calls malloc, then we most likely have another 32 bytes of overhead that malloc adds (depending on the specific malloc implementation). That will bring up the total overhead to 3.2 MB.

Fortunately, we can get around it the same way malloc does. Bookkeeping information is very useful in debug mode, but there is no need for it in release mode (the executable that will actually be shipped to the manufacturer). So in release mode, we do not need to keep any information at all—no allocation header and no end marker. And malloc will also not keep any extra information, so our overhead has completely disappeared.

```
void * operator new (size_t size, Heap * pHeap) {
#ifdef _DEBUG
    // Same implementation as before
#else
    return malloc(size);
#endif
}
```

```
void operator delete (void * pMemBlock, size_t size) {
#ifdef _DEBUG
    // Same implementation as before
#else
    free (pMemBlock);
#endif
}
```

The only drawback is that all the error checking will be gone in release mode. That means that the memory system will not immediately detect a memory overrun, or that passing an invalid pointer to be deleted will cause all sorts of bad things to happen. Whether this is acceptable or not depends on your particular situation—the type of game you are writing or the platform you are targeting. (See Chapter 16 for more information about crash-proofing your game and what to do in release mode when errors occur.)

MEMORY POOLS

With the memory manager so far, we can have an instant representation of where memory is being spent, track down memory leaks, and avoid any unnecessary overhead. One thing we have yet to address is the performance issue. When we set out to write the memory manager, one of the main motivations was to improve performance over direct calls to new and delete. So far we have replaced new and delete calls with malloc and free (which is probably what the libraries did in the first place), but we have not improved performance any. The solution to most allocation performance problems is the use of memory pools.

Recall that the expensive part of the default implementation of heap memory allocation was finding the block of memory to return. Especially when the memory is heavily fragmented, the search algorithm might have to look through many different blocks before it can return the appropriate one.

Conceptually, a memory pool is a certain amount of pre-allocated memory that will be used to allocate objects of one size at runtime. Whenever one of those objects is released by the program, its memory is returned to the pool, not freed back to the heap. This approach has several advantages:

- **No performance hit:** As soon as memory is requested from the pool, first free pre-allocated block is returned. There are no calls to malloc and no searching.

- **No fragmentation:** Memory blocks are allocated once and never released, so the heap does not get fragmented as program execution progresses.
- **One large allocation:** We can pre-allocate blocks in any way we want. Typically, this is done as one large memory block from which we return small subsections. This has the advantage of further reducing the number of heap allocations, as well as providing spatial coherence for the data being returned (which might improve performance even more by improving data cache hits).

The only disadvantage is that pools will usually have some unused space (slack space). As long as the pools are reasonably sized and are only used for dynamic elements, that extra space is well worth the benefits.

One added advantage of memory pools is that we can wipe all objects in a pool at once, without calling their destructors. Obviously, this should not be done carelessly, but if we make sure nobody outside the pool is referring to those objects, the pool could just wipe that memory and forget about those objects. The reason for doing this is simply efficiency; wiping all objects at once could be much faster than destroying each one individually. That is quite useful in games to either clear large chunks of memory when exiting a level or to destroy a several related small objects that need to disappear at once (particles, pathfinding nodes, etc).

Implementation

First, we will create a class that represents a memory pool, and then we will hook it up to our memory system. The first thing that the memory class needs to know is how large the objects that will be allocated from it are going to be. Since this is not going to ever change, we will pass it in the constructor. In addition, the two fundamental operations we will perform on the pool are going to be allocating and freeing memory. Here is the first, barebones version of a memory pool class declaration:

```
class MemoryPool {
public:
    MemoryPool (size_t nObjectSize);
    ~MemoryPool ();

    void * Alloc (size_t nSize);
    void Free (void * p, size_t nSize);
};
```

We need to come up with a scheme for managing many similarly-sized memory blocks, return one in the `Alloc` call, and put it back to be managed when it is returned in the `Free` call. We could pre-allocate all those memory blocks and keep a list of pointers to them, get the first one in the list in the `Alloc` call, and return it back to the list in the `Free` call. Conceptually, this is very simple, and it avoids doing dynamic heap allocations at runtime; but it also has several problems. The main one is that we are increasing the memory overhead per allocation. Now an allocation requires an entry in the list of free objects. It also means that all the pre-allocated objects are allocated individually, not as a large memory block, so we also incur whatever overhead the operating system requires for multiple, small allocations.

There is a solution that solves all those problems, but it requires getting our hands a bit dirty: handling memory directly, casting memory addresses to specific data, and other unsightly things. It is well worth the trouble, though; in the end, it will require no extra overhead, and all the memory will be allocated out of large, contiguous memory blocks, which is exactly what we were looking for. Besides, all that complexity will be hidden under the memory pool class, so nobody using it will have to know how it is implemented in order to use it correctly. As a matter of fact, once we are done, if we have done our job correctly, nobody will even need to know there is a memory pool class at all.

Let us start by allocating one large memory block. We will think of that block as made up of contiguous, similarly-sized slices of memory. Each slice will be exactly the size of the allocations we will be requesting from this pool (see Figure 7.4a).

At the start, before any allocations are done, all memory in the block is available, so all slices can be marked as free. In order to do that, we will create a linked list of free slices. Since the memory block has already been allocated, but we have not given any of that memory to the program, we have a lot of unused memory lying around, so we might as well put it to good use. Instead of wasting memory with a separate list, we will double up the first two double words from each slice as the `next` and `previous` pointers for a list element, and we will link all the slices in one doubly linked list (see Figure 7.4b).

The rest is simple. Anytime a new request comes to the pool class, we grab the first element in the free slice list, fix up the list, and return a pointer to that slice. Whenever memory is freed, we add that memory to the head of the free slice list. After a few allocations, the slices will be out of order in the list; but it does not matter. We are not causing any memory fragmentation, and we allocate and free memory blazingly quickly (see Figure 7.4c).

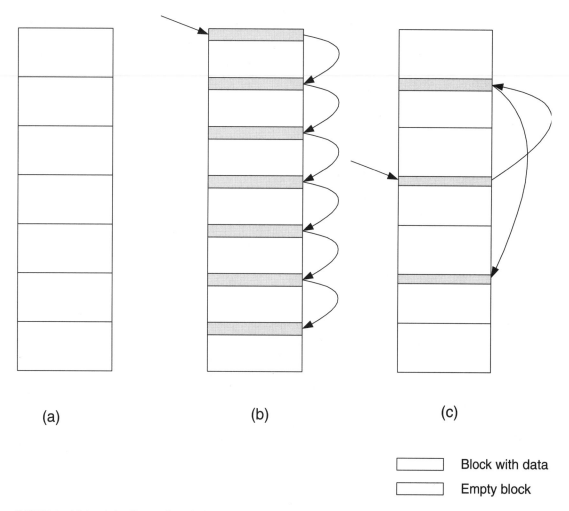

(a)   (b)   (c)

☐ Block with data
☐ Empty block

FIGURE 7.4   (a) A newly allocated pool object. (b) A pool object with the linked list connections. (c) A pool object after being used for a while.

The first question that comes to mind after reading how the pool class works is, what if we need more memory? The answer is simple. We allocate a similar memory block to the first one, and we link them together along with the rest of the free blocks.

Then the question becomes, how big should those memory blocks be? This is a much harder question to answer. It will totally depend on the type of allocations we are performing and on the behavior of the program that uses the memory pool. On one hand, we do not want to waste a lot of space by having a really large block that will never be completely used; but on the other hand, we do not want to have many little memory allocations all the time.

The best course of action is to pick some default. For example, each pool will create a block that can hold 512 slices. (We do not really need a power of two for anything here, but it will make the programmers feel better; feel free to change it to anything else you want.) Once we have memory pools hooked up to our memory manager, we can report how much wasted space there is and tweak them accordingly. We might also want make sure that the allocated blocks of memory are multiples of the memory page size or some other significant size that might make our lives easier and the allocations faster. In Win32, it makes sense to make each block a multiple of four kilobytes and allocate that memory directly, bypassing `malloc` and all its overhead.

As soon as we start dealing with memory allocation, the alignment issue comes up again. In some platforms, for best performance, the structures we access should be aligned to a specific memory boundary. In Win32, for example, it is best to align allocations to 32-byte boundaries. If we have decided to create a pool to allocate objects that are 78 bytes in size, it would make sense to create slices that are rounded up to the next 32-byte boundary—in this case, 96 bytes; that way, all the memory returned from the pool will be 32-byte aligned. At least we should consider adding an option to the heap class to enforce some specific alignment. That extra wasted memory is also worth reporting through the memory manager, so we are always aware of where all the memory is going at all times.

Hooking It up

Right now, the memory pool class does a lot of things, but it is still not particularly useful. It only allocates raw memory, so we cannot even allocate an object through it. Also, it is rather cumbersome to use, since we need to explicitly get the pool we want and then call `Alloc` with the number of bytes we need.

Let us improve that by hooking it up through the class-specific `operator new` and `operator delete`. To make sure all objects of a particular class use the pool for their allocation, we need to create a pool static member variable and then override `operator new` and `operator delete` in order to use it to allocate the memory they need.

```
// MyClass.h
class MyClass {
public:
    // All the normal declarations...

    static void * operator new(size_t size);
    static void operator delete(void * p, size_t size);

private:
    static MemoryPool * s_pPool;
};


// MyClass.cpp
MemoryPool * s_MyClass::pPool;

void * MyClass::operator new(size_t size) {
    if (s_pPool==NULL) {
        s_pPool = new MemoryPool(sizeof(MyClass));
    }
    return s_pPool->Alloc(size);
}

void MyClass::operator delete(void * p, size_t size) {
    s_pPool->Free(p, size);
}
```

Every time an object of type `MyClass` is created, it will use memory from a memory pool. This is not bad, but it is still a bit tedious to have to type all that for every class that we want to have use a pool. We can clean it up a bit more by wrapping up all the common statements in a macro. Now we can write the class as follows:

```
// MyClass.h
class MyClass {
public:
    // All the normal declarations...
    MEMPOOL_DECLARE(MyClass)
};

// MyClass.cpp
MEMPOOL_IMPLEMENT(MyClass)
```

This is much neater. Just by adding those two lines, we can make any class use our memory pools.

Finally, to really integrate pools with the memory manager, each pool can contain a heap and register all of its allocations through the heap. Now all the allocations, pooled or not, will appear correctly in the pool display. The source code on the CD-ROM (\Chapter 07.MemoryMgr\MemoryMgr.dsw) contains the macro definition in the source code and the final version of the memory pool macros, including their integration with the memory heaps.

Generic Pools

What if we have an inheritance hierarchy of objects, each with a slightly different size? Any class that inherits from MyClass will attempt to use the same memory pool object, and since its objects will most likely have different sizes, it will assert as soon as you try to instantiate an object. Clearly, we cannot just inherit from it and hope that things will work out.

Fortunately, it is often the case that most objects that need to be pooled are simple structures that are not intended to be inherited from. In that case, what we have seen so far will work perfectly. Some examples of objects of that type are handles, messages, and nodes of a spatial structure (e.g., BSP, quadtree).

On the other hand, we might have an inheritance hierarchy of game objects, all of them of varying sizes, that we would like to pool because they are allocated very often during program execution and are affecting performance. For this situation, we can create a generic memory pool allocation system. Instead of every class having a memory pool of its own, the memory manager can have a fixed set of memory pools—about five or six. Previously, each pool was used to allocate objects of a particular size. Here we will use them to allocate objects of that size or smaller. When a pooled memory allocation request arrives, the memory manager finds the heap with the smallest object size that will still fit the request and allocates it from there.

Clearly, this scheme will result in even more wasted memory, but it is sometimes worthwhile if we have many different objects that need to be created at runtime. Tweaking the sizes and numbers of the generic pools is crucial to having good performance and as little wasted space as possible. In addition, it is usually not worthwhile to create heaps for allocations larger than four kilobytes or so, since those allocations happen infrequently during gameplay, and operating systems are usually quite efficient at allocating large memory blocks.

Notice that generic pools can live side by side with regular pools and nonpooled memory allocations. We can choose what type of allocation behavior we want on a per-heap basis, so we should always be able to choose the best tool for the job.

IN CASE OF EMERGENCY . . .

You have decided to use dynamic memory allocation in your game. You implement a memory manager, a pool system, and you add it to your game engine. You get all the flexibility of dynamic allocations with almost none of the drawbacks. Unfortunately, there is one situation you must be ready to handle: running out of memory.

It is tempting to ignore it, but we have to face the facts. Unless you are extremely careful of how and when every single dynamic allocation happens, the player can probably put together a situation where so many dynamic allocations happen at the same time that the system runs out of memory—not a pleasant situation. There are two main strategies to deal with it: prevent memory from ever running out, or deal with it once it happens.

Perhaps the most natural way of handling these situations is to avoid running out of memory in the first place. We can accomplish this by adding some feedback on systems that require dynamic memory allocation based on the current amount of free memory. For example, the number of particles a particle system puts out could be scaled back as soon as a minimum amount of free memory is reached. If the amount of memory continues to decrease and reaches a critical point, we could stop putting out particles altogether. The game might not look as pretty, but at least it will not crash. Besides, we are counting on the large amount of allocated memory being something temporary, and that it will go down in a few frames, at which point all particle emitters will go back to normal. We can set up similar feedback with the sound system, the AI calculations, or any other system that allocates dynamic memory and can be scaled back without breaking the game.

Alternatively, we could let the system run out of memory and then deal with it. That is going to be a little bit more complicated. First of all, we do not have the luxury of checking for low memory anywhere we want. We will know it when the new call fails, and we will need to handle it there.

A common strategy is to have some spare memory allocated at the beginning, perhaps 50 KB or 100 KB. Whenever we run out of memory, the first thing we do is to free that spare memory we put aside. This should give us enough breathing room while we try to fix the situation.

Now we can handle it in a variety of ways. We could give up, just finish the level, and send the player back to the main menu. This is not ideal—but again, it is better than a crash. We could also try to do some digging around in the memory pools and free any memory that is not currently used, or even try to compact some of the entries in the pools to free some memory.

Independent of how you decide to handle the low-memory situation, an invaluable tool that you can add to your game is a memory stress-test mode. When in that mode, all available memory, except for a small amount, will be allocated. Your game should be able to continue working in that situation. If you added a feedback mechanism to some of the systems with dynamic memory allocation, you should be able to see it kicking in and observe its consequences. If you want to make your game totally bullet-proof, take over all available memory and see if the game continues to run.

CONCLUSION

In this chapter, we have presented the problem of memory allocation and different ways of dealing with it. One of the simplest ways is to use static memory allocation exclusively. This spares us the problems of memory fragmentation and the performance of dynamic memory allocation, but at the cost of being quite inflexible and wasting a lot of memory. Static memory allocation will tend to fall short in situations with a lot of interaction and dynamic worlds.

Dynamic allocation is a much more flexible solution, but at the cost of some added complexity. We have to deal with the problems of memory fragmentation, running out of memory during the game, and the performance of the actual allocation. We presented the source code for a memory manager system that allows easy integration into existing source code to keep track of how dynamic memory is allocated and also to provide us with some debugging aids.

Finally, we saw how using memory pools can allow us to use dynamic memory allocation without performance or memory fragmentation problems. We also saw some sample source code that can be used to easily put any class into a memory pool of its own.

SUGGESTED READING

The following book has several interesting insights on overriding new and delete operators:

Meyers, Scott, *Effective C++ Second Edition*, Addison-Wesley, 1998.

Here are some good articles on dynamic memory allocation:

Ravenbrook, *The Memory Management Reference*. http://www.memorymanagement.org/.

Johnstone, Mark S., and Paul R. Wilson, "The Memory Fragmentation Problem: Solved?" *Proceedings of the International Symposium on Memory Management*. ACM Press, 1998.

Hixon, Brian, et al. "Play by Play: Effective Memory Management." *Game Developer Magazine*, February 2002.

The following is another interesting article covering memory pools, but with an emphasis on a small memory footprint:

Saladino, Michael, "The Big Squeeze: Resource Management During Your Console Port" *Game Developer Magazine*, November 1999.

A very good and detailed explanation of a custom small-object allocation system can be found in:

Alexandrescu, Andrei, *Modern C++ Design*, Addison-Wesley, 2001.

Something worth a look, as a starting point, is the Boost pool library:

C++ Boost Pool library, http://www.boost.org/libs/pool/doc/index.html.

STANDARD TEMPLATE LIBRARY—CONTAINERS

IN THIS CHAPTER

- STL Overview
- To STL, or Not to STL?
- Sequence Containers
- Associative Containers
- Container Adaptors

This chapter is not intended to teach you all you need to know about the C++ Standard Template Library (STL). A whole book would be necessary for that and fortunately, other people have already written them. If you have not used the STL before, check out some of the introductory STL books listed at the end of the chapter and then come back.

The next two chapters of this book are going to concentrate on how to use STL effectively for game development or for any situation that requires high-performance programming. You are expected to know basic concepts, such as the difference between a vector and a list, and how to use an iterator to traverse all the elements in a container. That should be enough to get you through this chapter, although the more hands-on experience you have had with the STL, the more you will understand the problems we are trying to solve, and the more you will appreciate the solutions.

In Chapter 8, we will first ask ourselves whether or not we should use the STL in our projects. Then we will examine each major type of container in detail to become familiar with their performance and memory trade-offs, which will become crucial during game development. Chapter 9 will deal with algorithms and a few advanced topics, such as custom allocators.

STL OVERVIEW

This is a quick refresher on the basic STL concepts. If you have never used the STL, it would be best if you read some of the introductory readings listed under Suggested Reading at the end of this chapter, and try to get some hands-on experience. Also, you should have some rudimentary understanding of templates to get the most out of this chapter (see Chapter 4 for a review of templates). This chapter is more of a quick brush-up to get us all on the same wavelength.

The C++ Standard Template Library is a collection of classes providing *containers* to store data in different structures, *iterators* to access the elements in containers, and *algorithms* to perform operations on containers. All the classes are generic through the use of templates, so they can be adapted for use with any of our own classes.

There are several different types of containers, each with different operations and memory and performance characteristics. Choosing the right one for the job is a crucial step. The main two types are sequence containers, in which the elements are stored in a specific order, and associative containers, in which the order of the elements is not preserved.

```
// Adding three elements to a vector of integers
vector<int> entityUID;
entityUID.push_back(entity1.GetUID());
entityUID.push_back(entity2.GetUID());
entityUID.push_back(entity3.GetUID());
```

Iterators allow us to access the different elements in a container. All containers have two very important functions that return two different iterators: begin() returns an iterator to the first element, and end() returns an iterator past the last element. Notice that end() does not return an iterator to the last element, but to the one past it. This is a very important convention throughout STL. Most functions that specify a range of elements will require passing the iterator to the first element and past the last element in the range. This might seem odd at first, but it will make things a lot simpler when we are iterating through all the elements in a container or implementing an algorithm.

Once we have an iterator to a part of the container, it is possible to use it as a starting point to get to nearby elements. It is always possible to at least access the next element from a given iterator. Not all iterators have the same amount of functionality implemented, but sometimes it is possible to get the previous element, or even a random element, depending on the type of iterator.

```
// Traverse the vector of UIDs
vector<int>::iterator it;
for (it = entityUID.begin(); it != entityUID.end(); ++it) {
    int UID = *it;
    // Do something with the UID
}
```

The STL provides a set of standard algorithms that can be applied to containers and iterators. They are all rather basic algorithms that are usually combined to obtain the results we are looking for in our code. There are algorithms to find elements in a container, copy them, reverse them, sort them, and so forth. As with all the STL code, the algorithms have been highly optimized, and they will typically use the best available implementation instead of a more straightforward, slower one.

```
// Reverse the entire vector of UIDs
reverse (entityUID.begin(), entityUID.end());
```

All the classes and functions provided by the STL are wrapped up inside the namespace std. That means that you will have to prefix all the

STL names with `std::` or add a `using namespace std` statement to the top of the .cpp file where you will be using them.

To STL, or Not to STL?

When embarking in a new project, programmers should ask themselves whether they should use STL or not. You might think you know the answer to that question, given that this book has two whole chapters dedicated to it, but let's look at STL one point at a time and try to come up with a reasonable answer. If you have used STL before and are a convert, feel free to skip this section and dive right into the meat of the chapter.

Code Reuse

One of the biggest arguments in favor of using the STL is obvious. It is a large body of code that has already been written for you. People have implemented several different types of containers and algorithms, debugged them, ported them to your platform, and made it available either for free or for a reasonable amount of money.

Most of the code available is for the truly basic building blocks of any game or tool, such as lists, hash tables, sort algorithms, and searches. Do you really want to spend time writing those from scratch? Because the STL is mostly made out of templates and templatized functions, it is possible to integrate them seamlessly with your code base. You will not have to change all your list elements to inherit from some base class, or make any other intrusive changes; the code is a straight drop-in.

The code base has been debugged for several years, and many projects all around the world have used it to good effect, including other game projects. In other words, it is going to be a solid piece of code. If you have problems with anything in particular, chances are somebody had the same problems already, and there is a solution for it. The active online community can be a great resource for trying to work around any glitches you may find.

You also get all the source code along with it. Unfortunately, that is not as useful as it might sound, because the source code is nearly unintelligible to the casual reader. It is a tangled nest of highly customizable, optimized template code, full of includes and defines. Do not expect a neat little function that shows how a vector works. Instead, you will be treated to several implementations, depending on your platform and current configuration, all templatized and using preprocessor macros. Hitting the books or browsing through online discussion forums is often a better approach than wading through thousands of lines of code to solve a particular problem. Making your own changes is an even more daunting proposal. But if worse comes to worst, you can always go to the source and find out exactly how something is implemented.

Another advantage that cannot be ignored is that a good deal of the rest of the world is using STL. New hires can get up to speed faster if they do not have to learn a different internal set of classes for things like lists or sorting. Also, some libraries might become available that are designed to interface effortlessly with STL.

Performance

Now we get to the issue burns in most programmers' minds: performance. Game programmers are particularly concerned about performance, perhaps obsessively so. Does STL deliver the goods when it comes to performance?

The short answer is a resounding yes. Remember that STL has been improved by hundreds of users over the years. Some very smart people have taken it upon themselves to tweak every ounce of performance they can from particular containers or algorithms for each platform—all transparently for you.

If you have a hard time believing that such generic and elegant code can compete with your homemade programs, fire up your compiler and give it a try. Usually, you will find that STL will outperform a quick implementation by a huge margin, and it will be usually no slower than your best effort after spending days or weeks tweaking and optimizing the code.

But it is possible to beat STL performance. Usually, this entails either deeper knowledge of the data you are manipulating or specific hardware platform knowledge that STL does not have (maybe because the port to your specific platform is rather new and has not had time to mature and become faster). How many times are you going to need that extra bit of performance? Usually not often, and perhaps not in the whole course of a project. If the time ever comes, then you can replace a particularly slow part of the code with your own homemade functions. Until then, STL will result in a more robust, faster program than it would be without it.

One thing to take into account is how truly empowering STL can be. Having a whole set of fundamental data structures and algorithms at your fingertips is quite an experience. With STL, the basic elements of a problem are not pointers and memory buffers, but nodes in a list or entries in a set. Solving problems becomes a lot more natural, and better solutions are usually found.

For those of you still concerned about performance, keep this in mind: working with STL will often result in much more efficient algorithms, because of the ease of using advanced data structures and algorithms. The same solution implemented at a lower level will often be done with a simpler, much less efficient algorithm just because it was the easier one to write. With STL, we can take a bunch of elements, throw them in a hash table, and search them later on in constant time. Without it, a lot of programmers might simply put them in a fixed-size array, search for them in linear time, and keep their fingers crossed that we never add more elements than the maximum size of the array.

While STL can offer superb performance, it can also be the source of major slowdowns if it is not used properly. With the added complexity comes added responsibility in the part of the programmer. Something as simple as choosing the wrong data structure for the operations we want to perform in it can be a performance killer. More subtle problems include dynamic memory allocation for a particular container, or even extra copies introduced by copying elements. To use STL effectively, especially in a performance-sensitive environment such as games, it is important to understand what is going on underneath the hood and to choose the right tool for the right job.

Drawbacks

So is there anything bad about STL? Are there reasons we should not choose it for all our games and tools? Unfortunately, there are a few.

The most notable drawback is that debugging sometimes becomes quite hard. You can pretty much forget about stepping into some of the container operations or algorithms. The STL's heavy use of templates makes it very difficult (or impossible) for the compiler to allow good interactive debugging and breakpoints. But that is not so bad; after all, the code has supposedly already been debugged, and we should not have to get our hands dirty. The main issue is in just viewing the contents of the containers we have created. It is often impossible to see what an iterator is pointing to, or simply to see all the elements in a vector. It is possible, but it certainly takes some coercing of the debugger to do it.

The error messages generated by the compiler when using STL are not something you want to deal with often, either. They are usually long, multiline cryptic messages, often pointing to places that are not even in the code we wrote, just because we mistyped the class in a container we are using. It definitely takes some experience and patience to parse those messages correctly, and find the (usually trivial) bug that was causing them.

The last major drawback is memory allocation. STL is intended for a general computing environment with large amounts of memory and not much of a penalty for memory allocation. While that is most often the case when we are developing tools, it is not always the case on our target game platform, especially consoles. Fortunately, it is possible to provide custom memory allocators to specific containers, which allows us to control how and when memory is allocated. We will cover allocators in more detail toward the end of the chapter. Integrating STL into our own memory management also requires some extra work, either by providing more allocators or altering some of the global memory allocation functions to use our memory system. Fortunately, development can start on a game without the need to do either one of those things up front. Only once development is well underway it is necessary to deal with some of the lower-level memory issues.

Overall, there is absolutely no reason not to use STL in all your tools. You should also really consider using STL in your game code, and only decide to roll your own functions if STL simply will not do. Many PC and console games have already shipped that take full advantage of all the power STL has to offer.

SEQUENCE CONTAINERS

Sequence containers are so called because their distinguishing characteristic is that they store their elements in a specific order. Because the elements are in a specific sequence, it is possible to insert and remove elements at particular points in that sequence (e.g., at the beginning, the end, or anywhere in the middle).

Vector

Perhaps the simplest and one of the most used containers is the *vector*. Elements can be added or deleted anywhere in the sequence, although with different performance characteristics, depending on their specific position, as we will see in a moment. A vector provides bidirectional iterators. That is, we can access any element forward or backward from a given iterator. In addition, a vector's elements can be accessed in random order, just like a plain C array:

```
vector<int> entityUID;
// Fill it up
if (entityUID[5] == UID) //...
```

Apart from its similarity to an array, there is no hard limit to the number of elements that can be added to a vector. When working with an array, the normal technique is to try to guess the maximum number of elements we will ever need at once, and allocate an array of that size. Whenever we attempt to add one more element to the array, we first check that we are not exceeding its maximum size. If the array is already full, in the best case we will get an error, and hopefully the program will deal with it correctly. In the worst case, the program will go ahead and try to add the element anyway, causing memory corruption or a page fault, and an immediate crash. Using vectors instead of arrays makes all these problems disappear.

Typical Implementation

Vectors hold all their elements contiguously in one large block of memory. That block of memory will usually have some spare room for future elements. Each element is copied at the right offset, without adding any pointers or additional data (other than some padding, depending on the platform). Since all the elements in a vector are of the same type and consequently of the same size, the location of a vector can be calculated from its index in the sequence and its size.

In addition to the block of memory that holds the element, a vector has a small header with a pointer to the beginning of the elements and some other information, such as the current number of elements and the size of the currently allocated memory block. Figure 8.1 shows a typical implementation of a vector container.

Performance

Inserting or deleting elements at the end of the vector is very efficient, just like with an array. The STL documentation guarantees a performance cost of O(1). All that it tells us is that the insertion time does not depend on the size of the array. But how fast is it, really? Constant-time insertion will not be of much use if it takes 30 ms to insert an element. Fortunately, it is as blazingly fast as it can be, and the only cost involved is in copying the element in place.

However, inserting or deleting elements anywhere else, other than at the end, becomes a more expensive operation, since it requires copying

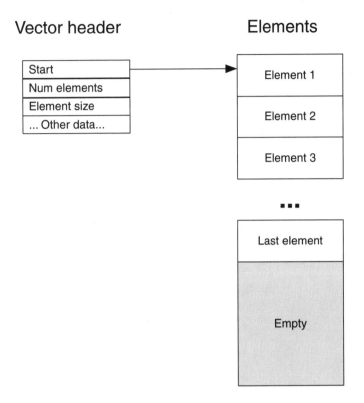

FIGURE 8.1   Vector implementation.

all the elements from the insertion point until the end and shifting them up or down by one. That is not to say that it is not possible to insert or delete elements in the middle of the sequence. The vector class is prepared for that; it is simply not the most efficient of all containers for that particular operation.

Also, inserting elements at the end of a vector might cause the allocated memory block to run out of memory. This will cause some reallocation and copying of all the elements, as we will see in the Memory Usage section. With some care, this can be completely avoided in loops that require high performance, so it should not be a consideration when looking at the overall performance of a vector.

A vector might still be the best container to use if our program adds or deletes elements from different positions very infrequently, or if the number of elements in the sequence is very small.

Traversal of all the elements in the container is as fast as it is going to get. A well-written traversal loop will be just as efficient as the same traversal on an array.

```
vector<int>::iterator it;
for(it=entityUID.begin(); it!=entity.UID.end(); ++it) {
    int UID = *it;
    // Do something with the UID
}
```

Memory Usage

As we saw earlier, vectors hold all their elements in one large block of memory. That memory block has to be large enough to hold all its current elements, with some extra room for future elements. As more elements are added, there is less extra space, until at some point a new element will not fit in that memory block anymore. At this point, the vector allocates a larger memory block, copies all of its current elements to the new block, adds the new element, and deletes the previous memory block. Usually, this new memory block will be twice the size of the previous one. This will give it a lot of room for expansion without the need for allocating new memory very frequently, or allocating too much memory and wasting space.

Notice that there is no mention of shrinking. A vector never gets any smaller by itself. So if at some point it grows to be really large, and then most of the elements are removed, there will be some unused allocated memory.

The astute reader might have already noticed something a bit disquieting in the previous paragraphs. Whenever the vector reaches its size limit, new memory is allocated, and all of its elements are copied over to the new location. So what happens if we have a pointer to some element when that happens? We are totally out of luck. A vector makes no guarantees about the validity of pointers or even iterators after an insertion. The same situation arises if we delete or insert an element into the middle of the sequence, and we have to shift all the remaining elements up or down by one. If we need to refer to specific elements, even after those operations, we should keep their indices and access them through the operator[] function.

Allocating a new memory block and copying all the elements in the sequence to the new location might not be cheap, either. The more elements we have and the more expensive they are to copy, the worse off we are. Is this something we have to worry about? Yes, it probably is. Fortunately there are a few things we can do to alleviate the problem.

First is to pre-allocate enough entries in the vector to avoid doing a lot of allocations. Remember that every time the vector runs out of memory, it doubles in size. So if it starts with 16 elements, it allocates 32, then 64, then 128, and so on. If we know we are going to need at least 800 elements, we will have six allocations (and copies) for sure. We can bypass that by pre-allocating 1,024 elements through the reserve() function. But reserve does not change the number of elements in the vector (like resize does), it just changes how much memory is allocated for the whole vector and future elements.

Vectors might often be filled with a lot of values that are used during a computation and then discarded. If this happens frequently, it will mean that we are constantly allocating and freeing the vector (possibly multiple times if we are not using reserve). A good solution in this case is to keep that vector static and clear all of its elements before each use. Clearing the elements does not free any memory; it marks the vector as empty and calls the destructor for each element (assuming there is a destructor to call).

One really handy characteristic of a vector is that all of its elements are stored sequentially in memory; that is, there is just one block of memory allocated, and all the elements are located next to each other as part of that block. Several good things come out of that. First of all, traversing all the elements will result in good data cache consistency. This is more important for some platforms than others, but in extreme cases of thousands of elements, it will probably be noticeable, even on a PC. The second advantage of the sequential arrangement is that the contents of a vector can be passed straight to a function that takes a pointer to an array of elements as a parameter. It is a simple optimization that can be done to interface with functions that do not use STL. For example, a pointer to the contents of a vector could be passed to a 3D API function as an array with vertex data. Use this carefully, and make sure that the function itself does not try to add or delete elements from the array, or the vector will get out of synch with its contents.

Recommendation

Use vectors everywhere you can, given their performance characteristics. There is almost no reason to use arrays anymore, so use vectors instead of arrays, unless memory is so tight that you cannot afford the extra few bytes that a vector requires. This applies even in cases where the maximum number of elements is known ahead of time. Using vectors everywhere gives you a bit of extra flexibility, it does not require you to keep track of the number of elements separately, and it uses the same interface as all other vectors in the game.

Vectors have a lot of ideal properties for high-performance programming, so you should always start by considering whether a vector is appropriate for a given application, and only move to other, more complex containers if it is not sufficient (see Table 8.1). Situations that come up during game development that could be best implemented using vectors include:

- The list of all the weapons the player can cycle through
- The list of all the players currently in the game
- Some pre-allocated buffers to receive network traffic
- A list of vertices with simplified geometries for collision detection
- The list of children in a tree node (if the children are reasonably static or there are only a few children)
- The list of all animations a game entity can play
- The list of all components a game entity holds
- The list of points along a path for camera movement or AI path calculations

Table 8.1   Vector Summary Table

Insert/delete element at the back	O(1)
Insert/delete element at the front	O(N)
Insert/delete element in the middle	O(N)
Memory allocation	Rarely, only to grow
Traversal performance	Fastest (like C array)
Sequential memory access	Yes
Iterator invalidation	After an insertion or deletion
Memory overhead	12–16 bytes total

Deque

For those readers who are not familiar with the data structure deque, it is pronounced "deck," and it stands for "double-ended queue."

A *deque* is almost identical to a vector, but with slightly different performance characteristics. Like a vector, it provides random access to any of its elements, and it is also possible to insert and delete elements from anywhere in the sequence, although at different costs. What makes a deque unique is that it provides fast insertion and deletion to the beginning as well as to the end of the sequence.

Typical Implementation

A deque is similar to a vector in that it keeps all its elements in large memory blocks. However, the main difference is that it has several memory blocks, not just one. As more elements are added (to the back or the front), a new block is allocated, and the new elements are added there. Unlike vectors, there is no need to copy existing elements to the new block, since the old memory block is still valid.

To keep track of those memory blocks, a deque has several pointers to each of them. As the number of memory blocks increases, more pointers are stored. (You can think of this list as a vector of pointers to the memory blocks.) The rest of the deque header is made up of bookkeeping information: number of elements, pointer to the first element in the sequence, pointer to the last element, and so forth. Figure 8.2 shows a typical implementation for a deque container.

Performance

As with a vector, inserting or deleting an element at the back of the sequence is a very fast operation (O(1)). Also, just like a vector, inserting or deleting an element from the middle of the sequence is a relatively slow (O(N)) operation.

However, as mentioned earlier, the main difference between a deque and a vector is that inserting or deleting an element at the beginning of the sequence is just as fast as doing it at the back. This makes deques perfect data structures for implementing FIFO (First In, First Out) structures, such as queues.

A deque usually keeps its elements in several memory blocks, instead of just one like a vector. Within each of those blocks, elements are arranged sequentially in memory, so the benefits of cache consistency still apply to that block. However, when accessing an element in a different memory block, performance will degrade a bit. Even so, since those blocks are relatively large, the traversal of all the elements in a deque is not much slower than in a vector. The rest of the operations are usually either a bit slower than or just as fast as with a vector.

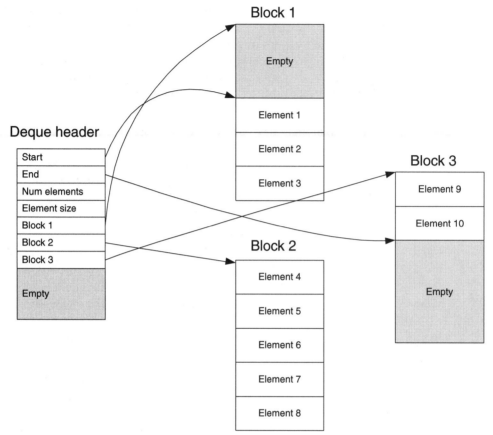

FIGURE 8.2   Deque implementation.

Memory Usage

Memory allocations will happen periodically during normal usage of a deque. Clearly, if we keep adding elements to a deque, new memory blocks will be needed and allocated. Similarly, removing elements will eventually cause some memory blocks to be freed.

The less intuitive part is that even if the number of elements stays relatively constant, a deque will continue to cause memory allocations. If objects are added at the back and removed from the front, new blocks will need to be added at the back, and old, empty blocks will be removed from the front. In a way, we can imagine the deque as 'sliding' along in memory, even if it always stays the same size.

Because of the dynamic nature of a deque, there is no equivalent toa `reserve()` function to pre-allocate memory for a fixed number of elements.

The last important thing to know about a deque is that it might allocate a 'large' initial memory block. In some implementations, that initial block might be as high as 4,096 bytes, so keep this in mind if you need to create many deques simultaneously.

Recommendation

Because of the lack of control over its memory allocation and the unpredictable allocation pattern, a deque might not be a good container for environments with tight memory budgets or expensive memory allocation. If you are dealing with a small number of elements, a vector is probably a better choice, even when paying the extra copying penalty every time an element at the front is removed. Otherwise, you might want to consider a list, possibly with a custom allocator.

The uses of a deque are not as numerous as those of a vector in game development (see Table 8.2). Even so, here are some situations that arise in game development where a deque might be a good choice:

- A queue to store game messages that need to be processed in FIFO order
- A queue to traverse an object hierarchy in a breadth-first manner

Table 8.2   Deque Summary Table

Insert/delete element at the back	O(1)
Insert/delete element at the front	O(1)
Insert/delete element in the middle	O(N)
Memory allocation	Periodically, during normal usage
Traversal performance	Almost as fast as a vector
Sequential memory access	Almost; several sequential blocks
Iterator invalidation	After an insertion or deletion
Memory overhead	Header of 16+ bytes; initial memory block could be 4 KB

List

The list container is another sequence container, but it has very different characteristics from vectors and deques. A list provides bidirectional iterators, which means that given the iterator to a certain element in the list, we can access the next or the previous element. However, it does not provide random access to its elements like the previous two containers we have seen. Any algorithms that require random access will not be able to be applied to a list. What we lose in flexibility we gain in performance and convenience for certain operations. Like a vector or a deque, it is possible to insert and delete elements from any position, as long as we have an iterator referring to that position.

Typical Implementation

A list is implemented as a doubly linked list of elements. The main departure from vectors and deques is that the elements, instead of being lumped together in a large memory block, are individually allocated as nodes in that list. Each node will also contain a previous pointer and a next pointer.

The list also has the usual header information, with a pointer to the first element, the last one, and possibly some other information. A typical implementation of a list container is shown in Figure 8.3.

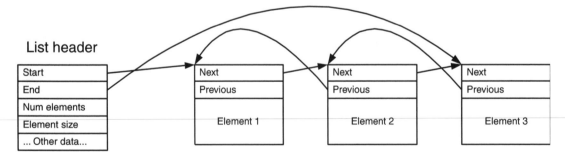

FIGURE 8.3   List implementation.

Performance

As you might have guessed, the big advantage of a list is that it does not have a performance penalty for inserting or deleting elements in the middle of the sequence. Any insertions or deletions, anywhere, are all constant time, since all they require is fixing up some pointers. Of course, we need to have an iterator referring to the location where we want to perform our operation, and getting there might not be constant time.

Traversal of the elements in the sequence is much slower than a vector. To traverse the sequence, the program must read the pointer at each node and access a different location somewhere else in memory, which causes poor data cache consistency. This results in a significantly slower traversal, possibly an order of magnitude slower than with a vector. Do not panic, though; keep in mind that the traversal time is usually not the largest performance drain. So even if it is greatly increased, it might not be very noticeable. It will depend on your particular application.

Any operations that involve rearranging the elements in a sequence (such as sorting) will probably be very efficient when using a list, since there is no need to copy the elements to a new location, just fix their pointers. The larger and more expensive it is to copy the elements of the sequence, the more gains we will get by using a list.

Memory Usage

A list is totally different from the other sequence containers. The other containers allocate large blocks of memory and try to copy as many elements as possible in them. A list will allocate a small amount of memory for each element, and that small block of memory will become a node in the list.

The advantages are that we do not disturb the nearby elements when we insert or delete one in the middle of the sequence. It also means that iterators and pointers to elements are preserved, even in the presence of insertions and deletions. This makes many algorithms very convenient to implement.

The drawbacks of such an arrangement are that almost every operation causes a memory allocation. This can be a big hit in platforms with slow dynamic memory allocation, but it can be easily alleviated with a bit of work by creating a custom allocator.

Nodes are not laid out sequentially in memory. They are dynamically allocated at different times during execution, so they could be scattered all over memory. That could cause some severe performance penalties due to bad data cache consistency. Fortunately, we can improve the cache consistency through the use of a custom allocator, as described earlier. So not only does the custom allocator avoid the constant allocation of dynamic memory, it also improves performance by making the nodes more likely to be near each other. But the allocator will not make this issue go away completely, and in the worst cases, even with a custom allocator there could be almost no spatial coherence.

Another drawback of a list is the extra memory consumption. A list node will typically require an extra 8–12 bytes per node. This might not be an issue for PC platforms, but the extra memory consumption can add up to a significant amount in consoles with limited memory if we have a lot of very small nodes.

Recommendation

Lists are a well-rounded, general sequence container. It would be very tempting to use them exclusively and forget about vectors and deques. However, their poor performance when iterating through their elements and the constant memory allocations, make them poor candidates for high-performance situations. It is best to consider lists only when we have determined that vectors and deques are not well suited for the problem at hand.

Interestingly, even though it is not part of the standard, several STL implementations provide a different sequence container: slist. It is just like the list, but it is implemented as a single-linked list with the usual tradeoffs. There is less memory per node (no need for a back pointer) and slightly less pointer management, but it is impossible to move back from a node, so the iterators provided by slist are only forward iterators. Additionally, slist can have some unexpected performance characteristics, since some operations rely on accessing previous elements (e.g., deleting an element in the sequence). It is best to only use slist if the minor memory savings are very important. Otherwise a normal list is a better all-around choice. A few of the many uses for lists during game development are (see Table 8.3):

- A list of all game entities, with many insertions and deletions throughout the course of the game
- A list of possible objectives evaluated by the AI, from which some will be chosen and removed
- A list of all meshes that we want to render in this frame, to be sorted by material and render state

Table 8.3   List Summary Table

Insert/delete element at the back	O(1)
Insert/delete element at the front	O(1)
Insert/delete element in the middle	O(1)
Memory allocation	With every insertion or deletion
Traversal performance	Much slower than a vector
Sequential memory access	No
Iterator invalidation	Never
Memory overhead	8–12 bytes plus 8–12 bytes per element

ASSOCIATIVE CONTAINERS

Sequence containers preserve the relative positions in which the elements are inserted and deleted from the table. Associative containers forego that characteristic, and instead focus on being able to find a single element from the containers as quickly as possible.

Finding a particular object in a sequence container usually requires O(N) time, since we need to look at every single element in the sequence. In the case of a vector or a deque, if the elements are already sorted, then it could be possible to find an element in O(ln N) time by using a binary search, since they provide fast random access to any element. However, to take advantage of this, we need to keep the sequences sorted in a particular order, which is not necessarily what we want, and which is rather expensive to maintain as new elements are added and old elements deleted.

Associative containers provide us with either O(ln N) or even O(1) time to find specific elements. Usually, elements are keyed off some particular data for fast lookup through the data; sometimes the elements themselves are their own keys.

Set and Multiset

A set provides a container that is very similar to a mathematical set: it contains some objects, without saying anything about their order. An object simply is or is not in a set.

It should be possible to check whether two objects added to a set are not equal. In particular, they should have the operator< defined, or we should provide a function as part of the template to compare the equality of two of the objects.

New objects are added by calling insert() and are removed by calling erase(). To find if a particular element is present in the set, we call the function find(), which will find the element in O(ln N) time. The template declaration for a set is:

```
set<Key, Compare, Alloc>
```

Key is the type of the element we want the set to contain, and Compare is a functor that will be used to compare the elements as they are inserted. We will see how the last parameter, Alloc, works in the next chapter, STL—Algorithms and Advanced Topics. As usual, not all parameters are necessary, and the template will provide a default allocator and a default comparison function. Specifically, it will attempt to use the operator< on the elements themselves, so you only need to provide a comparison functor if the elements do not have an operator< already defined, or if you want to do some different type of sorting.

```
set<int> objectives;
objectives.insert(getObjectiveUID());
//...

if (objectives.find(objectiveUID) != objectives.end()) {
    // That objective was completed. Do something
}
```

The set container will only keep one instance of each similar object. So inserting the same object multiple times will not change the set. A multiset, on the other hand, will keep multiple copies of the same object if it was inserted multiple times. A multiset also has some extra functions to deal with, having multiple elements such as count(), which returns how many of a particular element there are in the container.

A set can be the perfect container for taking some data and removing all redundant entities. We can just throw them all in a set and read them back. This will be much more efficient than doing an $O(N^2)$ pass through the list, looking for duplicates, especially as the number of elements grows larger.

We can also use the fact that we can pass our own comparison function to create more interesting applications. Imagine that we have a set of points in 3D space, and we want to collapse all points within a certain distance of each other. One quick solution would be to create an equality function to compare two points, but only consider two points equal if they are within a minimum distance of each other. We can then create a set of points that uses that equality function, throw all the points in, and then read them back out.

```
struct PointNearbyLess {
    bool operator()(const Point3d & pt1,
                        const Point3d & pt2) const
    {
        float fDist = ::Distance(pt1, pt2);
        return (fDist > POINT_COMPARE_THRESHOLD);
    }
};

typedef set<Point3d, PointNearbyLess> PointCollapseSet;
PointCollapseSet pointSet;
// Insert points in pointSet...
```

Notice that we did not actually create an equality function, but rather an inequality function—or more specifically, a 'less than' function. This is because STL uses the 'less than' comparison rather than equality in its set implementation. Actually, STL will often check for equality of two elements, not by applying operator ==, but rather by using:

```
!(k1 < k2) && !(k2 < k1)
```

So we will write 'less than' functions very often when working with STL.

Sets and multisets are called sorted associative containers because in addition to being associative containers, they will store the elements in a certain order (based on the comparison function). That means that in addition to being able to find any element quickly, we can iterate through all the elements in that given order. Not all associative containers will have this property.

Typical Implementation

As the containers get more complex, implementations from STL version to STL version vary more. What is described here is just a typical implementation that we can use as a basis for our discussion about performance and memory usage. If you are using an obscure STL implementation or a strange target platform, you might want to check the source code to verify that things are implemented in roughly this way.

Sets and multisets are usually implemented as a balanced binary tree to facilitate O(ln N) searches of its elements. Each element is in its own node, as in the case of a list, but now they are arranged in the form of a binary tree, and they are ordered based on the comparison function provided with the template. A possible implementation of a set container is shown in Figure 8.4.

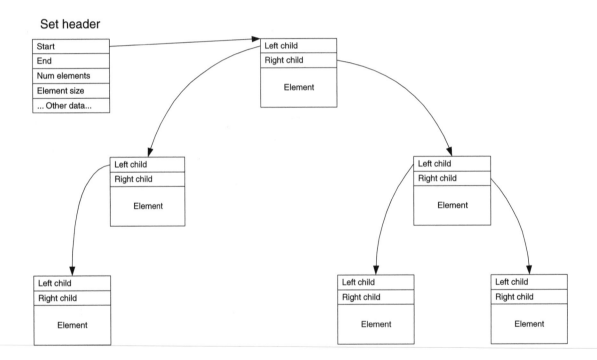

FIGURE 8.4   Set implementation.

Performance

The strength of a set is that we can very quickly find out whether an element exists in the set or not. How quickly is very quickly? A set will usually be implemented as a balanced binary tree, so it will usually require on the order of O(ln N) comparisons. To that we have to take into account how expensive the comparisons actually are. Comparing two integers is very straightforward, but comparing two large matrices or strings can be much more time consuming.

Clearly, sets pay off whenever there are a lot of elements in the set. We can use them for convenience even with a very small number of elements, but at that point, a vector and a simple linear search could be just as fast.

Another alternative, especially if the contents of the set do not change frequently, is to store the elements in a vector, sort them, and then use binary searches every time we want to find out whether or not an element is already present. All of the cost associated with the initial filling and sorting of the vector would be quickly amortized if it is frequently queried but its contents never change.

Inserting new elements requires knowing whether more elements of that type already exist, so it will be at least as expensive as a normal search through the elements, which is $O(\ln N)$. In addition, the insertion might cause some small rearrangements of the tree to keep it balanced. Most implementations will try to minimize the insertion cost by using red-black trees or some other well-known algorithm to keep the tree balanced, so the extra cost should not be very noticeable.

Traversing through all the elements in a set is a matter of following pointers, as in the case of a list. There might also be a slight extra cost because the elements are arranged in a tree, but the overall performance should be very similar to a list.

Memory Usage

If the exact memory usage of a container is of prime importance to you, then associative containers might not be the best choice. Because they are implemented as balanced binary trees, every insertion requires the allocation of a new node, and removing an element causes its node to be deleted. Fortunately, rearranging the tree to keep it balanced does not cause any extra allocations.

Recommendation

Sets and multisets are not the type of containers we need in everyday use. But whenever there is any application that needs to cull out all redundant instances of all items, they are a very good solution to the problem. (Depending on your specific situation, a map, which we will see in the next section, might also be a good solution.) Some of the frequent uses of a set are to (also see Table 8.4):

- Keep a set of collision normals so we do not process the same one multiple times.
- Keep a set of objects that we are reading from disk. Those objects are read in date order (older to newer), and newer objects can override older ones. Putting them in a set as we read them will automatically check whether they already existed and will override the old ones.

Table 8.4   Set and Multiset Summary Table

Insert/delete elements	O(ln N)
Find an element	O(ln N)
Memory allocation	With every insertion or deletion
Traversal performance	A bit slower than a list
Sequential memory access	No
Iterator invalidation	Never
Memory overhead	8–12 bytes plus 8–12 bytes per element

Map and Multimap

Maps are another type of associative container, so their primary objective is to provide very quick search operations for particular elements. They are very similar to sets, but with an added twist. In the case of sets, the elements themselves are the keys that were used to sort and search the elements of the set. In the case of a map, there are two separate pieces of data: the element and the key, which is used to search in the map.

Alternatively, you can think of a map as an array, but instead of using integers to index into it, you can use any type of data. Conveniently, maps even provide a custom operator[] that allows us to use the array syntax to access its elements. The specific template declaration for a map is:

```
map<Key, Data, Compare, Alloc>
```

Here Key is the data type that will be used for the map keys, Data is the data type for the actual elements, and Compare is a functor that will be used to compare and sort keys as they are inserted into the map.

The difference between maps and multimaps is easy to guess. It is the same as between sets and multisets; a map can only have one of a particular key, but a multimap can have multiples of the same key. Notice that the difference only applies to keys, not to the elements themselves. It is certainly possible to have multiple copies of the same element with different keys in a plain map.

The applications of a map are many, but one of the ones that comes up frequently is the quick lookup between some arbitrary number and a piece of data. Consider, for example, an architecture where each game entity in the world has a unique ID, and those IDs are 16-bit numbers, so the range is between 0 and 65,536. We will definitely want to have a way to go from ID to the entity it corresponds to.

One possibility is to traverse all entities, checking the ID for each one until we find the one we are looking for, or until we run out of entities. Considering that there will probably be many game entities, and that this is something that will happen many times per frame, this approach will quickly break down and become way too expensive.

A different approach would be to create an array (or a vector) of pointers with $2^{16} = 65,536$ elements. Every time a game entity is created, we fill the element in the array with an index corresponding to its ID, with the pointer to that entity. Going from IDs to entities is a piece of cake, since we only need to look up the correct array element. The problem is that the array will take a fair amount of memory. If pointers are 32 bits, the array itself will take 256 KB, independently of how many objects there are in the game world. And this might seem wasteful already, but things get worse. Maybe 256 KB does not sound like much, but game entity IDs are not necessarily limited to 16 bits. It is more likely that they will be 32 bits or more. An array large enough to hold that many pointers would need 16 GB. That amount of memory should sound a lot more scary than 256 KB. Clearly, we need a different approach.

Maps are the perfect solution. We can create a map with the key as an integer and the elements as pointers to game entities. We can still access the map with the same syntax as the array in order to get the entity pointer, and the operation will be relatively efficient. What is more important, we will only use as much memory as the entities we add to the world.

Maps and multimaps are also sorted associative containers, so it is possible to traverse all the elements in a map in the order in which they are stored. As in the case of sets and multisets, that order is not the order in which they were inserted, but the order resulting from applying the Compare functor to the keys.

Typical Implementation

Maps and multimaps are implemented just like sets, using balanced binary trees. The only difference is that the keys to access and sort the elements are a different object, instead of being the element itself.

Performance

The performance of maps and multimaps is exactly the same as for sets and multisets, except that all comparisons are done on the keys, not on the elements. If you have large or expensive elements and very simple keys, this can be a significant advantage. On the other hand, if you have more complicated key types, such as strings or other complex objects, comparing two of those keys will be slower and will slow down the overall search.

A couple of words of warning about operator[] defined for a map. On the surface, it looks like a very convenient notation to access map elements, just like with a vector or an array. The first thing that we need to realize is that if we choose to use it, operator[] is not as fast on a map as it is on a vector. Even though it gives us the illusion of constant-time random access to any element, it still needs to find the element in O(ln N) time, underneath.

The next interesting bit about operator[] is what happens when we try to access an element that does not already exist. If we are writing to an element that does not exist, then the new element gets added to the map with the key we used to access the map.

```
// A new entry is added to the map as we would expect
map<int, string> playerName;
playerName[0] = game.GetLocalPlayerName();
```

However, what happens if we are attempting to read an element with a key that does not already exist? Surprisingly, the result is that a default element is added for that key, and its value is returned.

```
// Try to get the name of player 0, even though there is
// no such player. A new player gets added!
map<int, string> playerName;
const string & playerName = playerName[0];
// Now playerName[0] == ""
```

So if you are just trying to find out if an element is already in the map, you should use the `find` function, which will return an iterator to that element if found, or an iterator to `.end()` if it was not found.

Finally, if we want to add a new element to a map, it will be slightly more efficient to use the `insert()` function rather than the `operator[]`. This is because using `operator[]` usually causes several temporary copies of the key-element pair to be created and copied before they are finally inserted in the map. When calling `insert` directly, you are creating those copies explicitly, and there is as little copying as possible involved. However, when updating the contents of an existing element, using `operator[]` ends up being slightly more efficient than calling `insert()` again with the same key to override the existing element.

Memory Usage

Maps have a very similar memory usage pattern to the sets, so the same comments about many memory allocations and hard to predict behavior apply.

Recommendation

Maps are often used as fast dictionaries when we need to go from a handle, a unique ID, or a string to a certain object. They can also be thought of as arrays that can be indexed by types other than integers, including complex data types, such as strings or other more complicated objects.

Maps are a very useful concept, but hashed maps (see the next section, Hashes) provide the same functionality with better performance. Consider using hashed maps when dealing with a lot of elements unless your STL implementation does not provide them, or you have very tight memory requirements (see Table 8.5). Some applications of maps are:

- Maintaining a dictionary of unique IDs to their corresponding game entities. That allows the game to avoid using pointers to entities, which can disappear at any time.
- Translation between strings and integers: for example, translating between player names and their player ID.

Table 8.5   Map and Multimap Summary Table

Insert/delete elements	O(ln N)
Find an element	O(ln N)
Memory allocation	With every insertion or deletion
Traversal performance	A bit slower than a list
Sequential memory access	No
Iterator invalidation	Never
Memory overhead	8–12 bytes plus 8–12 bytes per element

Hashes

There is one type of associative container that did not make it in the standard, but it is available under several STL implementations. It is not just one container, but a whole family of them: the hashed associative containers.

The hash family of containers consists of `hash_set`, `hash_multiset`, `hash_map`, and `hash_multimap`. As you can probably guess, those containers are very similar to `set`, `multiset`, `map`, and `multimap`. They are so similar, in fact, that they do not look any different from the user's point of view. The only difference is in how they are implemented, and the performance and memory consequences that they have.

All the associative containers we have seen so far are implemented as some sort of balanced binary tree. This sort of organization allows reasonably fast access to any element in the containers, which is the primary goal of associative containers. In this case, 'reasonably fast' means O(ln N), but many times we can do better.

Hashed containers have the same rules as their corresponding binary tree containers, but they are implemented with hash tables. That means that given the right keys and the right hash table size, finding an element can be as fast as O(1). Unfortunately, it means that if things are not set up correctly, performance can be as bad as O(N), in which case the balanced trees would be faster.

Fortunately for most cases, performance of a hashed container will be very close to O(1). It is a bit like quick sort; theoretically it could be pretty slow, but for most random sequences, it is usually the fastest sort algorithm. The template declaration for a `hash_map` looks a bit more complicated than for a plain map:

```
hash_map<Key, Data, HashFcn, EqualKey, Alloc>
```

Key and Data are the same as with a map; the data type of the keys and the elements the container will hold. HashFcn is a functor that takes a reference to a key and returns a hash key of type size_t. This is the function that does the actual hashing, and the container just takes care of inserting elements in the right position based on their hash value. EqualKey is another parameter that is different from a map. Unlike a map, the hash table does not care whether two keys are smaller than each other; it just cares about whether they are exactly equal, and that is what this function does. By default, hash_map will try to use operator== on the keys.

The template declaration for hash_set and hash_multiset is the same except that it does not have a Data parameter, since the Key doubles up as both key and data.

Typical Implementation

Hashed containers are implemented as a traditional hash table. There is a set of buckets (usually allocated contiguously in memory, just like a vector), each holding a pointer to a linked list of elements that belong to that bucket.

Adding new elements is a matter of running the key through the hash function, which then points to the correct bucket and inserts the element into the list. The actual order of the elements in the list is not important.

Finding an element follows a similar process, but instead of adding an element, once we find the bucket where that element should be, the whole list is traversed, looking for the element we want. Ideally, that list should be as short as possible and ideally should only have one element. Figure 8.5 shows a typical implementation of a hashed associative container.

Performance

We already talked about the performance of hashed associative containers in their description since, after all, performance is their main distinguishing characteristic from the other associative containers. As we saw, in the ideal case, finding an element in the hashed container is a very fast, O(1) operation. However, as with any hash table, things can go wrong. The hash function takes care of generating an internal hash key from the key of the element we are inserting. The overall performance of the container will completely depend on how well this function performs. A good hashing function will generate a good spread of keys and avoid having many elements in the same hash bucket.

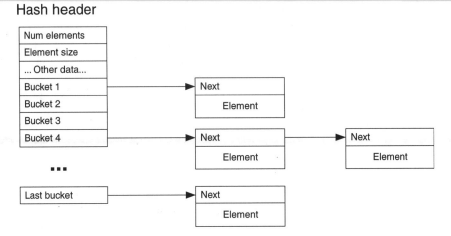

FIGURE 8.5   Hashed associative container implementation.

However, it is possible that a very particular set of keys will all map to just a few hash buckets, slowing down the performance of most operations linear to the number of objects O(N). Fortunately, most of the time, the default hash function provided with the hash templates is enough, especially if your hash keys are simple integers or strings.

Memory Usage

What about memory usage? Not surprisingly, hashed containers will allocate and free dynamic memory quite often. Elements are still node based, just like with the sorted associative containers; so inserting a new element requires allocating new memory, and removing an element frees memory.

In addition to the nodes themselves, hashed containers need to also allocate all the buckets. The buckets themselves should be pretty small, but keep in mind that you will most likely have about one bucket per element, possibly more. If the elements in the hash table are also small, then the buckets could make the total memory consumption double or triple. For larger elements, the memory overhead introduced by the buckets is not as large a percentage.

Interestingly, hashed containers have some functions to deal with buckets directly. The function bucket_count() returns how many buckets are currently allocated, and resize() works just like with a vector, but it sets the number of buckets instead of the number of elements. That way, if you know you will need a minimum number of elements in the hash table, you could resize() it to the right number of elements and avoid extra allocations and copies of buckets while the hash table is growing.

Recommendation

For a large number of elements and with a good hash key, hashed containers can be much faster than sorted associative containers. The only drawbacks are that hashed containers do not keep the elements in any particular order, and that they can take more memory. If you want maximum performance, you can live with those restrictions, and are reasonably sure you can come up with a good hash key. Then hashed associative containers are the perfect tool.

If performance is not a top priority, then using a sorted associative container might be a less risky move. With a sorted associative container, we do not have to worry about strange data distribution that might cause really bad runtime performance; and it is part of the STL standard, which will make it easier to port to different platforms.

Since performance is often crucial in games, hashed containers are used more often than regular sorted associative containers (see Table 8.6). Some of the situations in which a hashed associative container is useful are:

- Maintaining a dictionary of unique IDs to their corresponding game entities. This allows the game to avoid using pointers to entities, which can disappear at any time. It is the same example we presented for the case of a map, but since this is often a query that is done many times per frame, it is worth using a hashed container to achieve the best possible performance.
- Performing a fast lookup between class unique IDs and class information. This can be used to implement a very efficient RTTI system (see Chapter 12, Runtime Type Information).

Table 8.6   Hashed Associative Containers Summary Table

Insert/delete elements	O(1) - O(N)
Find an element	O(1) - O(N)
Memory allocation	With every insertion or deletion
Traversal performance	A bit slower than a list
Sequential memory access	No
Iterator invalidation	Never
Memory overhead	Very implementation dependent; easily 8–16 bytes per element for a well-distributed hash table

Container Adaptors

So far, we have seen all the containers provided in STL. Some of them were expected, such as vector (which is nothing more than a resizable array), list, or set. Some of them were not as well known, such as a deque or a multimap. But what happened to some of the other, very basic data structures? Does the STL provide a stack or a plain queue?

Let's think about the operations necessary to support a stack. All that is required is to push elements at the top of the stack, and remove them from the top. Any of the sequential containers can do that. So a stack would be a more limited container than any of them.

If the STL implementation had provided a stack container, how should that stack be implemented? Should it be like a vector, and when it grows past a certain size, should it reallocate memory and grow? Or should it be more like a list, where every element is a node? Or maybe a deque, and use page-based allocations? All those possible implementations are valid, and we might need different versions of the stack for different applications.

So instead of just giving us one stack implementation, the STL provides adaptors. Adaptors give an existing container a new, more restrictive interface, without adding any functionality of their own.

Why provide an adaptor to restrict what we can do with a container? It seems like we do not need an adaptor at all. If we want to treat a vector just like a stack, we can do so by ourselves in the code. In fact, this is true. There are two mains reasons for using a container adaptor:

- By declaring a data structure as a stack, we make very clear to everybody reading the code what we intend to do with it and what rules it will follow. It conveys more information than just using a vector.
- In addition to telling other programmers what we intend to do with that data structure, we are also telling the compiler, which will not let us sneak by one single operation that does not belong to the stack interface. If we had used a vector, it would be too easy to accidentally peek at the second item on the stack, which would break the rules we set for that data structure.

Stack

The simplest type of container adaptor is the stack. As we just saw, the main operations we can do on the stack are to add and remove elements from the top, as well as see what the top element is.

Because the stack is more restrictive than any of the sequence containers, it can be used on any of them. Clearly, the performance and memory characteristics of the stack will be the same as for the container it uses. By default, a stack is implemented using a deque. The following code implements a game event system in which the last event added must be resolved first.

```
// Create a stack using a deque for game events
stack<GameEvent> eventStack;
eventStack.push(currentEvent);
//...
// Resolve all events in the stack
while (!eventStack.empty()) {
    GameEvent & event = eventStack.top();
    event.Process();
    eventStack.pop();
}
```

If we decided that the underlying deque implementation was not good enough for our purposes, and we would rather use a vector, the only necessary change is in the definition of the eventStack variable.

```
// Create a stack using a stack
stack< vector<GameEvent> > eventStack;
```

Queue

The queue is another very popular data structure that is apparently missing from the STL containers. Again, like the stack, it is simply a restricted version of a container. In this case, the only operations allowed are adding elements at the back and removing elements from the front. We cannot add, remove, or even access other elements in the sequence.

By default, a queue uses a deque for its implementation, but it is also possible to use a list. Surprisingly, it is not possible to use a vector, even if we are fully aware that the performance of removing elements from the front is not particularly good. This is because vectors do not have a push_front function, which is required by the queue adaptor.

```
// By default the queue is using a deque
queue<Message> messages;
messages.push(getNetworkMessage());
//...
// Process all messages in the order they were received
while (!messages.empty()) {
    const Message & msg = messages.front();
```

```
        process(msg);
        messages.pop();
    }
```

To use the same code implemented as a list, we can declare the queue to use a list container.

```
    // Now the queue is using a list
    queue< list<Message> > messages;
```

Priority Queue

A priority queue is very similar to a plain queue; elements can be added only at the back and removed only from the front. The difference is that the element that is ready to be removed from the front is always the one with highest priority, not the one that was inserted first.

Unlike other container adaptors, the `priority_queue` adaptor adds a bit of functionality. Whenever elements are added to the container, they are sorted based on the priority function. This is something we could have easily done ourselves; so in a way, it is not adding anything new. It is just wrapping some higher-level functionality into the adaptor.

By default, the priority queue uses a vector as its underlying representation. It can also be used with a deque, but not with a list, since it requires random-order access to elements for efficient insertion of sorted elements.

Also by default, the comparison between elements, which is what determines the priority of an element, is done by using `less<Type>`. If we want a different comparison function for our priority, or if our elements do not have an `operator<` defined, then we must provide our own comparison function.

The following code snippet shows a priority queue whose priority is based on distance. Something like that can be used often in a game, where we want to prioritize the sounds we hear from the camera or the lights that affect an object, or even the game entities that an AI entity needs to process to decide what to do next.

```
        struct EntityPos {
            EntityPos(uint nUID, const Point3d & pos);
            uint    nUID;
            Point3d pos;
        };
        template<typename T>
        class CloserToCamera
        {
```

```
public:
    bool operator()(const T & p1, const T & p2) const;
};

bool CloserToCamera<typename T>::operator()(const T & p1,
                                            const T & p2) const
{
    const Point3d & campos = GetCurrentCamera.GetPosition();
    Vector3d camToP1 = p1 — campos;
    Vector3d camToP2 = p2 — campos;
    return (camToP1.length() < camToP2.length());
}


priority_queue<EntityPos, CloserToCamera<EntityPos> > entities;
// Fill all the entities we might want to consider
entities.push(EntityPos(nUID,pos));
//...
// Now process entities in order of distance to the camera until
// we run out of time, or maybe a fixed number of them
while ( WeShouldContinue() ) {
    uint nUID = *(entities.top()).nUID;
    entities.pop();
    // Do something with that entity
}
```

CONCLUSION

In this chapter, we have seen that there is very little reason not to use the STL in your development, both for development tools and for the game code itself. However, you have to be very aware of all the performance and memory implications when using different containers. There are some containers that will be wholly inappropriate to use for certain tasks, and there might even be some really low-level code that should not use STL containers at all. There are two major types of containers: sequence containers and associative containers.

Sequence Containers: Sequence containers allow the user to specify the order in which the elements are stored. They all allow insertions and deletions from any part of the sequence, but with very different performance characteristics. The sequence containers are:

- vector: It is like a resizable array. Elements are stored sequentially in a memory block that is resized whenever there is need for more memory. Inserting or deleting elements anywhere else other than the end is usually slow.

- `deque`: It is similar to a vector, but it allows very efficient insertion and deletion from the front as well as the back. It is implemented by allocating several memory pages, and elements are stored sequentially in each of those pages.
- `list`: A list allows very efficient insertion and deletion from anywhere in the sequence at the cost of extra memory per element and more memory allocations. Elements are not stored sequentially in memory, which causes more data cache misses when traversing large lists.

Associative Containers: Associative containers provide fast searches for a particular element. As a tradeoff, associative containers maintain elements in their own order, instead of in the order specified by the user.

There are two flavors of associative containers: sorted associative containers and hashed associative containers. Each of the four types of associative containers is available in both flavors.

Sorted associative containers are typically implemented as balanced binary trees. Elements are actually stored in the order used by the container. Access to elements is guaranteed to be logarithmic time ($O(\ln N)$).

Hashed associative containers are implemented as a hashed table. As a consequence, elements are not stored in any particular order. Access to any element can be as fast as constant time, but the worst case is a painfully slow linear time ($O(N)$). The associative containers are best summarized with a table:

Table 8.7   Associative Containers

CONTAINER	CAN HAVE MULTIPLE INSTANCES OF THE SAME ELEMENT	THE KEY IS THE ELEMENT ITSELF	IMPLEMENTED AS A HASH TABLE
set	no	yes	no
multiset	yes	yes	no
map	no	no	no
multimap	yes	no	no
hash_set	no	yes	yes
hash_multiset	yes	yes	yes
hash_map	no	no	yes
hash_multimap	yes	no	yes

Adaptors: In addition to the different containers, the STL provides container adaptors. They present a new interface on top of an existing container and are used to implement other popular data structures. The three container adaptors present in the STL are `stack`, `queue`, and `priority_queue`.

SUGGESTED READING

These are some introductory books about the STL. Some of them go into quite a bit of detail, but they all start from scratch.

> Musser, David R., Saini, Atul, *STL Tutorial and Reference Guide*, Addison-Wesley, 1996.
>
> Austern, Matthew H., *Generic Programming and the STL*, Addison-Wesley, 1999.
>
> Josuttis, Nicolai M., *The C++ Standard Library*, Addison-Wesley, 1999.

Meyers' is one of the few STL books that deals with the ins and outs of actually using the STL in your programs effectively. After you are done with this chapter, and if you are hungry for more nitty-gritty details, it is highly recommended.

> Meyers, Scott, *Effective STL*, Scott Meyers, Addison-Wesley, 2001.

For everyday work, it is handy to have some good STL references, especially online:

> SGI's STL reference, includes hashes and other nonstandard containers, http://www.sgi.com/tech/stl/.

STL—ALGORITHMS AND ADVANCED TOPICS

Chapter 8 covered the basics of STL—the containers. Even if you decided to only use containers in your programs, the STL would already be worthwhile. You get a set of highly varied data structures that are optimized and thoroughly debugged.

However, there is more to the STL than just containers. This chapter will cover the different types of premade algorithms that can be used on containers, the string class, and even some advanced topics that can be very useful for game development, such as writing custom allocators and keeping track of STL memory.

FUNCTION OBJECTS (FUNCTORS)

Before we dive into the details of algorithms, we need to quickly cover *function objects* (or *functors*). We actually saw them briefly last chapter, but they will become a lot more relevant as soon as we start talking about algorithms.

Function Pointers

Let's take as an example a situation that is similar to how we used function pointers in Chapter 8. Imagine that we have a container and we need to determine how the elements will be sorted. If we want total flexibility in how we sort the elements, it is clear that we need to write some sort of function that takes two elements and determines which one is 'larger' than the other. So what is the best way to pass this function to our container code?

Traditionally, this would have been done with a function pointer. The following code illustrates the point by creating a comparison function that compares two numbers based on their absolute values. Then a function pointer is created that can be passed around to other functions.

```
bool LessAbsoluteValue (float a, float b)
{
    return (fabs(a) < fabs(b));
}

bool (*mycomparison)(float, float);
mycomparsion = &LessAbsoluteValue;

// Now we can pass mycomparison to any function that takes
// function pointers of that type.
```

Function pointers might look ugly and messy, especially once you start piling up the parentheses and pass them as function parameters. For example, here is the declaration of a possible function that sorts a vector of floats, given any comparison function, and takes a pointer to the comparison function as an argument:

```
void sort (bool(*cmpfunc)(float, float), vector<float>);
```

We usually get around the messy code—and most important, the difficulty in parsing function parameters quickly—by using a `typedef` on the function pointer type.

```
typedef bool (*ComparisonFunct)(float, float);
ComparisonFunct mycomparison = &LessAbsoluteValue;

void sort (ComparisonFunct, vector<int>);
```

This code is a bit better. So far, we have been assuming we know the type of the elements we want to sort. If we want to make it work on any type of element, we should use templates. The syntax for a templated function pointer becomes even uglier, and to make things worse, C++ does not allow templated typedefs. To get around that, people wrap the `typedef` inside a templated class, which gets the job done at the expense of more code and more complexity.

Functors

It is no surprise that the STL chose a different route. Passing functions to containers and algorithms is something that is used extensively throughout the STL, so it is important that it be as simple and clear as possible.

The STL solution is to use function objects, also known as functors. A functor is anything that can be called as a function. Typically, functors are objects that have `operator()` implemented, but a function pointer or even a function itself can be considered a functor, and therefore can be used with STL.

```
class EvenNumbersFirst {
public:
    bool operator()(int a, int b) const {
        return (fabs(a) < fabs(b)); }

};
```

If we need to make the same function work for different data types, we can treat it just like any other template. In this particular case, the only data types it will work for are ones that are acceptable parameters to the function `fabs`, so it is rather limiting.

```
template <typename T>
class EvenNumbersFirst {
public:
    bool operator()(T a, T b) const {
        return (fabs(a) < fabs(b)); }

};
```

Using this new, templated function with the STL's own `sort` function is now easy. In this case, we specify that we want the comparison function to work on floats.

```
sort(sequence.begin(), sequence.end(),
    EvenNumbersFirst<float>);
```

Apart from the pure convenience of passing them as arguments, functors have several other advantages. The first is convenience, again. A functor is an object, and therefore it can also contain some member variables or other helper functions. If the function we are encapsulating in a functor is complex and would benefit either from some associated data or some extra functions, they can all be made part of the same functor.

For example, imagine that our function needs some reference number that it will use in all its calculations. This number can be made a member variable and used every time it is needed. If we are using several instances of the same functor simultaneously, they can each have their own different reference numbers. Accomplishing the same thing with function pointers would usually require a global static variable, or a stack of them, and the function would need to be aware of the existence of other similar functions, which would make the program unnecessarily complex.

The other advantage of functors is in performance. When using a function pointer, there is no way the compiler can do anything smart about that call. It has to wait until the last second and make the appropriate call at runtime. These types of functions are often very small and are called very often, so the overhead can be significant.

When we use functors in conjunction with a templated class or templated function, we are telling the compiler what specific function we want to call. That way, the compiler is able to optimize the code and can often inline the function with the templated code. For small, often-called functions, this can be a significantly performance improvement.

Functor Adaptors

One situation that comes up often is that we want to pass a function that is already a member function of a particular class. We cannot just pass a pointer to it (remember that member functions take a 'hidden' parameter that is a pointer to the object they are acting on), so it appears that the only solution is to create a wrapper functor class that just calls the function we want. This would do the job, but it is more work than it should be for something so simple. Fortunately, the STL provides us with functor adaptors.

Functor adaptors are templates that let us use existing member functions as functors, and they can be used in any place where we could use a functor. Obviously, the function called should have the same number and type of parameters that the calling code expects, just like with any functor. Functor adaptors come in three flavors:

- `mem_fun`: Works on member functions through a pointer
- `mem_fun_ref`: Works on member functions through an object or a reference
- `ptr_fun`: Works on global functions through a function pointer

As an example, imagine that we are trying to sort some elements again, but this time they are objects, not just integers. Specifically, they are scene nodes, and we are trying to sort them to minimize render state changes and render them as fast as possible. If there were a global function that would compare two scene nodes and decide which one should be rendered first, we could just pass a function pointer into the sort function and be done with it. But what if the sort function were a member function of the scene nodes themselves? This is the right time to use a functor adaptor.

```
vector<SceneNode *> nodes;
//...
sort(nodes.begin(), nodes.end(),
    mem_fun(&SceneNode::RenderFirst));
```

Notice that we used `mem_fun` because the container had pointers to objects. If we had actually stored `SceneNode` objects directly in the vector, then we should have used `mem_fun_ref`, instead.

Strictly speaking, `ptr_fun` is not necessary most of the time. In addition to binding the functions to a functor, the functor adaptors also do some extra work behind the scenes by defining a few `typedefs` that are used by some algorithms. If you try to pass a function pointer directly to one of those algorithms, you will get a syntax error, which can be fixed by using the `ptr_fun` adaptor.

ALGORITHMS

A large portion of the STL is made up of *algorithms*: templated functions of common operations that are performed on containers. Because the functions themselves are templated, they can work with any data type, and because they work on existing containers, they know how to traverse them and modify them.

There are four broad categories of algorithms, depending on their behavior. The breakdown is a bit arbitrary, but it is better than listing hundreds of unclassified functions. Besides, if you know what you are looking for, it is very easy to zero in on the appropriate algorithm based on these categories.

Many algorithms will take two iterators to the same container as parameters. The first iterator points to the first element in the sequence that we want to apply the algorithm to, and the second iterator points (as is the custom with STL) to one element past the end of the sequence to which we want to apply the algorithm.

Several algorithms require that a value be passed as a parameter, and they will use that value to perform some operation on the container, such as to search for it, replace it with something else, or count it. Most of those algorithms have a variant of the same function that takes a *predicate* instead of a value. A predicate is a function that returns `true` or `false`, and it is usually implemented as a functor. The predicate versions of the algorithm functions give us more flexibility in operating on a whole range of elements determined by the predicate, instead of matching only one. The version of the algorithm that takes a predicate is usually named like the original version with `_if` appended to the name; so it is very clear at a glance which function is used, instead of relying on polymorphic function calls.

This section will list the STL algorithms used most often in games and give some examples of specific situations where they could be applied. For a comprehensive list and description of all the algorithms, refer to one of the STL references listed in Suggested Reading at the end of this chapter.

Nonmutating Algorithms

Nonmutating algorithms, as the name implies, work on a container but do not modify its contents in any way. For example, searching for an item or counting the number of items are nonmutating algorithms.

Find

Probably the most common nonmutating algorithm is `find`. It will iterate through all the items in a sequence (between the two iterators we pass as arguments) and look for a specific item.

The `find` algorithm has a linear-time performance, because it does not assume anything in particular about the container it accessed, and so it needs to look through every element until it finds the one we are looking for. Associative containers offer better performance for finding specific elements; so in that case you should use the member function `find` instead of the standalone algorithm, which will take into account how the associative container is organized and search the element in O(ln N) time, instead.

The `find` algorithm should be used when you need to search for an element in a sequence container that is not ordered. You should only do this infrequently, or with a small number of elements in order to avoid needless performance degradation. For example, we could search through the player list or through the different personalities the local player has set up, but we should probably avoid using this algorithm to search for a particular game entity in the world.

```
list<string> PlayerNames;
//...
// Make sure the player name is not taken for this session
if (find(PlayerNames.begin(), PlayerNames.end(),
    wantedName) == PlayerNames.end() ) {
    // Name was taken, do something
}
```

There is a predicate version of this algorithm, called `find_if`. It will look for an element in the sequence that makes the predicate `true`. For example, the following code looks through a list of game entity IDs for those with a value less than 10,000 (possibly because IDs under that range are reserved for other purposes).

```
class LessThan10K {
public:
```

```
        bool operator(int x) const { return x < 10000; }
};

vector<int> GameUIDs;
//...
vector<int>::iterator it;
it = find(GameUIDs.begin(), GameUIDs.end(), LessThan10K());
if (it != GameUIDs.end()) {
    // We found at least one
}
```

For_each

The for_each algorithm simply executes a particular function on each element of a sequence. As you would expect, the range of the sequence is passed through two iterators, and the function is passed through a functor.

As an example, let's take a very common situation in game programming. Our task is to call the Update function of all our game entities for a particular frame. That will give them the chance to run the AI, update their position, start new animations, and so forth. The most natural way we would think of for accomplishing this would be by setting up a for loop:

```
// EntityContainer is a typedef for the specific container
// of the game entities.
EntityContainer::iterator it;
for (it=entities.begin(); it!=entities.end(); ++it) {
    GameEntity & entity = *it;
    entity.Update();
}
```

Now, we can accomplish the same thing using the for_each algorithm:

```
void Update (GameEntity & entity) {
    entity.Update();
}

for_each (entities.begin(), entities.end(), Update);
```

This is only marginally clearer, because it does not use a loop, but it requires us to create a whole new function. The reason for the new Update function is that, as previously discussed, we cannot pass member functions directly as functors. Fortunately, we can get around that by using mem_fun_ref. Now our new code looks like this:

```
for_each (entities.begin(), entities.end(),
    mem_fun_ref(&GameEntity::Update) );
```

That is better, but is it really that much better than a plain `for` loop? Frankly, no. They are largely equivalent, and the `for` loop might have an edge in that more people will be able to understand it without any problems, but `for_each` is more concise and a bit less error prone. Your choice comes down mostly to personal preference.

However, `for_each` has one extra advantage that might be of particular interest to game developers—performance. It is possible for the algorithm `for_each` to take advantage of the underlying implementation of the container it is applied to and perform a faster traversal than is possible with a plain for loop with iterators. This is very dependent on the specific container and the STL implementation; so if you are interested in that extra bit of performance, you should do some timings on your target platform. One thing is sure, `for_each` is never going to be any slower than any loop you can write by hand.

Count

If you just wanted to know how many elements that are in the container, you would use the member function `size()`. This algorithm does not just count all the elements; it counts all the elements that match a particular value.

Imagine we have a vector of game entity UIDs, and over time, as entities are removed, we set their entries to zero instead of just removing them. Every so often we want to count how many entries are set to zero. Yes, we can do this with another `for` loop, but the algorithm `count` is the perfect tool:

```
int numZeros = count(UIDs.begin(), UIDs.end(), 0);
```

Probably, a more useful version of `count` is its predicate variant: `count_if`. Instead of counting the number of elements with a particular value, we can count the number of elements that make the predicate true. The following code uses `count_if` to count the number of enemy units within a certain distance of the player. We can then use such a value to change the music tempo or to flash some warning on the screen, alerting the player to a large number of enemies headed her way.

```
class IsEnemyNearby
{
```

```
public:
    bool operator()(const GameEntity & entity)
    {
      return (entity.IsEnemy() &&
            ::dist(player.GetPos(),entity.GetPos())<RADIUS));
    }
    static float RADIUS = 100.0f;
};

int nNearbyEnemies = count_if(entities.begin(),
                              entities.end(),
                              IsEnemyNearby());
```

Obviously, be careful with any such function that traverses all elements in a container. If the number of game entities in your world is very large, you probably want to do a fast cull of all the entities that are not roughly within distance of the player before you attempt to traverse them all.

Other Nonmutating Algorithms

The remaining nonmutating algorithms are: `adjacent_find`, `mismatch`, `equal`, and `search`. They are not used as often as the ones we saw in the sections above, but it is still worth knowing them and keeping them in mind for when they are the best tool for the job at hand. Refer to the Suggested Reading at the end of this chapter for references to a full description of each of them.

Mutating Algorithms

Mutating algorithms work on a container and change its contents. They do not include sorting algorithms, which are a different type of STL algorithms. Mutating algorithms can be used to copy values, reverse the order of some elements, change their order, and so on.

Copy

The copy algorithm copies all the elements in a range specified by two iterators to another range, possibly in a different container. If we just want to copy all elements in a container to another container of the same type, the easiest way is to simply copy the whole container.

```
vector<int> highScores;
//...
vector<int> newScores = highScores; // Copies all the scores
```

The copy algorithm comes in handy when we need to copy only a specific range, or when we want to copy across different types of containers.

```
// Only copy the first 10 scores (assume there are at least 10)
list<int> newScores;
copy(highScores.begin(), highScores.begin()+10,
    newScores.begin());
```

Notice that copy only takes three iterators. The first two denote the start and end of the source range to copy from, and the third denotes the start of the range to copy to. There is no need to specify the end of the destination range, since the number of elements is already determined by the first two iterators.

As long as certain conditions are met, copy works with overlapping ranges. Elements are copied one at the time, so as long as the beginning of the destination range does not overlap the source range, and everything will work as expected.

If you need to copy between two overlapping ranges, where the first element of the destination is part of the source range, you need to use the variant copy_backward, which will start from the end of the sequence, avoiding the overlapping problem.

Swap_ranges

The algorithm swap_ranges is similar to copy. It takes the same parameters to specify the same ranges, but instead of copying one range into another, it just swaps the elements of the two ranges.

Remove

We finally come to one of the most useful and least intuitive algorithms in the STL. You would imagine that the following call would perhaps remove all the elements that have the given value in that range:

```
remove (first, last, value);
```

Almost, but not quite. The remove call does not actually remove any elements. Instead, it puts all those elements that match value at the end of the sequence and returns a new iterator, newlast, such that there are no elements equal to `value` in the range `first` to `newlast`. This is an important point, so let's go through a simple example.

```
vector<int> test;
test.push_back(3);
test.push_back(1);
test.push_back(4);
test.push_back(1);
test.push_back(5);
test.push_back(3);
test.push_back(1);
test.push_back(8);

remove(test.begin(), test.end(), 1);
```

The call to `remove` will return `test.begin()+5`, because it removed three elements from the sequence, and now all the elements between `test.begin()` and `test.begin()+4` are guaranteed not to be equal to 1. Specifically, the first five elements of the sequence are now 3, 4, 5, 3, and 8. What about the remaining three elements? Are they the three ones we removed? The standard says that they are undefined, so they could be anything. In practice, they are usually the same elements that were in the original sequence; they just have not been modified, but they are most definitely not the elements that were removed.

So once again, `remove` will not remove anything from the container; the number of elements will be the same. Its name is somewhat misleading, but there is no other name that better expresses what the algorithm does.

What if we really wanted to remove those elements from the container? Then we should call the `erase` function in the container, which actually takes care of totally eliminating a range of elements from the container. In the example above, to reduce the container to just the elements that are not equal to the value we pass, we would write:

```
vector<int> newEnd = remove(test.begin(), test.end(), 1);
test.erase(newEnd, test.end());
```

Once we are comfortable with the idea, we can put it all in one line. This is the way you will see it used most often:

```
test.erase(remove(test.begin(), test.end(), 1), test.end());
```

As you can probably imagine, the `remove` algorithm has a predicate variant called `remove_if`, which matches not only a value, but the functor evaluated at each element.

Ordering Algorithms

There is a whole set of mutable algorithms whose only function is to change the order of the elements in a sequence. Again, these are not sorting algorithms (see Sorting Algorithms, in the next section). Ordering algorithms include:

- `reverse(first, last)`: Reversing all the elements in a sequence, it puts the first one at the end, the second one second to last, and so forth.
- `rotate(first, middle, last)`: It rotates all elements in a range. Another way to think of it is as a shift with wraparound. The elements in that range will be shifted until the middle element is at the first position, and any elements that were shifted out one way are added in from the opposite end.
- `random_shuffle(first, last)`: It shuffles all the elements in that range. The possibilities for games are quite obvious—not just for card games, but every time we need to randomize a set of events ahead of time, and we have to make sure they are all used (as opposed to just picking one at random every time).

Other Mutating Algorithms

There are a fair number of mutating algorithms, some more useful than others. Algorithms that are not specifically covered in this chapter include `transform`, `replace`, `fill`, `generate`, `unique`, and `partition`. Several of those algorithms have slight variations. Again, refer to a comprehensive STL reference for all the details.

Sorting Algorithms

Sorting is an important operation in game programming. It happens more often than we think. From a simple sort of the players on the scoreboard based on the number of points they scored, to the sorting of possible threats for an AI unit, to the sorting of meshes to minimize state changes before passing them to the renderer—sorting functions are important tasks. The STL has a whole range of algorithms to help us with sorting, although the main workhorse will be the sort algorithm, itself.

Before the STL was developed, our only choice was using qsort from the standard C library or rolling our own sort functions. The standard C qsort ended up being a very efficient implementation most of the time, but with a rather ugly and type-unsafe syntax that required function pointers to take void pointers.

At the core of all sorting function is the generic algorithm sort. It sorts all the elements in a range by applying operator< to compare them or using a functor passed as an argument. The sort algorithm is implemented by using quicksort, which will result in average sort time of $O(N \ln N)$, but could be as bad as $O(N^2)$ in some situations.

Because sort requires random access to any of the elements, it can only be used with containers that provide random access (e.g., vector, heap, or a custom container with that property). The following code snippet sorts a vector of player pointers, based on their high score:

```cpp
class HigherScore {
public:
    bool operator()(const Player & p1,
                    const Player & p2) const {
        return (p1.GetScore() > p2.GetScore());
    }
};

vector<const Player *> players;
sort(players.begin(), players.end(), HigherScore());
```

An important characteristic of the sort algorithm is that it is not stable. This means that two elements with the same sort order might end up in different relative positions with respect to each other after the sort. This is usually not an issue for most situations in game development, but it is important to be aware of it in case it becomes a requirement at some point.

If a stable sort is required, we should use the stable_sort algorithm. It has the same interface as sort, but it guarantees that the sort will be stable. Unlike sort, it runs slower, in $O(N (\ln N)^2)$ time, so only use it when a stable sort is really necessary.

Sometimes we have a really large number of elements, but all we care about is the sort order for the top X elements. In that case, we can use partial_sort, which does exactly that: it sorts the top X elements, puts them at the beginning of the sequence, and leaves the rest of the sequence in an unspecified order. The performance of `partial_sort` is O(N ln X), which is much better than the regular `sort` algorithm when we only want to sort a small number of top elements.

The STL offers several other sorting-related algorithms, such as to merge ordered sequences, determine if a sequence is ordered, or work with heaps.

Generalized Numerical Algorithms

Finally, the STL offers a small set of numerical algorithms that operate on containers. These algorithms do not frequently come up in game development, but they could come in handy one day, so it might be worth knowing how to use them.

- `accumulate(first, last, init)`: This algorithm performs a sum of all the elements in the specified range. The initial value is set to `init`. By default, it performs the sum of the elements, but it can perform any binary operation we pass as a functor.
- `partial_sum(first, last, output)`: It computes the partial sum of a range and stores it in a separate container. A partial sum is defined as the sequence of numbers created by adding all the elements up to the nth element for each of the output elements. As with `accumulate`, we can also provide our own binary operator to replace the default addition.
- `adjacent_diference(first, last, output)`: It calculates the difference between adjacent pairs of elements and stores them in the sequence pointed to by `output`. As usual, we can pass any binary operator to replace the subtraction.
- `inner_product(first1, last2, first2, init)`: At first, this might seem like something very useful for game development. After all, the inner product is the same thing as the dot product, and we are doing that constantly over the code, from camera movement to plotting paths for the AI, to lighting equations. Unfortunately, it is not as useful as it might seem. Most of the dot products in game development will be done on specialized vector classes, not on generalized STL containers. Still, the algorithm does exactly that. It performs the inner product of two different ranges. It is also possible to pass custom functors to replace the default addition and multiplication with other operations.

Some STL implementations will offer additional algorithms not covered in the standard. If cross-platform portability is not a big issue for you (or your STL implementation is available in all your target platforms) you might want to investigate which extensions they provide and whether they fit your needs.

STRINGS

The STL also offers a class that has been long-needed in C++: the *string* class. In this section, we will see why strings are useful and how to use them effectively.

No Strings Attached

Unlike most languages, C and C++ do not have a native concept of a string. Instead they have to make do with arrays of characters and conventions, like marking the end of a string with a NULL character. Unfortunately, working with arrays of characters is very inconvenient.

Arrays need to be created large enough to hold the intended string. When the string changes dynamically, this can create a real problem: how large is large enough? For example, a function that retrieves the full path for a file and copies it into an array that we pass as a parameter requires that the array be large enough to hold the whole string. To achieve this, each operating system comes up with some maximum constants, like MAX_DIR_PATH, that set an upper limit in the length of a file path.

```
char path[MAX_FILE_PATH];
GetFilePath(filename, path);
```

This same situation happens often. When we get the contents from a Web page, we do not know how large that Web page is before we start downloading it. So all sorts of convoluted functions have been devised to make sure the functions work with fixed-size character arrays.

To make things even worse, character arrays are very error-prone. The only way to know where the string ends is by setting the last character to be NULL, or simply zero. This means that the number of characters allocated in the array is always at least one more than the length of the string itself. This leads to a lot of fudging around with +1 and -1 in the code to convert between length and array size.

And what happens when somebody gets confused by a +1 in the code, or simply tries to read or write past the end of the array? All sorts of things can happen, depending on the platform and depending on how lucky we are. If we are fortunate, the program will crash right away, as soon as we try to access anything past the end of the array. Then we can immediately fix the problem and prevent any future headaches. If we are not so lucky, the program will continue to work as usual, and every so often it will cause weird crashes or subtle bugs—the kind that don't repeat themselves and are impossible to track down. These bugs are the feared buffer overruns. If we accidentally write past the end of an array, but that memory location was used by some other part of our program, nothing will crash, but we will have corrupted some potentially crucial data. Maybe it will be just corrupted graphics, maybe the AI will act weird, or maybe the program will crash once in a blue moon. It gets worse, though. Every time we make a change, the strange behavior will also change, or even temporarily disappear. Even something like adding a simple printf to track down the problem could cause the problem itself to change. This is without a doubt one of the most frustrating and time-consuming bugs a programmer can encounter. Anything we can do to avoid it is a big bonus.

What about performance? If char arrays are so painful to work with, at least they must be very efficient. Unfortunately, not. Getting the length of a character array requires counting all its characters until we hit the NULL character, so it is not particularly fast. Concatenating two strings usually requires allocating new memory and copying both strings to a different location unless somebody had the forethought of creating one of the arrays large enough. They are not even that good at saving memory, since arrays will often be larger than the strings they need to hold in order to avoid running out of space.

The String Class

C++ had the chance to fix this sorry state and introduced the string class in the STL. Strings address all the major problems of the character arrays:

- Strings will grow larger transparently when needed, so our program will never run out of space or produce buffer overruns when writing to them.
- We do not have to worry about the size of the allocated memory versus the length of the string.

In addition, the string class provides a lot of functions that were previously available through the C library for string manipulation. The advantage is that this time we can treat strings as objects, and the syntax is a lot cleaner and more self-evident.

```
string text1 = "This is an example string";
string text2 = text1;        // We can copy them
string text3 = text1 + text2; // Append them
if ( text3 == text2 )        // Compare them
    //...
```

But how well does string mesh with C-style char arrays? Pretty well. The people who designed the string class clearly had that in mind, so we can easily go from a string to a character array by using the c_str function on the string class. The returned character pointer can be used like any char array.

```
string text = "Yada, yada, yada...";
char oldstyle[256];
strcpy (oldstyle, text.c_str());
```

One thing to note is that c_str returns a const char pointer. That constness should never be cast away, since it would allow other parts of the program to modify the contents of the string without the string's knowledge. If you need to go from a char array to a string, then you should create a new one, or assign the contents of the array to an existing string. This will cause the contents of the character array to be copied, but it is the safest way.

One operation that was not mentioned in this discussion is how to write to the string—not just add another string, which is easy to do by splitting and concatenating the string. Writing an integer or a float, or some other data type is a bit more complicated. If we were using char arrays, we would use the handy sprintf function and freely write to it.

```
char txt[256]; // Let's hope it's large enough!
sprintf(txt, "Player %d wins with %d points and
        an accuracy of %.2f.",
            player.GetNumber(), player.GetScore(),
            player.GetAccuracy());
```

C++ purists might cringe, but even though sprintf might be type-unsafe and a bit ugly, it gets the job done. To accomplish the same with a string, we are encouraged to use streams.

```
ostringstream oss;
oss << "Player " << player.GetNumber() << "wins with" <<
        player.GetScore() << "points and an accuracy of " <<
```

```
            player.GetAccuracy();
    string txt = oss.str();
```

This version is type-safe, and it is supposed to accomplish the same thing. Unfortunately, specifying the exact formatting is not as straightforward, so in the previous example we left out that we only want to display two digits after the decimal point in the player's accuracy.

The most important drawback is that it requires that we buy into the whole stream paradigm for doing input and output. This is fine, and there are many advantages to streams, but not everybody is ready to take that step. Strings without streams are a bit crippled when it comes to writing to them.

An alternative is to write to a character array like we did before, and then convert the existing array to a string. This is not the most elegant solution, and it will cause the extra performance hit for converting from an array to a string, but it will work.

Fortunately, the Boost library provides an alternative, the Format library. The Format library gives us the ability to format the contents of a string in a more direct way by using a format string. There are several variations, but one of the types of format strings supported is the `printf` style, with which a lot of programmers will already be familiar. We can finally write to strings directly like we used to do with character arrays, with the only difference being that now we use percent signs to separate the arguments instead of commas.

```
    string txt = boost::io::str(
            format( "Player %d wins with %d points and
                an accuracy of %.2f." %
                player.GetNumber() %
                player.GetScore() %
                player.GetAccuracy() ));
```

By now you might be wondering why the `string` class is part of the STL. From all we have seen so far, it does not look like a template. Actually it is. The class `string` is just a `typedef` for a template:

```
    typedef basic_string<char> string;
```

The template is `basic_string`, and it can work with characters or with any other type of element. For example, another useful string type is one that contains wide characters (`wchar_t`), which is very useful for localizing our game in different parts of the world where they use different character sets than ours. There is also a typedef for that type of string, called wstring for wide-character string.

Technically speaking, a string is just another container, like a vector or a list. However, since it is typically used for completely different purposes, we consider it a separate type of template for the purposes of this book.

Performance

If you are used to dealing with char pointers for passing strings, you might need to adjust to using string. When working with char pointers, to pass the text as a parameter to a function, we only pass the character pointer itself. That is a very efficient operation, because only the pointer is copied. With strings, things are a bit different; we have to be careful how we pass them as parameters. If we just pass the string by value, it will create a copy of the string object and its contents, which could be very wasteful of memory and performance. To avoid that, we should pass them by reference most of the time and probably by const reference, unless we want the function to modify the contents of the string.

The same thing applies to returning a string from a function. If we assign the value returned by the function to a const reference, we avoid making any extra copies. Otherwise the contents of the string will be copied if we try to assign it to a new string. The following code illustrates both cases.

```
// Bad code! We are making two copies of the contents
// of the string!
void SetHighScore(string name);

string playerName = player.GetName();
SetHighScore(playerName);

// Much better version. No copies involved.
void SetHighScore(const string & name);

const string & playerName = player.GetName();
SetHighScore(playerName);
```

Another common performance penalty was already mentioned in the previous section; every time we convert a character array into a string, it involves allocating a new buffer and copying all the characters to the string. This might not be necessary if the original array was not going to change, but most implementations will go ahead and copy its contents anyway. It becomes more of a problem when a code base is using both character arrays and strings. Fortunately, converting from a string to a character array is completely free.

Even if we are only using strings, using string literals as a function argument will also usually cause its contents to be copied into the string objects. For example:

```
void SetPlayerName(const string & name);
// Will usually cause a new string buffer to be created and the
// contents of the literal to be copied to it, passed to the
// function, and then discarded. Pretty wasteful!
SetPlayerName("Player1");
```

On the other hand, we should not have many string literals hard-coded in the game. Most of that type of data should be read from resources created by the artists and designers. Things like text, especially, should come from an outside source to make localization easier.

Actually, it might turn out that there is not much of a performance penalty for passing strings by value in your particular STL implementation. Remember, for good or for bad, there is a huge amount of variation between STL implementations, even though they all adhere to the standard. So it is possible that your implementation is using reference counting and copy-on-write (CoW). Unfortunately, even though reference counting makes copying strings much more efficient, it has its own share of problems that can lead to totally unexpected results. This is especially true in multithreaded environments. If your string implementation uses reference counting, you might want to disable that feature, switch to another STL implementation, or consider one of the alternatives presented toward the end of this section.

Memory

Memory usage can be a concern if you are using many strings in an environment that is very tight in memory. Every string is allocated with a bit of extra padding so that concatenation operations are quite efficient without requiring the string to be reallocated and copied. Unfortunately, if you have no plans to ever increase the size of the string, that is just wasted space. Exactly how much space is allocated for padding is implementation-dependent, but it usually is around 16 bytes or 32 bytes—not enough to worry about under normal circumstances, but it will add up if you are using thousands of strings.

To make things more interesting, some STL implementations also use a memory pooling scheme. That means that allocating several strings will not necessarily cause many memory allocations, but it also means freeing some strings will not necessarily free all the memory they were using. This is an advantage most of the time, since it allows for much faster string-creation operations. On the other hand, if you were already tight in memory, this will make things worse, particularly if at some point during program execution (during level loading, perhaps) your string use spikes up considerably and then goes back to normal. At that point, the amount of memory reserved for strings will be much larger than necessary.

In addition, each string will have a fixed overhead. Depending on the implementation, the overhead can be anywhere from 4–16 bytes. Those extra bytes are used to keep track of bookkeeping information, like start address or length of the string.

Alternatives

If the `string` class does not suit your needs, before you revert to using `char *` again, there are a few alternatives. The classes `rope`, `vector<char>`, and `CString` are worth considering.

Rope

The first alternative is the `rope` class. It is not part of the standard, but it is provided by several implementations. Like the `string` class, it is really a templated class, so it is possible to specify what type of elements you want to work with and to specify an allocator: `rope<type, alloc>`.

The rope class is intended to work with very large strings as a unit. It accomplishes this by storing the string data in several memory blocks instead of just one consecutive one. In particular, assignment, concatenation, and substring operations are much faster for large strings. On the other hand, doing single-character operations on a `rope` is much more expensive. Also, converting them to character arrays is a much more expensive operation than it was with the `string` class. Clearly the `rope` class is not going to completely substitute for the `string` class. But it might be worth considering for very specific circumstances.

Vector<char>

A string is little more than a sequence container for characters, so why not use vector<char>? We are already familiar with its syntax, its performance, and its memory utilization characteristics, so it seems like a good candidate.

There is no explicit call to convert to character arrays, but with a few tricks, you can get a pointer to the sequential memory block where the characters are stored. As long as all your operations maintain a NULL character to indicate the end of the string, everything should work fine.

The best thing about vector<char> is that you know there is no reference counting or CoW going on under the hood, so the integrity of your text data is guaranteed. Sometimes this is the best alternative for people who want to avoid their own string implementation but do not want to switch STL versions.

The main drawback of this approach is its lack of many string-specific functions, such as replacement or substring operations. It is possible to implement all of them in terms of more basic STL algorithms and vector functions, but you have to write them yourself, and you will end up with a different syntax than what people are used to for the string class.

CString

The Microsoft Foundation Classes (MFC) introduced the CString class to solve all the problems of manipulating char * arrays. The CString class evolved along a very different path than the STL string class and is not compatible with the STL, but to its credit, it was created many years before the string class saw the light of day.

CString is not template-based, since there was no decent support for templates when it was created, but it does everything you could ever need from a string class. If anything, it does a little too much, and it has often been criticized for its kitchen-sink approach and bloated interface.

The most common complaint about CString is that it is tied to MFC and the Windows platform. That is not totally true, since there are some implementations available that let you use it without bringing in a single MFC header file or library, but they are still dependent on the Win32 API. That alone might rule it out for your application if you are targeting anything other than Windows-based platforms.

Even if you are only using Windows, unless you are tied to a large body of code that uses CString extensively, there is almost no reason not to switch to the standard and portable STL string class.

ALLOCATORS (ADVANCED)

There might come a time when the STL memory allocation strategy is just not enough. That could be for many different reasons. Maybe the constant allocation and freeing of memory when dealing with node-based containers is fragmenting memory or causing major performance hiccups. Maybe we need to keep better track of where memory is going, as we saw in Chapter 6. Maybe we need to keep elements of a container allocated contiguously in memory to improve data cache consistency. Maybe we want to create some elements temporarily on the stack and then release them without any penalties. If that time arrives, the answer lies in using custom allocators.

Notice the qualifiers in the previous paragraph: There *might* come a time . . ." and "if that time arrives. . . ." Do not automatically assume that the STL memory allocation is not going to be good enough. Depending on your platform and your requirements, you might never need to change your allocation strategy. If so, you can count yourself lucky. In any case, it is a good idea to peruse this section, just to be aware of potential problems and how to go about solving them if you ever need to write your own custom allocators.

At its core, a custom allocator is simply an object that allocates and frees memory when requested. It does not sound all that different from overriding `new` and `delete` in a class, but that is not the case. Unfortunately there is quite a bit of baggage that comes along with allocators, and things are made even worse by compilers' lack of language features or specific workarounds.

In practice, allocators will be implemented slightly differently in different platforms, so a full, working allocator is not provided on the CD-ROM. Instead, the best way to write a custom allocator is to start with the default allocator of your STL implementation and change the specific parts related to the new memory allocation strategy.

As an example, let's create an allocator that uses our own memory heaps, like the ones described in Chapter 6, to keep better track of where memory is being allocated. Every time there is an allocation, we want to call the new version of `operator new` with the correct heap.

So we dig out the standard STL allocator, copy it somewhere else, and attempt to modify its allocation and deallocation functions to call our overridden `new` and `delete` operators. This might be an initial attempt:

```
template<typename T>
MyHeapAllocator {
public:
```

```
pointer allocate(size_type nNumObjects,
                 const void * hint = 0) {
    return static_cast<pointer>(new(nNumObjects*sizeof(T),
                                    pHeap));
}
void deallocate(pointer p, size_type nNumObjects) {
    delete(p, nNumObjects*sizeof(T));
}
//...
};
```

There is a slight problem here. How do we pass pHeap into the operator? Ideally, we would like the allocator to keep a pointer to the heap we want to use and pass it to new every time there is an allocation. Here comes the first quirk of STL allocators: allocators should not have any per-object state. So we cannot keep a pointer to the heap. To get around that, we need to create a quick wrapper class around our heap and use that class as a parameter into the allocator template. Here is a new attempt at writing the allocator:

```
class HeapGraphics {
public:
    static void * allocate(size_t nNumBytes) {
        return new(nNumBytes, s_pGraphicsHeap);
    }
    static void deallocate(void * p, size_t nNumBytes) {
        delete(p, nNumBytes);
    }
};

template<typename T, typename Heap>
MyHeapAllocator {
public:
    pointer allocate(size_type nNumObjects,
                     const void * hint = 0) {
        return static_cast<pointer>(Heap::allocate(
                        nNumObjects*sizeof(T), pHeap));
    }
    void deallocate(pointer p, size_type nNumObjects) {
        Heap::deallocate (p, nNumObjects*sizeof(T));
    }
    //...
};
```

This new version respects all the rules of allocators and allows us to allocate all memory from our own heap. The only drawback is that we need to create one wrapper class for every heap we want to use, which could be a nuisance. As has been mentioned, though, STL allocators are not perfect.

The actual workings of the insides of allocators are a bit more involved, but from a user's point of view, this is all you need to know to get up and running at writing your own custom allocators. Refer to some of the sources listed in Suggested Reading at the end of this chapter for some interesting reading on allocators.

WHEN STL IS NOT ENOUGH (ADVANCED)

Ironically, after spending several whole chapters discussing how STL can be a real benefit to your game project, we are going to wrap it up by discussing alternatives. Let's be very clear about one thing: STL is a great starting point. There is very little reason not to use it to get things up and running. If used carefully, as explained in this chapter as well as Chapter 8, you will be on your way to shipping a game or creating tools with some solid data structures and slick algorithms, without the need to implement them from scratch. The less time you spend on trivial work, the more time you can spend improving gameplay, researching new techniques, or even taking a break. And if you are developing for the PC, then that is probably all you will have to worry about.

However, there might come a time when the STL is just not good enough, particularly if you are developing for a console with much more limited resources than a PC. The most common reason is lack of fine control over memory allocation. Maybe you already fiddled with the non-trivial task of creating custom allocators, and you are still not satisfied with the memory allocation patterns of STL containers. Maybe you want to reliably release the memory in a `vector`, or you want more control over the block sizes of a `deque`. Hopefully this is motivated by something you saw that was interfering with your game. Do not just assume that more control over memory is a good thing; if it is not detracting from the game in any way, then do not waste your time. Only look for alternatives if it is slowing down your game at crucial moments, or if your game is using more memory than you think it should.

Another of the common complaints about STL, and templates in general, is code bloat. Some compilers are more prone to this than others, but it is possible for the same template to be created over and over for use in different classes, causing a large growth in the final executable size.

Finally, another reason that we have not even considered so far is the increase in compile times. Do not forget that STL is made out of templates, and templates are nothing more than code that is generated at compile time, so that is more work for the compiler. The more work that the compiler needs to do, the longer the compile step will take. The longer the turnaround time from making a trivial change to getting the game up and running, the more costly and cumbersome development becomes. If this situation arises and you suspect that it is being caused by overuse of STL, then it might be time to consider an alternative. However, first make sure that STL is really the cause. A lot of project developers are careless about their physical structures and how header files are included (see Chapter 15, Dealing with Large Projects, for some possible explanations for slow compilations).

So what should we do about these situations? Is there a better library out there? Unfortunately, not yet. Probably the best thing to do is to provide your own custom containers.

It might come as a bit of a shock to get a recommendation for writing your own containers after hearing all about the virtues of STL, but given the circumstances, it is probably the best solution. But do not totally give up on STL and start writing your own container classes.

Have a look at your code base. Think about what parts of STL you use most often or which ones give you trouble. Chances are that 90% of your STL use is limited to a couple of containers—maybe vectors, some sort of maps, and possibly strings. That does not mean you are not using STL for the rest, but these are probably the bread and butter of your everyday STL usage.

A good approach then is to only replace those containers that are used often, or the ones that you are having trouble with. You can continue using the rest of the STL normally in your code; you do not need to give it up completely. For example, you could create your own version of `vector` and call it `myvector`, or `array`, or whatever you want. It can have an interface that is very similar to the STL vector: you still have `push_back`, `clear`, `resize`, and `reserve`. But you can also add new functions that let you more carefully control how memory is allocated and freed. You can also provide custom versions of your containers to fit your needs. For example, you could provide a bare-bones `vector` that has minimal overhead, so you can use it in each of the thousands of game entities in your world.

You can also provide iterators to access your container, and if you are careful about how those iterators are implemented, you might still be able to use a good part of the STL algorithms on your own container. So in a way, you are not totally replacing STL; you are augmenting it, and you can use pieces of it even with your new containers.

Again, this is not a task to be undertaken lightly. Do not underestimate the amount of effort require to make a robust, solid container that fits your needs and is more efficient than the STL version. Take your time when deciding if you really need it and what exactly needs to be different. Until then, continue using STL, and maybe the time to replace it will never come.

Conclusion

In this chapter we saw the other 'half' of the STL. We started with one of the building blocks of STL, functors, which are a more flexible way of passing functions around than just using function pointers. Then we covered the four types of algorithms the STL provides:

- Nonmutable algorithms, which work on a sequence of elements but do not change their contents. They are used to find elements, count them, iterate through all of them, and so forth.
- Mutable algorithms, which modify the elements in a sequence, but without sorting them. They are used to copy ranges of elements, remove them, or alter their order.
- Sorting algorithms, which order a sequence of elements and perform other related tasks.
- Numerical algorithms, which are just a few algorithms that perform numerical computations on the elements in a range.

Next, we saw the STL `string` class and its companion, the `wstring` class for wide characters. They have a few minor quirks, but they make life a lot simpler when dealing with text strings, and they are better solution than using `char *` most of the time.

Finally, we briefly covered how to deal with the STL when we need more than the STL offers by default. We first saw how to write custom allocators for our containers and what we can expect to get out of it, and then we saw under what circumstances it might make sense to write our own versions of containers instead of using the STL ones.

Suggested Reading

The following book has great all-around tips. Specific to this chapter, it has some very good advice on functors, a discussion about strings and `vector<char>`, and STL algorithms:

Meyers, Scott, *Effective STL*, Addison-Wesley, 2001.

Below are some excellent books on general algorithms. You will find that many of the STL's algorithms are explained in detail here, including how they are implemented and what the consequences are. Incidentally, you will also find a good description of most data structures used in the STL containers.

Cormen, Thomas H., et al., *Introduction to Algorithms*, McGraw-Hill, 1990.

Knuth, Donald E., *The Art of Computer Programming*, 3rd ed., Addison-Wesley, 1997.

Here are some good resources about string classes, their implementation, and related libraries.

Strings in SGI STL, http://www.sgi.com/tech/stl/string_discussion.html.

C++ Boost Format library, *http://www.boost.org/libs/format/index.htm.*

Allocators are a tricky subject. There are not a lot of references out there, possibly because it is so platform-dependent. Some good starting sources are:

Meyers, Scott, *Effective STL*, Addison-Wesley, 2001.

Treglia, Dante, et al., *Game Programming Gems 3*. Charles River Media, 2002.

Josuttis, Nicolai M., *The C++ Standard Library*, Addison-Wesley, 1999.

Josuttis, Nicolai M., User-Defined Allocator, *http://www.josuttis.com/ cppcode/allocator.html.*

Again, here is a great overall STL reference:

SGI's Standard Template Library Programmer's Guide, http://www. sgi.com/tech/stl/.

SPECIAL TECHNIQUES

There is more to putting a game together than writing some C++ code and making it run quickly. The way in which that code is put together can have important consequences for the rest of the project. Game development has some particular tasks that come up over and over in every game: creating objects, saving the state of the game, writing plug-ins for tools, and so forth. Finding the most effective way of implementing each of those tasks can take many years of trial and error.

This last part of the book is intended to be a guide for specific techniques that have proven effective during the development of actual games. Often, more than one technique will be presented in a chapter, along with a discussion of the merits of the different techniques. By studying these techniques, you will be able to add them to your repertoire and use them appropriately in your project.

ABSTRACT INTERFACES

Abstract interfaces are an extremely useful concept. They allow us to completely separate the implementation of a class from its interface. All of a sudden, this opens the door for many possibilities that were previously out of our reach, such as swapping implementations at runtime, extending the behavior of our program after it ships, or allowing our classes to behave in different ways by implementing specific characteristics.

This chapter explains how abstract interfaces can be implemented in C++, and shows how to take advantage of them effectively in our games and tools. Chapter 11 will present a specific use of abstract interfaces: plug-ins.

ABSTRACT INTERFACES

The primary objective of a class is to represent a concept, encapsulating how it is implemented and sparing the irrelevant internal implementation details to its users. Ideally, only the interface describing the public functions for a class should be exposed outside of that class.

Unfortunately, C++ is not quite that clean. No doubt in part due to its C heritage, C++ exposes a lot more than just the public interface to the outside world. A C++ class is described in a header file, and any part of the program that uses that class also includes its header file. But in a header file, there is much more than just the class interface; it contains any other includes necessary for that header file to compile correctly, the declarations of all its protected and private functions, and the list of all its member variables, whether they are public or not. Granted, the compiler will not let any part of the program touch anything other than its public functions and member variables, but the information about implementation details will 'leak' out into other parts of the program.

So why is this a big deal? Usually, this information leakage is not too much of a problem. After all, that is how C++ classes were designed from the start, and they are perfectly usable. However, sometimes we need better encapsulation. By increasing the decoupling between a class implementation and the code that uses it, we might be able to achieve any of the following things:

- We can change class implementations without having to modify any other code, just with a recompile and relink step. Imagine being able to select one of several different pathfinding implementations to test and measure, and determine which one is best for your current game, or try several spatial partitioning algorithms (octrees, quadtrees, BSP trees, etc.), just by swapping out class implementations.

- We can change class implementation at runtime, which takes things a step further, but it is still possible with a good separation between interface and implementation. This could be particularly useful for selecting a rendering system at runtime that is based on the user's hardware or the rendering system selected from a menu.
- We can provide new implementations after the game has been released. Imagine shipping the game, and then extending it by adding new units, new behaviors, or new game types, all as additional downloads. This is possible if the program is prepared for it from the beginning. The same method can be applied to your tools (either internal, or released with the game), which can be extended through plug-ins instead of being forced to release new executables (see Chapter 11, Plug-Ins for detailed information).

An abstract interface is a particular type of organization that separates the interface and the implementation parts of a C++ class. It allows us to achieve any of the previously mentioned goals by being a little careful with how things are organized.

In addition to those specific goals, decoupling the game code from the objects it manipulates is a worthwhile goal in itself. It creates cleaner, easier to maintain code than if objects were referenced directly. It also provides cleaner division lines between different parts of the code, which allows several programmers in the same team to work more easily together at the same time on the same code. Without that decoupling, programmers could more often be stepping on each other's toes and interfering with each other's work.

Abstract interfaces are not a new concept or a concept that is only applied to game development; it is a useful general programming technique. Some companies have created APIs based around the concept of abstract interfaces and even provided their own standardized abstract interface functions and macros. Microsoft's COM is one such API that relies heavily on the use of abstract interfaces. As a matter of fact, COM can do all the things that we are going to develop by ourselves in this chapter.

Why take the time to write our own abstract interfaces when we can just use COM? Mainly, because most of the time we want the basics, without any of the baggage. We are probably not going to be doing any remote process invocation or any of the advanced features that COM (and some of its successors, like COM+) provides. Also, abstract interfaces are such a simple concept that it is worth learning in isolation first. If we later realize we would rather use COM, we will have a much better understanding of how to use it effectively. Finally, a major blow against using COM is that it is platform-dependent. Nowadays, there is no single platform dominating the game market. PCs are a small part of the game market, which is currently dominated by consoles. Even among consoles, there are several totally different platforms. By creating our own platform-independent version of abstract interfaces, we can easily reuse our code on any platform we wish as long as we have a C++ compiler.

GENERAL C++ IMPLEMENTATION

An abstract interface in C++ is a class that only has pure virtual functions—no implementation, no member variables, nothing else. Recall that pure virtual functions are marked with a =0 at the end of their declaration, and that they indicate that a derived class must provide an implementation in order to be able to create any objects of that class. A simple abstract interface class would look like this:

```
// IAbstractInterfaceA.h
class IAbstractInterfaceA {
public:
    virtual ~IAbstractInterface() {};
    virtual void SomeFunction() = 0;
    virtual bool IsDone() = 0;
};
```

It does not even have a corresponding .cpp file, since it has no implementation of any kind; it is simply a description of the interface. Notice that the class name was prefixed by the letter I to indicate it is an abstract interface. It is by no means necessary to use the prefix, but it is a convenient notation to help remind us that the class we are dealing with is an abstract interface. To create an implementation based on that interface, we would inherit from it and provide an implementation for all of its functions.

```
// MyImplementation.h
class MyImplementation : public IAbstractInterfaceA {
public:
    virtual void SomeFunction();
    virtual bool IsDone();
};
```

Notice that the functions are not pure virtual anymore. That is because we are about to provide an implementation for them in the .cpp file.

```
// MyImplementation.cpp

void MyImplementation::SomeFunction() {
    // ...
}

bool MyImplementation::IsDone() {
    // ...
    return true;
}
```

Now anybody can select this class and use it in the rest of the program without worrying about what specific implementation they are using.

```
IAbstractInterfaceA * pInterface = new MyImplementation;
//...
pInterface->SomeFunction();
if (pInterface->IsDone()) // etc ...
```

This is just a general case, and so far it does not look all that useful. It almost looks like an extra layer of indirection for no reason, making our program less clear and harder to maintain. We can put that indirection to good use, and then it will pay off. Let's look closely at some particular uses of abstract interfaces and how they can be effectively used in games. As with a lot of things, the details are the hardest part, so we will describe the exact implementation and figure out how to solve a few tricky problems along the way.

ABSTRACT INTERFACES AS A BARRIER

The first, most straightforward use of abstract interfaces is simply to act as an insulation layer between the class implementation and the rest of the program. Let's look at an example.

We will create the layout for a graphics renderer. There will be two types of graphics renderers: OpenGL and Direct3D. Clearly, this can be extended to have any other types, depending on your platform and your program needs. Our goal is to make it so the program that uses the renderer does not need to know which one is being used, and can run with either type without any modifications. In addition, we would also like to be able to switch renderers at runtime.

This is a perfect application for an abstract interface. Here is the C++ source code for a possible interface for the graphics renderer:

```
// GraphicsRenderer.h
// This is the abstract interface class
class IGraphicsRenderer {
public:
    virtual ~IGraphicsRenderer() {};
    virtual void SetWorldMatrix(const Matrix4d & mat) = 0;
    virtual void RenderMesh(const Mesh & mes) = 0;
    // ...
};
```

Those are just two representative functions. In a real situation, we would need to decide what other functions the renderer would expose in order to deal with materials, render states, shaders, lights, and so forth. Now we can provide two bare-bones implementations based on that interface: one for D3D and one for OpenGL.

```
// GraphicsRendererOGL.h
#include "GraphicsRenderer.h"
#include <gl.h>
class GraphicsRendererOGL : public IGraphicsRenderer {
public:
    virtual void SetWorldMatrix(const Matrix4d & mat);
    virtual void RenderMesh(const Mesh & mes);
    // ...
}
```

```
// GraphicsRendererD3D.h
#include "GraphicsRenderer.h"
#include <d3d.h>
class GraphicsRendererD3D : public IGraphicsRenderer {
public:
    virtual void SetWorldMatrix(const Matrix4d & mat);
    virtual void RenderMesh(const Mesh & mes);
    // ...
}
```

Their corresponding .cpp files provide the implementation for each of the functions in the abstract interface. As long as the rest of the program only works with the graphics renderer through an `IGraphicsRenderer` pointer, changing implementations is easy. We just need to create the type of renderer we want and pass a pointer to it for the program to use.

```
IGraphicsRenderer * g_pRenderer = new GraphicsRendererOGL();
// ...

// Now we don't care which renderer we're using.
g_pRenderer->SetWorldMatrix(ObjectToWorld);
g_pRenderer->RenderMesh(mesh);
```

There is nothing stopping us from changing the type of renderer at runtime either; just create a new object and tell the system to use it instead of the old one. The only difficult part is in doing the necessary adjustments in the renderer itself to maintain the selected preferences, such as video mode, textures, and geometry. From the abstract interface point of view, the operation is simple.

Headers and Factories

There is one extra beneficial side effect of the way we have organized the renderer. Notice that both `GraphicsRendererOGL.h` and `Graphics-RendererD3D.h` include one (and possibly more) platform-specific header file. This is needed because the header files of the specific implementations are filled with details about how they are implemented. They probably contain structures, enums, and macros that are OpenGL- or Direct3D-specific, so the header files must be included.

If the graphics renderer had not been designed with an abstract interface, the program would be using the OpenGL or the Direct3D renderer directly, which means the rest of the program would be forced to include the platform-specific header files for each renderer. This is not necessarily a bad thing, but it has a few drawbacks:

- Those header files are usually not small. They can include other header files that in turn and have a lot of structures, classes, or macros. If every file that uses the renderer is forced to include that chain of header files, compile times will be significantly degraded. Using an abstract interface gives both a cleaner design from a programming point of view and faster compile times. It is one of those win-win situations.

If you are using a compiler with precompiled header support or some other way of including many header files only once, the compile times will be further reduced. Unfortunately, that approach makes the next drawback even worse.

- Any code that includes the platform-specific renderer files will have access to any of its contents. This makes it very easy for unrelated parts of our program to start becoming dependent on OpenGL or Direct3D, and we will not realize it until we try to switch to a different platform. At this point it could cost us a lot of time and grief, and possibly a missed deadline. It can start as an innocent use of a macro that happens to be defined in d3d.h. Then the use of a typedef, followed by calling a helper function to set up a matrix . . . and before we know it, our code is totally locked to one particular platform without us realizing it because we are not explicitly including the Direct3D header file in our program.

This situation is explored in more detail in Chapter 15 (Dealing with Large Projects), which deals with the physical structure of a project. However, some part of the code needs to include the implementation header files in order to be able to create those objects and pass them to the rest of the program. This can be restricted to just one .cpp file, so it is usually not a problem.

We can take it a step further and encapsulate the implementations even more by using a *factory*. A factory is a very simple design pattern that allows the creation of related objects. In our case, it will allow us to create any of the different implementations for the renderer without even needing the implementation header files.

The following code shows how a the renderer would be created through our factory class. Notice that we are not dealing directly with the specific class implementations GraphicsRendererOGL and Graphics-RendererD3D, but rather we are just asking for them by name from the factory function.

```
GraphicsRendererFactory factory;
IGraphicsRenderer * g_pRenderer;

// This creates an OpenGL renderer
g_pRenderer = factory.CreateRenderer("OpenGL");

// This creates a Direct3D renderer
g_pRenderer = factory.CreateRenderer("Direct3D");
```

The actual implementation of the factory is straightforward; it checks the name that is passed to its `CreateRenderer` function and does a `new` in the correct implementation of the renderer. Now only the factory class needs to include the implementation header files for each of the renderers. The rest of the code does not need to know they even exist.

We have now totally separated the implementation from the interface. As you can imagine, such a clean break is a perfect boundary for separating that code into another library (static or dynamic). The only thing the library exposes is the abstract interface and the factory to create new implementations. Everything else can remain well hidden underneath.

Real-World Details

There are a few more interesting C++ implementation details that are worth mentioning. These are not details dealing with the concept of abstract interfaces, but purely with how they are implemented in C++ in the most effective way.

The first one is that all functions in the abstract interface are virtual. Clearly, we want to call the functions of the derived classes through a pointer to the abstract interface, which is the whole point. So we must declare all functions in the abstract interface as virtual.

In addition to being virtual, they are pure virtual (indicated by the `=0` next to the function declaration). This means that the compiler will not let us create an object of that type until somebody has provided an implementation for that function. It is not necessary to declare them as pure virtual, but it certainly is a good reminder to implement all the functions required by the interface.

You may have noticed the appearance of the virtual destructor in the previous example, even though we did not make any comment about it. Now, did you notice something a bit strange about that destructor? For those of you who missed it, here is the destructor in the abstract interface again:

```
class IGraphicsRenderer {
public:
    virtual ~IGraphicsRenderer() {};
    //...
};
```

The first thing to observe is that the abstract interface itself has the declaration for a destructor. And not only that, but it is a virtual destructor.

The reason for making the destructor virtual is the same as for making all of its other functions virtual. At some point, the program is most likely going to delete the object pointed to by the abstract interface pointer. If the destructor were not virtual, it would call the destructor for the abstract interface and leave it at that. None of the destructors of the derived classes would ever be called. By making it virtual we ensure that we call the destructor for the specific implementation we are using.

The other interesting point is that the destructor, unlike the rest of the functions, is not pure virtual. As a matter of fact, the two curly brackets to the right of the destructor are an inline empty function body. So we are providing an empty implementation for the destructor. This has to do with keeping the compiler happy. Without it, the compiler will complain about linker errors, since destructors work slightly differently than normal functions.

We could have made the destructor pure virtual and provided an implementation for it like this:

```
virtual ~IGraphicsRenderer() = 0 {};
```

Or we could have made it pure virtual and hidden the empty function body in a .cpp file. All those things are functionally equivalent, but with the drawback that we force all derived classes to provide a destructor. Some of them might want to do that anyway, but some of them might not, so it is a better solution to not make it pure virtual and let the derived classes decide for themselves whether they need a destructor or not.

Finally, one question comes up often while working with this type of abstract interface. Can an abstract interface provide some partial implementation? At first this might seem an odd idea. Why would we want to provide partial implementation? After all, the whole point of an abstract interface is to separate the interface and the implementation. Unfortunately, in practice things are not quite so clear cut. Sometimes we will want to create many different implementations of an abstract interface, but with all of them implementing a few functions in the exact same way. It would be very convenient if the abstract interface could implement them directly.

The short answer is that is acceptable to do that in a few cases. If it is just one simple function, then it is probably fine. It is probably still a good idea to label that function as pure virtual; that way it will force the derived class to explicitly call the parent implementation and avoid some of the multiple inheritance ambiguity.

As things get more complicated, and we want to have many different functions implemented in the interface, then we need to back off and reconsider our design. The more implemented functions we add to the abstract interface, the less it becomes an abstract interface. Many of the problems we were hoping to solve come back: tighter coupling, header files leaking into the rest of the program, and so forth. A better solution would be to keep the pure abstract interface, create one class that derived from it that provides all the common functionality, and then create the rest of the specific implementations deriving from that intermediate class (see Figure 10.1).

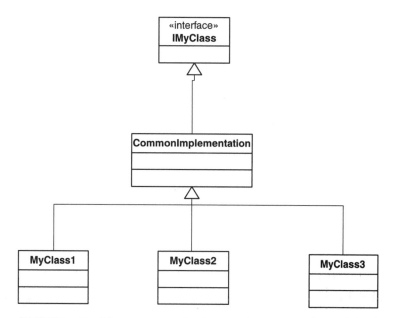

FIGURE 10.1   Providing a common implementation to many classes derived from an abstract interface.

ABSTRACT INTERFACES AS CLASS CHARACTERISTICS

In the previous section, we saw how an abstract interface could be used to totally separate interface and implementation, and allow us to switch implementations with ease. In this section we will look at a different aspect of abstract interfaces. Here we are not concerned with switching implementations, but with hiding the identity of an object behind abstract interfaces, so the same code can manipulate objects of any class, even of a class that did not exist when the game shipped.

The general idea is simple: our program will not be hardwired to use any objects of a specific class. Instead, every time we need to perform an operation on a object, we ask that object if it has an implementation that matches what we want to do; if so, we call the appropriate functions.

For example, consider the situation where we want to render all the objects in the world. Not all objects are renderable; some of them have purely logic functions, such as switches, counters, or flags. Using abstract interfaces, we could go through every object in the world, ask it whether it is renderable or not, and if it is, call its render function. This sounds very simple, but again, the details will be a bit tricky. (Incidentally, there are much more efficient ways of rendering the scene than checking every single object in the world, so do not take this as an example of a good architecture. We are using it as an example purely for simplicity.)

Implementations

Let's quickly review how we would implement the above example without abstract interfaces.

Hardwired Types

The first option is to hardwire the object type in the calling code and traverse all the objects in the world, checking each object for its type. Whenever we find an object of a type that we know we want to render, we call its render function. However, this approach is exactly what we are trying to avoid, because it is hardwired to specific object types.

```
// Pseudo code of a render function using hardwired
// object types
void RenderWorld () {
    for (each object in the world) {
        if (object is enemy ||
            object is environment object ||
            object is effect ||
            object is terrain ||
            object is sky ||
            //... etc ) {
                object.Render();
        }
    }
}
```

This approach will work, but as you can see from the source code snipped, it is clumsy, error prone, and not very maintainable. Whenever we add a new object type, we need to remember to also change the function that checks whether something should be rendered and add it there, not to mention all the other functions throughout the program that use the same logic to do other types of processing, such as AI, collision, and physics. It basically makes it impossible to add a new object type without changing the whole program.

Leave It up to the Object

A better approach would be to let the object itself decide whether it should be rendered. We can do that just as easily without abstract interfaces. All the object needs to do is implement a function that returns a Boolean indicating whether it should be rendered or not. Then in our pass through all the game objects, we call that function and render it or not based on the result.

```
// Pseudo code of a render function asking each object
void RenderWorld ( void ) {
    for (each object in the world) {
        if (object.IsRenderable)
            object.Render();
}
```

Clearly, this is a much neater solution than our previous one. It is still not perfect, though. The main drawback is that every object needs to implement the IsRenderable function along with all the functions that will be called to render it if needed (in this case, just Render). In itself it is not a big deal, but as more characteristics like this one are added, the more functions all objects will have to support, even though they will often be empty and meaningless for that particular class, since not every class will need them. Imagine if we start adding similar functions for collision, manipulation, or movement. All the classes will be quickly cluttered up with useless functions.

Even worse, imagine that after we have dozens, maybe hundreds of different types of objects, we decide to add one more type of characteristic, such as whether or not the object makes sounds. Now we need to modify all our existing objects and create a new function that returns whether it should play sounds or not. Certainly, it will be easier if all the game objects inherit from a common root, but things are not always that way (or we might only want half of them to return false and the other half to return true). There is no clean way to do that with this approach.

Abstract Interfaces

An even better solution would be one that would allow us to implement and declare only the functions that will be used by a particular class. That is one of the things that abstract interfaces and inheritance allow us to do. The pseudocode for the rendering function using abstract interfaces looks like this:

```
// Pseudo code of a render function using abstract interfaces
void RenderWorld ( void ) {
    for (each object in the world) {
        if (object implements Renderable interface) {
            IRenderable * pRend;
            pRend = object.GetInterface(IRenderable);
            pRend->Render();
        }
    }
}
```

An object that does not implement a particular interface does not need to do anything about it. As a matter of fact, it does not even need to be aware that a rendering interface even exists, which is good, because it means we will be able to extend things more easily later on.

Notice also that an object is not limited to implementing just one abstract interface. We could create a new object that implements as many abstract interfaces as we want; it just needs to inherit from each of them and implement the correct functions. Since we are inheriting from abstract interfaces, most of the potential problems of multiple inheritance are not an issue anymore. This is arguably one of the best uses of multiple inheritance in C++. This is how an actual class that implements the IRenderable interface would look:

```
class IRenderable
{
public:
    bool Render() = 0;
    // ...
};

class GameEntityPhysical : public GameEntity,
                           public IRenderable
{
public:
    bool Render();
    // ...
};
```

Query Interface

So far, we have glossed over one major detail: how can we tell if an object implements a particular interface? One possible answer is to use dynamic_cast, as we did in Chapter 2, to find out if an object inherits from a particular class, and if so, get the correct pointer to that parent class. This will work fine as long as we are willing to have runtime type information turned on in the compiler options. That is not always desirable, since many times we would rather replace the standard RTTI with our own system to have better control over the memory used and the performance of the queries.

In that case, instead of relying on RTTI being enabled, it makes sense to provide a special function to determine whether objects inherit from a particular abstract interface. (This function will be different from the default custom RTTI system that will be described in Chapter 12.) We are trying to do two things here. The first one we have already discussed; the function needs to tell us whether an object implements a particular abstract interface. The second goal is a bit more subtle; it needs to return a pointer to the object, but the pointer must be of the type of the abstract interface.

As you may recall from our discussion on multiple inheritance in Chapter 2, an object that uses multiple inheritance will have several vtables merged into one, and correctly casting from one type to another requires changing the original pointer by some offset. The calling code cannot cast the pointer correctly, since it does not know the type of the referenced object; so it is up to the object itself to deal with the casting. A very convenient place for doing the casting is in the same function that checks if an interface is available.

Here is a very simple implementation of that function. It is called QueryInterface because it answers the question of whether a particular interface is implemented by an object or not. If the interface is present, it returns a correctly cast pointer to that interface; otherwise it returns NULL.

```
    void * GameEntityPhysical::QueryInterface(Interface
interface)
        const
    {
        if (interface == IRENDERABLE) {
            IRenderable * pRender =
static_cast<IRenderable*>(this);
            return (void *)(pRender);
        }
        return NULL;
    }
```

Notice that we first cast the this pointer to the type of pointer we want, and then we return it as a plain void pointer. Even though it looks like an unnecessary step, that casting will most likely change the actual value of the pointer. Without it, the returned value could not be safely cast to the correct interface type.

Clearly, every class that inherits from an abstract interface must implement this QueryInterface function. It also needs to be called by the program independently of what class it is, so it is usually best to put that function in a parent class, even if that is the only member function available.

This function also assumes that somewhere there is a list of unique identifiers for each interface. In this example, the unique identifier was IRENDERABLE. It is possible to use strings instead of unique numbers, but this will result in poor performance at runtime, and QueryInterface could end up getting called many hundreds or thousands of times per frame. For most purposes in our own programs, a simple list of sequential numbers is plenty. If we want to let other people extend our system and add new interfaces, a method for guaranteeing the uniqueness of interface identifiers is required. Microsoft's COM system uses a system very much like this, as well as a method to have unique identifiers.

If we find ourselves creating many QueryInterface functions, we could easily wrap all of the functionality in a few macros to make it easier to add to new classes. When using those macros, creating a new QueryInterface function is simple:

```
QUERYINTERFACE_BEGIN
    QUERYINTERFACE_ADD(IRENDERABLE,IRenderable)
QUERYINTERFACE_END
```

Adding more interfaces just requires inserting several QUERY-INTERFACE_ADD macros after the first one. This is how the rendering function from the previous examples would use QueryInterface:

```
// Render function using QueryInterface
void RenderWorld () {
    for (each object in the world) {
        void * pInterface;
        pInterface = object.QueryInterface(IRENDERABLE);
        if (pInterface != NULL) {
            IRenderable * pRend;
            pRend = static_cast<IRenderable*>(pInterface);
            pRend->Render();
        }
    }
}
```

Extending the Game

One of our goals at the beginning of this chapter was to extend the game after it has shipped. How exactly do we apply abstract interfaces to accomplish that?

The first thing we need to realize is that we might not need to change the code at all. A lot of the additions to a game after it has shipped could be done solely by adding new data files. If the game has been architected so it is mostly data-driven, it should be possible to do many new things by just providing new data files: new levels, new game types, new characters, or new special powers. If you had planned on user extensibility of your game, they will have an easier time creating new content for your game if they can just add new data with the provided tools, rather than having to write C++ code.

If it becomes necessary to release new code along with the new data, sometimes the executable itself can be replaced or patched. That updated executable could be compiled with the latest classes. So using abstract interfaces for this purpose is not an absolute necessity, although it still has its share of benefits from a development point of view, simply by decoupling the game code as much as possible from the objects it manipulates.

A different approach is to release new functionality in the form of new components for the game, possibly along with new data, but no updated executable. This would be particularly appropriate if you are making a lot of different bits of content available, and you expect the players to only download the ones in which they are interested. For example, in a tycoon-style game, you could provide hundreds of different new game units for download, each of them with some data (new graphics, animations, and sounds), along with some new code that would be hidden behind abstract interfaces. The original executable will be able to deal with these new objects as if they had been part of the original set of objects with which the game was shipped.

The game normally creates game objects through a game object factory. It passes the game object type, and the function returns a game entity of the correct type.

```
GameObjecType objType = LoadObjectType();
GameEntity * pEntity = factory.CreateObject(objType);
```

The factory knows about the different object types and the classes that should be instantiated in each case. It looks like something along these lines:

```
GameEntity * GameObjectFactory::CreateObject(
                        GameObjectType type)
{
    switch (type)
    {
    case GAMEOBJECT_CAMERA:     return new GameCamera;
    case GAMEOBJECT_ENEMY:      return new GameEnemy;
    case GAMEOBJECT_TERRAIN:    return new GameTerrain;
    case GAMEOBJECT_PROJECTILE: return new GameProjectile;
    }
    return NULL;
}
```

The key to extending the game after shipping is to avoid having those object types hardwired in the game object factory. Instead, the factory can be extensible. It does not know anything about game object types and classes at first, and other parts of the code must register an association between a particular object type and a class to create.

Whenever the game detects any new components (Chapter 11 will delve into more detail about plug-ins), those components are loaded and initialized. The first thing they do as they are initialized is to register any new game object types with the new classes that the component provides. Now, as the game attempts to load a new level that uses some of the new game objects, the factory will create them correctly, and the rest of the game will treat them like any other object through their abstract interfaces.

ALL THAT GLITTERS IS NOT . . .

So far, this chapter has been expounding on the benefits of using abstract interfaces. Chapter 11 will continue that trend by delving into another abstract interface application—plug-ins. However, abstract interfaces are not the be-all and end-all solution for every problem. Even though they increase decoupling between the implementation and the code that uses it, which is always something to aspire to do in our programs, they have their own set of problems. It is just as important to know when to avoid abstract interfaces as when to use them.

The first and foremost problem is the added complexity. If an abstract interface is not needed, all it does is add another layer of complexity. It will make the program more difficult to understand, maintain, and change in the future. In programming, usually the simplest approach that does everything we want is the best solution.

The second problem is closely related to the first one; code that uses abstract interfaces is more difficult to debug. If we break into the debugger while the program is running, and we attempt to view the elements of an object pointed to by an abstract interface pointer, chances are its contents will be empty. The debugger cannot show anything there because an abstract interface has no implementation. In order to see its contents, we must cast the pointer by hand to its correct type (assuming we know the object type it points to).

The final drawback of abstract interfaces is performance. Remember that every function present in an abstract interface, by the nature of an interface, has to be declared virtual. This means there will be a slight performance penalty for calling it (which is not very important), plus it will never be able to be inlined. (This is of much greater importance for a tiny function. Refer to Chapter 1 and Chapter 5 for the performance implications of virtual functions.)

The consequences of the last problem is that abstract interfaces need to be placed carefully. The most important aspect to consider is whether it makes logical sense where the abstract interface is laid out. Then the performance implications need to be considered. If the abstract interface is located at too low a level, then it will be called many times per frame, resulting in performance degradation. By moving it to a slightly higher level, we could dramatically reduce the number of calls to the interface and have no impact in the overall performance.

To continue with the example of the renderer, a bad design would be to have the abstract interface deal with individual polygons. Many hundreds of thousands of polygons are rendered every frame, maybe even millions. Paying that extra cost every single time a polygon is rendered would be wasteful. Instead, the renderer could deal with geometry at a higher level, such as meshes, and a whole group of polygons could be rendered at once with only one call to the abstract interface.

CONCLUSION

In this chapter, we have seen the concept of an abstract interface and what some of its uses are. We first learned how to create an abstract interface in C++, using a class without implementation and pure virtual functions. Specific implementations of the abstract interface inherit from the interface and provide their own implementation.

Then we saw how an abstract interface can be used as a barrier to isolate the implementation from the code that uses the interface. Doing so allows us to switch implementations on the fly much more easily, and it also provides some extra encapsulation that results in fewer physical dependencies between files.

Next we looked at abstract interfaces as characteristics a class can implement and how we can create code that does not rely on specific class types. Instead, that code checks for implemented abstract interfaces, and works on them if they are found. This is the basis for being able to create new class types after the game ships without having to release a new executable.

Finally, we had a look at some of the drawbacks of abstract interfaces, and under what circumstances is better to avoid them, or at least to be cautious with them.

SUGGESTED READING

Here is a good introduction to the concept of abstract interfaces:

> Llopis, Noel, "Programming with Abstract Interfaces," *Game Programming Gems 2*, Charles River Media, 2001.

This very enlightening read on the internals of COM takes a progressive approach and develops the COM API from scratch, showing the reasoning at each step:

> Rogerson, Dale, *Inside COM*, Microsoft Press, 1997.

The book below is a detailed look at the status of component software, which is the whole idea behind writing a program as independent parts that are tied together through the use of abstract interfaces or other similar mechanisms.

> Szyperski, Clemens, *Component Software: Beyond Object-Oriented Programming*, Addison-Wesley, 1999.

This excellent book covers the factory pattern, among many other fundamental patterns:

> Gamma, Erich, et al., *Design Patterns*, Addison-Wesley, 1995.

11

PLUG-INS

T his chapter explains the concept of plug-ins and how we can architect our programs to use plug-ins. You might choose to design some of your own tools so they can be extended through plug-ins, or maybe you want to simply write plug-ins for some of the popular modeling and texturing packages used in game development. In either case, this chapter will give you a firm understanding of how plug-ins are implemented and how a program should be structured to use them.

THE NEED FOR PLUG-INS

Complex tools are more than one-shot deals. People will want to extend those tools, customize them, or add new functionality to fit their needs. However, putting every single possible bit of functionality in the tool is quite impossible, and it is also a bad idea. The program would quickly degenerate into an unmaintainable mess due to the thousands of different options, not to mention that it would balloon in size and features, and become a fine piece of bloatware that nobody wants to use.

A much more flexible approach is to use plug-ins. The program provides all the core functionality, everything that most users will want. The rest of the functionality can be provided through extensions called plug-ins. The users can choose which plug-ins they want and which ones they would rather not even load. Also, by allowing a tool to be extended this way and making a small API public, users or third-party companies can create their own plug-ins to take the tool exactly where they want it to go. Sometimes we will find ourselves writing plug-ins for other people's programs, and sometimes we will architect our code so other people can modify our own tools.

Plug-Ins for Other Programs

The artists at your company are very excited. They have just received Version 13.75 of their favorite modeling package. Shivering with anticipation, they install it and fire it up. It is an instant hit; it is exactly what they had been waiting for. It has this feature and that feature, and the other one. . . . Wait, no, it does not have *that* feature. "But we really needed *that* feature for our game! There is no way we will be able to create all the content in time without *that* feature!" the artists clamor. Fortunately, not all is lost. There are always alternatives.

One possibility is to use a different modeling program that has all the features they want. Does such a program exist? Probably not. Another option is to use several modeling programs. Hopefully, between all of them, they will have all the desired features. This is quite likely, but what about money? Modeling programs are not cheap. And what about interoperability? Can we save and load models from all of them? Then there's the question of expertise. Will the artists be able to use all the tools efficiently?

A third option is to write a tool from scratch. The tool could replace the modeling program, although it is highly unlikely we would be able to come up with a substitute for a thirteenth-generation modeling program created by a team of hundreds of people. Maybe our tool could just complement it. The artists can save their models on the full-featured modeling tool, load them in our little tool, and apply the extra features they wanted. Switching back and forth is a bit cumbersome, but it would probably work. The main issue is whether or not the artists can go back to their modeling program and continue working on their models after they has been processed by our tool. It is not always easy to make data go both ways. Will the information from our tool be overridden whenever the model is saved again in the original modeling package?

One last possibility is to extend the existing program. This would be ideal. The feature the artists want is pretty minor, so if we could only extend the modeling program, we would have the perfect solution. If it uses a plug-in architecture, then we are in luck. It is probably just a matter of implementing a couple of abstract interfaces and giving the plug-in to the artists. All it takes is one afternoon's work, and you have achieved hero status among the artists.

It turns out that game companies routinely extend off-the-shelf modeling programs to export models and textures in their own formats, to tag models with extra information specific to their game, to do special filters and conversions on their textures, and even to display how a model will look rendered with their game engine inside the modeling program. As a matter of fact, a lot of programs (not just modeling programs) are intended to be extended through user plug-ins—web servers, web browsers, .mp3 players, e-mail programs, compilers, and editors.

Plug-Ins for Our Programs

So hero status is good, and being able to write plug-ins for other programs is very useful, but what about our own programs? Why would we want to bother to add plug-ins? We have the source code, so we can just modify the programs anytime we want, recompile them, and release them with the new functionality.

The simple answer is that the tools will be easier to extend. Once the plug-in architecture is in place, it will undoubtedly be easier to write a new plug-in than to add basic functionality to the tool itself.

The other key point in support of using plug-ins is that the original tool is completely insulated from the contents of the plug-in. This makes it possible to have a generic tool, but add game-specific functionality to it later on without losing any generality. As an example, consider a resource viewer program. This is a program that allows us to browse the thousands of resources that a game usually needs, such as textures, models, animations, and effects. The program might natively know about some of the basic, generic resource types, like .tiff textures, VRML model files, and a few others. Then we can write new plug-ins to be able to browse our game-specific resources: platform-optimized mesh files, specially compressed textures, game entity objects, and so forth.

Such a generic tool could be used to display resources from several different projects, each of them with some custom resource types. If we were to add that functionality in the base tool, we would need to make the tool dependent on thoseprojects, as well as any future projects. And even worse, what if two projects interpreted the same resource in slightly different ways? By using plug-ins, the users can choose which resources they want the tool to display. The same goes for multiplatform projects. We could display resources created for specific platforms just by having new plug-ins for them, without ever having to touch the original tool.

One final advantage of using plug-ins is that one day you might decide to release your tool to the game community so they can create new content for your game. At that point, other people might want to extend the tool in the same way we extended the off-the-shelf modeling package. Shouldn't they get a chance to obtain hero status as well?

PLUG-IN ARCHITECTURE

ON THE CD

In this section, we will cover in detail how a plug-in architecture is set up, and we will go over some of the most interesting parts of the implementation. The source code on the accompanying CD-ROM contains a full Win32 sample program. You can find it in the folder \Chapter 11. Plug-ins\, and the Visual Studio workspace is pluginsample.dsw. You might want to refer to that code for all the details.

IPlugin

The whole plug-in architecture revolves around the abstract interface for a plug-in. (See Chapter 10 for a detailed explanation of abstract interfaces.) The abstract interface contains all the functions that the program will use to manipulate the plug-in.

As an example, let's create an interface for a set of plug-ins to export data from our tool. Here is one possible abstract interface for our plug-ins:

```
class IPluginExporter
{
public:
    virtual ~IPluginExporter () {};

    virtual bool Export(Data * pRoot) = 0;
    virtual void About() = 0;
};
```

The interface declares only the minimum set of functions necessary to interact with all of the exporter plug-ins. In this case, the program interacts with the plug-ins in only two ways. The first way is by calling the Export function and passing the appropriate data to export. Each plug-in will implement that function differently and export the same data in different formats.

The second way the program interacts with the plug-in is by calling the About function. About displays the plug-in's name, its build date and version information, and so forth. Having a function like this is extremely useful when dealing with plug-ins. Not only does it allow us to see what plug-ins are currently loaded, but it also lets us check that the plug-ins are the correct version. Since plug-ins can be copied and updated independently of each other and the main program, being able to check their version from within the program will save the users many headaches.

In this example, all the initialization is supposed to happen in the constructor and all the shutdown in the destructor, so there are no separate initialize and shutdown functions. When possible, this is the preferred way of dealing with initialization and shutdown, since it makes it impossible for an object to be successfully created, but not initialized. On the other hand, if the initialization can fail (e.g., if it has to access a file or allocate memory), then exception handling is needed to flag that error from a constructor (see Chapter 5, Exception Handling).

Creating Specific Plug-Ins

Creating an exporter plug-in for a specific format is just a fill-in-the-blanks exercise. Here is an example:

```cpp
class PluginExporterHTML
{
public:
    PluginExporterHTML (PluginMgr & mgr);

    // IPlugin interface functions
    virtual bool Export(Data * pRoot);
    virtual void About();

private:
    // Any functions specific to this implementation
    bool CreateHTMLFile();
    void ParseData(Data * pRoot);
    // ...
};
```

Along with the header file, we provide a .cpp file implementing those functions, and our exporter should work. There is nothing else to do. Notice that we did not have to change a single line in the original program.

Creating another plug-in to export a different format is just a matter of creating a new class that also inherits from IPlugin and filling in the blanks again with the new implementation.

```cpp
class PluginExporterXML
{
public:
    PluginExporterXML (PluginMgr & mgr);

    // IPlugin interface functions
    virtual bool Export(Data * pRoot);
    virtual void About();

private:
    // Any functions specific to this implementation
    // ...
};
```

Dealing with Multiple Types of Plug-Ins

So far we have seen how to make new plug-ins of the same type; in the previous example, they were all exporter plug-ins. Often a program will need to have more than one type of plug-in: one type to export data, another one to import data from different sources, another one to display new data types, or another one for user extensions. The possibilities are endless, so more than one plug-in type is clearly needed in more-complex programs.

The best way to organize several types of plug-ins is through inheritance. One abstract interface will contain the interface functions that are common to all plug-in types, such as initialization and shutdown (assuming you have explicit functions for those tasks), and getting the plug-in name, version, and any other relevant information. In our case, the base abstract interface for all plug-ins could look like this:

```
class IPlugin
{
public:
    virtual ~IPlugin () {};

    virtual const std::string & GetName() = 0;
    virtual const VersionInfo & GetVersion() = 0;
    virtual void About() = 0;
};
```

For each plug-in type, we will create a new class derived from IPlugin that adds the new functionality for that plug-in type. Notice that these new classes are still abstract interfaces, since they inherit from an abstract interface themselves, and they do not provide any implementation. Here are some possible classes for different plug-in types:

```
class IPluginExporter : public IPlugin
{
public:
    virtual ~IPluginExporter () {};
    virtual bool Export (Data * pRoot) = 0;
};

class IPluginImporter : public IPlugin
{
public:
    virtual ~IPluginImporter () {};
    virtual bool Import (Data * pRoot) = 0;
```

```
};

class IPluginDataViewer : public IPlugin
{
public:
    virtual ~IPluginDataViewer () {};
    virtual bool Preprocess (Data * pData) = 0;
    virtual bool View (Data * pData, HWND hwnd) = 0;
};
```

To create a specific plug-in, we need to inherit from one of these specialized types of plug-ins. Then we need to implement both the general IPlugin functions as well as the functions specific to that type of plug-in. The resulting inheritance tree can be seen in Figure 11.1.

FIGURE 11.1   Inheritance tree with multiple plug-in types.

Loading Plug-Ins

So far we have been talking about plug-ins, and describing their interfaces and implementations, but we have not mentioned how they do their magic—how they get loaded at runtime. For plug-ins to get loaded at runtime, they clearly cannot be part of the program that uses them. Otherwise, as soon as the program as been compiled, we would not be able to add any new plug-ins. Instead, they need to be compiled separately and then loaded on the fly.

In our Win32 example, the most straightforward way of loading plug-ins on the fly is through the use of DLLs (Dynamic Link Libraries). DLLs allow us to defer linking with the code inside the libraries until runtime. Only at that point, when we explicitly load a DLL, is that code made available to the rest of the program. This sounds like a perfect match for our needs.

To create a DLL, we must specify certain settings in our compiler. That way the target binary will be a dynamic-link library (.dll) and not an executable (.exe) or a static library (.lib). Depending on your compiler, you might also have a wizard that can set up a DLL project with a couple of mouse clicks.

Once we have created a DLL, we must decide what functions to export. Unlike other types of libraries, a DLL requires us to explicitly flag the functions, classes, or variables that we want to make available outside of the library. We would like to keep the number of exports from the DLL to a minimum, just to keep things as simple as possible. Instead of exporting the plug-in class itself, we will export a global factory function that will take care of creating the actual plug-in object. The following code exports the factory function:

```
#define PLUGINDECL __declspec(dllexport)
extern "C" PLUGINDECL IPlugin * CreatePlugin(
                            PluginManager & mgr);
```

With Visual C++, the way to export a function from a DLL is to add the keyword __declspec(dllexport) before the function declaration, which is what PLUGINDECL is defined to. As we will see in a moment, we define PLUGINDECL instead of adding __declspec(dllexport) directly so we can reuse the same header file when the DLL functions are imported instead of exported.

The other thing that might seem odd about the declaration of the factory function is the use of extern "C". This keyword tells the compiler not to decorate the function name in the usual C++ way. Instead, leave it undecorated, as if it were a C function. As a result, we will be able to look for that function later on using its normal name and not a name that has been mangled by the compiler.

Now, in addition to the actual plug-in implementation, every plug-in DLL needs to provide an implementation for the factory function. In most cases, this function is quite simple, as it just creates a new plug-in of the correct type.

```
PLUGINDECL IPlugin * CreatePlugin (PluginManager & mgr)
{
    return new PluginExporterHTML(mgr);
}
```

The DLL is ready to be used as a plug-in. One convenient trick often used by tools with many different types of plug-ins (or even by tools with only one type of plug-in, just to add more safety) is to rename the file. Instead of using a generic .dll extension, they are often changed to an extension that reflects the type of plug-in they are. For example, we could give exporters .exp extensions, or importers .imp extensions. With many different plug-ins, this little trick will prove quite convenient when trying to manage them by hand.

Plug-In Manager

So far we have described in detail how a plug-in is created, but we have not touched on how they are actually used. We have assumed that the program would magically load them and use them. This is the job of the plug-in manager.

The plug-in manager's only role is to deal with the plug-ins. Everything is quite straightforward, but it is a lot of bookkeeping and busy work. The objective is to make the rest of the program think that the plug-ins are just other objects; it will not know that the plug-ins were loaded dynamically.

ON THE CD

A design decision that needs to be made for each program that uses plug-ins is when exactly the plug-ins are going to be loaded. They could be loaded as soon as the program starts, when the user decides to load them, or maybe only individual plug-ins get loaded as the user selects them. Most programs attempt to load all the plug-ins whenever the program starts, as does the example on the CD-ROM (\Chapter 11. Plug-ins\pluginsample.dsw). Changing this is just a matter of calling the correct plug-in manager functions at a different time.

In our example, as soon as the program is loaded, the plug-in manager attempts to load all available plug-ins. It looks in a specific directory, and finds all the files with matching extensions to the plug-in type that with which we are dealing. This directory is usually relative to the executable and is usually something obvious, since the user will probably want to add or delete plug-ins directly. In our sample code we look in the ./plugins/ directory.

For every possible plug-in file that we find, we attempt to load it as a plug-in. The first step is to load the dynamic link library:

```
HMODULE hDll = ::LoadLibrary (filename.c_str());
```

The Win32 function `LoadLibrary` loads a DLL according to its file name. It returns a handle that we will need later on in order to free the DLL, or it returns `NULL` if there was an error attempting to load the DLL. At every step, we must check that the result was successful, since it is possible for some other random file to have the same extension as the plug-in we are looking for, or the file might be corrupted.

Remember how we declared the `CreatePlugin` function in the `IPlugin` header file? Here it is again, this time without leaving out the details:

```
#ifdef PLUGIN_EXPORTS
    #define PLUGINDECL __declspec(dllexport)
#else
    #define PLUGINDECL __declspec(dllimport)
#endif

extern "C" PLUGINDECL IPlugin * CreatePlugin(
                            PluginManager & mgr);
```

Now it becomes clearer that `PLUGINDECL` can be two different types of declarations, depending on `PLUGIN_EXPORTS`. Both the plug-in manager and the plug-in implementation itself need to include the `Plugin.h` header file, but the plug-in implementation needs to declare its function as a DLL export, and the plug-in manager needs to declared it as a DLL import. By using this little trick with the preprocessor, we can get away with using only one header file, and we avoid the maintenance headaches of having two separate header files with almost the same code. The next step, assuming the DLL was loaded correctly, is that we must look for the exported factory function.

```
CREATEPLUGIN pFunc = (CREATEPLUGIN)::GetProcAddress (hDll,
                            _T("CreatePlugin"));
```

The function `GetProcAddress` looks for the specified function in the exported function list from a certain DLL. We decided to call our factory function `CreatePlugin` for all the different plug-ins, so we can just look for that one function. Notice that we are able to look for the function by its plain name; this is because we chose to export it as `extern "C"`, which tells the compiler not to apply the usual C++ decorations in the symbol table.

Assuming the function is found, `GetProcAddress` will return a pointer to that function. Otherwise it will return `NULL`, and we will know that we do not have the expected DLL.

The plug-in manager is finally ready to create the plug-in. We call the factory function through the function pointer we just retrieved, and we should get back a plug-in of the correct type. Of course, the plug-in manager has no idea what that type is. It is hidden behind the `IPlugin` abstract interface:

```
IPlugin * pPlugin = pFunc(*this);
```

We pass `*this` as a parameter to the factory function, because it takes a reference to the plug-in manager. The plug-in needs to access the manager in order to interact with the rest of the program, as we will see in the next section. Finally, the plug-in manager keeps the pointer to the plug-in we just created in a list for the program to use whenever it is needed.

The rest of the plug-in manager functions are straightforward. We need some way for the program to enumerate the plug-ins. In our example, we just have one function that returns how many plug-ins are loaded, and another function that returns the plug-in corresponding to a particular index. Things are a bit more complicated if we have multiple types of plug-ins. In that case, the program needs to query for all the exporter plug-ins, all the importer plug-ins, and so on.

There is also the need for functions to load and unload plug-ins at run time. We at least want to unload all the plug-ins when the program exits so that all memory is freed correctly. To free a plug-in, all that is needed is to remove it from the plug-in list, delete the actual object, and unload its DLL by calling `FreeLibrary`. The function to unload the DLL takes as a parameter the DLL handle returned by `LoadLibrary`, so we must make sure we keep that handle along with the plug-in pointer itself.

Another very useful feature is to be able to reload all plug-ins (or just a particular one) without having to shut down the program itself. It is particularly useful during development to be able to quickly test several iterations of a plug-in, especially if loading the main program and the data set takes a while. To be able to do this correctly, it is not enough to just call a function to reload all plug-ins. We must be able to release a plug-in individually and then load it again at a later time. The reason is that as long as a DLL is loaded (through the function call `LoadLibrary`), its file will be locked by the operating system, which means we will not be able to replace it with the new version of the plug-in we have just compiled. So we must first unload the plug-in, update the DLL, and reload it again. All in all, it is usually still much faster than having to close, and start the program from scratch.

Two-Way Communication

So far the communication between the program and the plug-in has been highly unidirectional. The program calls plug-in functions whenever it is necessary. Is it time to export a file? Call the appropriate plug-in function. Do we need to display an object for which we have a plug-in? Call the render function. Everything is working perfectly.

There are some situations where we wish our plug-in to take a more active role, such as to add buttons to the toolbar or entries to the main menu. Maybe the plug-in needs to check the status of something periodically or intercept a message before the application gets to it. In order to do any of those things, the program has to be structured to allow the plug-ins to have that type of access.

The cleanest way to grant the plug-in access to other parts of the program is through the plug-in manager. All plug-ins already know about the manager, since we passed it as a parameter to their constructor, so we can easily extend it to become a gateway to the rest of the program.

At this point, we should decide what level of access we want to let the plug-in have. The more restricted the access to the rest of the program, the less dependency between the plug-in and the program (which means that the plug-in is likely to work with updated versions of the program), but also the fewer things it can do. Giving the plug-in free reign means that it has the ability to implement anything the plug-in writer has decided, but it also means that it has a much tighter coupling with the rest of the program and more potential for errors. A good rule to follow is to use the most restrictive approach that still allows the plug-in to do all the operations it requires.

The safer and more restrictive way is to do everything through the plug-in manager. The plug-in manager needs to anticipate the needs of all the plug-ins and have one function for every operation the plug-in will want to do. Since the plug-in manager is compiled with the rest of the program, it can have a more intimate knowledge of the different parts of the program, and the plug-in manager will be less likely to cause problems than a plug-in that accesses the program directly. Also, as the program changes and new versions are made available, the plug-in manager can be changed if necessary. If the plug-ins were accessing the program directly and there was a major architectural change, they would all become invalidated and would have to be updated and recompiled, which is exactly the situation we are trying to avoid.

ON THE CD

In the CD-ROM sample code (\Chapter 11. Plugins\pluginsample.dsw), the plug-ins communicate with the program in a very minimal way. They are exporter plug-ins, so they do not interact with the rest of the program very much. However, they do add a menu entry under the File | Export submenu. To do that they use a couple of functions in the plug-in manager to add and remove items from the export submenu. In that case, it is up to the plug-in manager to find a handle to the main frame, get the menu, find the correct submenu, and insert the items. Leaving that operation up to the plug-in has a lot of potential for problems, since it is tightly tied to the structure of the program.

The alternative is to grant the plug-in full access to the rest of the program. The plug-in manager can return a handle to the main window, or a pointer to some of the main objects, so the plug-in can manipulate them freely. It is a much riskier approach, but it allows maximum freedom in implementation and the potential to do things unforeseen by the original program.

Both approaches can be combined. A plug-in manager can provide many safe functions while allowing a 'back door' to give the plug-in full access to the program if it needs it. Most plug-ins will be well behaved and use the safe functions. If somebody absolutely needs to do something else, they have the ability to do so at the cost of making their plug-in more likely to break in the future.

PUTTING IT ALL TOGETHER

ON THE CD

The source code on the CD-ROM includes an example of a plug-in-based application. It consists of three different project files for Visual Studio in the \Chapter 11. Plugins\ folder:

- `pluginsample.dsp`: This is the main MFC application. It includes the plug-in manager class. It does not do anything in itself, other than to serve as a shell to demonstrate how plug-ins are hooked up.
- `PluginA\pluginA.dsp`: This is a simple exporter plug-in. To keep things simple, instead of exporting anything, it just displays a message box when the export function is called. It also has an "About" dialog box that is displayed when viewing the loaded plug-ins from the application.
- `PluginB\pluginB.dsp`: Another simple exporter plug-in

The plug-ins should be in the `./plugins/` directory relative to the application, and are loaded as soon as the application starts. It is possible to unload all of them, and load them again through a menu.

PLUG-INS IN THE REAL WORLD

We have seen in detail how to set up a plug-in architecture. But how do plug-ins perform in the real world?

Using Plug-Ins

Are they worth the complication? The answer is a resounding "Yes." Plug-ins are a great way of extending programs, and a lot of commercial products are designed to be extended that way. Some of products even take it to an extreme and provide all of their functionality through plug-ins so that the program itself is just a hollow shell, with the plug-ins doing all of the useful work.

That is fine for tools, but what about games? Here, extending functionality through plug-ins is less common. Many games are designed to be extended by users, but usually in the form of new resources and new scripts instead of new code. One of the main problems with offering a full plug-in approach is that of security. Once the plug-in is hooked up, it can do virtually anything to the game, or even the whole computer. It could be possible for malicious code to do many unpleasant things, from sniffing passwords and private information to deleting files on the hard drive. Script code, on the other hand, is usually very restricted in the type of operations it can do, so it is a lot safer to run game scripts of unknown origin than it is to run full plug-ins.

Debugging plug-ins may at first appear as something cumbersome or difficult to do, but in reality, it turns out to be extremely easy. Most debuggers will let us set breakpoints, and step into source code from a loaded DLL just as you would with the executable code itself. We just need to wait for the DLLs to be loaded before we set any breakpoints. That, combined with the fact that we can reload plug-ins without having to shut down the main program, makes debugging them a very pleasant experience.

Drawbacks

Not all is rose-colored in the world of plug-ins, however. Communication going from the plug-in to the main program is always slightly cumbersome, since it has to go through the plug-in manager (or get the correct objects or handles to access the program directly in some other way).

Plug-ins, by their dynamic nature, have difficulty dealing with global data. But since that is not a good practice anyway, removing global variables and offering singletons and objects for accessing that data instead solves most of the problems. Along those lines, it is sometimes a bit tricky to get plug-ins to use the right GUI resources, and we might have to jump through a few hoops to make sure all works as expected.

Also, plug-ins are particularly bad at interacting with each other. Two plug-ins that depend on each other might not both be loaded at once, or they might be loaded in a different order than expected. Usually, the safest approach is to make sure plug-ins do not depend on each other.

Apart from these drawbacks, the only other potential disadvantage of plug-ins comes as a consequence of what they are trying to solve. Because plug-ins are intended to extend a program after it has been compiled, the user must install and remove plug-ins directly or through some sort of install program. There is the potential that the plug-ins might be out of date or have mismatched versions. Fortunately, plug-ins are usually intended for one program only, so at least there is no problem with different programs installing conflicting plug-in versions in the same directory, which could result in DLL havoc, as sometimes happens with shared DLLs.

A good practice is to be very careful with the versioning of plug-ins. Always make sure the user can check the version number of a plug-in, and always check for correct versions of the program or other plug-ins with which your plug-in interacts.

Platforms

This chapter has been entirely devoted to plug-ins running in the Win32 platform. What if we are not developing for Win32? Even if our target platform is not Win32, often our development tools run on Win32, so all the details of this chapter are relevant. Both Linux and Apple operating systems have similar mechanisms to load dynamic libraries, so you just need to change the platform-specific details.

What about game consoles? Some of them have DLL support, but some of them do not. If you are working with one that does not support DLLs, you will have to do a bit more work to achieve the same results. You might be able to use segment loading (a technique that allows you to load and unload specific sections of code) plus some pointer fix-ups to use dynamically loaded code. Here it really pays off to export only the factory function, which needs to be loaded and executed only once and avoids the complication of exporting the full plug-in class. After the actual plug-in objects have been created through the factory, it can be used almost as if it were a normal object.

CONCLUSION

In this chapter, we covered the extremely useful technique of plug-ins. Plug-ins allow us to extend our programs without having to modify the original source code and having to recompile everything again. We can also use them to extend other people's programs, such as off-the-shelf art tools.

We saw how we could architect our program to support the use of plug-ins, how to organize the different plug-ins, how to manage them, and how to load them on a Windows platform. Plug-ins are still possible on other platforms that do not support DLLs if we use other methods to load code dynamically. These techniques are illustrated with the sample code for a working plug-in manager that can be found on the CD-ROM (\Chapter 11. Plugins\pluginsample.dsw).

ON THE CD

Finally, we saw how plug-ins are used in the real world, and what some of their advantages and drawbacks are.

SUGGESTED READING

For such a useful technique, there is surprisingly little published material on plug-ins. Some of the more detailed plug-in architecture descriptions come from the documentation of some of the major software packages that are intended to be extended through plug-ins, such as Discreet's 3D Studio Max, Adobe Photoshop, and others. Scanning through the API documentation for those packages can reveal many interesting details of real-world applications of plug-ins.

What follows is a really good reference for any Windows-system programming topic. It has some excellent chapters on DLLs.

Richter, Jeffrey, *Advanced Windows*, 3rd ed., Microsoft Press, 1997.

RUNTIME TYPE INFORMATION

IN THIS CHAPTER

A s games grow larger and more complex, the number of different classes involved during gameplay significantly increases. We might have thousands of objects of hundreds of different classes interacting with each other. In the middle of this chaos, sometimes we need to find out more information about the identity of the objects we are dealing with, such as the name of their class, or whether they inherit from a certain class or not. To achieve that we need some sort of *Runtime Type Information* (RTTI).

In this chapter, we will learn about the RTTI system that C++ provides, its uses, and its cost. We will then see why sometimes it makes sense to roll our own RTTI system, and we will present a very simple, yet powerful custom RTTI system that can be used directly in your code.

WORKING WITHOUT RTTI

In a game that was designed in an object-oriented way, all our game objects should be interacting with each other and with the player, using encapsulation and polymorphism. Everything happens at a fairly abstract level, and we never have to worry about what type of object, exactly, we are dealing with.

That is an ideal situation. The higher the level at which we can interact with objects, and the higher the level at which they can interact with each other, the fewer dependencies we introduce in the code. Consider the simplified hierarchy structure for a real-time strategy game as shown in Figure 12.1.

Most of the interactions between objects should happen through the GameEntity class. That is, a UnitTank should not know anything directly about a UnitResourceCollector. But we know what happens when a tank runs over one of our little resource collector robots. So how can we implement that without having the tank check if it is about to run over a UnitResourceCollector? Both the tank and the resource collector get a message saying they are colliding against another GameEntity object, without knowing the specific type. Then, each can see the velocity and mass of the other GameEntity object it is colliding against and decide if it takes any damage or not. In the case of our little resource collector robot, this should be enough damage to squash it flat.

The same technique can be applied for other types of interaction. For example, suppose our game has barrels full of highly flammable fluid. When a tank runs into one of them, the barrel detects the collision and causes an explosion that will damage all entities within a certain radius. If the damage caused by the explosion is enough to destroy the tank, it will

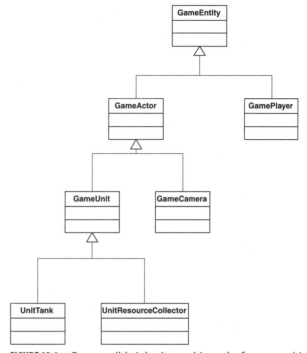

FIGURE 12.1   One possible inheritance hierarchy for game objects.

blow up in turn—all that without the tank ever knowing that what it collided against was an explosive barrel. The barrel also has no idea of what hit it, just that colliding object was enough to make the barrel blow up.

The main benefit of modeling object interactions in this way is that we do not introduce many dependencies in the code between all types of objects. Also, their interactions are generic enough that new interactions are bound to occur automatically as a result of how they were modeled. For example, now we do not need to do anything special about modeling a tank colliding with a car. Our generic way of handling collisions and damage will take care of that. If we need a land mine, it is very easy; a land mine is very similar to the explosive barrel. Whenever we add a new unit type, we can implement some generic ways of interacting with the rest of the world, and it should work just fine with all the other units.

USES AND ABUSES OF RTTI

Consider the alternative: the tank class specifically checks to see if it is interacting with some of the other object types in the game. It needs to know about barrels, about resource-gathering robots, and about every other unit in the game. Whenever it collides against anything, it needs to find out what type of object it is and then react according to that type of object. Any time we add a new type of object, we would need to make all existing types aware of the new one, and we would have to hand-code how they would each react to the new object. This sounds like a lot of unnecessary work. Sometimes it is more convenient, or even necessary, to find out exactly what type of object we are dealing with, perform a downward cast in the inheritance hierarchy, and continue using that object directly.

In our previous real-time strategy game example, imagine that the tank unit has the ability to combine itself with the aircraft unit to make a more powerful unit. To combine them, we need to land the aircraft and bring the two units together. If we just let the generic code handle it, they will probably blow each other up when they detect a collision. Instead, either the tank or the aircraft should have some special code in its collision-handler function that looks to see if it is colliding against another special unit. If it is, it then triggers the metamorphosis into the new unit. In a case like this, finding out exactly what type of object we are colliding against is very useful, but it is nothing more than a shortcut.

In a more real situation, we probably would like several other units as well as the tank to have the ability to combine themselves with other units to create new unit types. In that case, a better design would be to abstract that interaction through the `GameEntity` class. Maybe whenever any two units are brought together, they can send a message to each other, asking whether or not they can combine. If they can, the combination is triggered; but otherwise it is ignored and everything continues as normal. Maybe such a functionality could be better exposed through an abstract interface, as we saw in Chapter 10.

The moral to take from this example is that RTTI should be used carefully and sparingly. If you find yourself wanting to know the type of almost every object you interact with, that is usually the sign of a poor object-oriented design. You should consider this technique as a quick shortcut to be used sparingly, not as a major design technique. Over-reliance on runtime type identification will lead to entangled class dependencies and programs that are hard to maintain, add new features to, and debug.

What are some situations where using RTTI is a good idea? Object and player interaction could benefit from RTTI, sparingly. Maybe it could be used in the rare case in which we want to save the trouble of creating new abstract interfaces or adding some functionality to the base class when it should not really be there. The combination of two units is a good example—as long as it is just those two units that have the added functionality. Checking whether or not a node is a light when we are about to render a scene is an acceptable usage, also. As soon as the interaction between those objects becomes a common situation, the solution would be better handled by moving that functionality to a higher level in the hierarchy and avoiding RTTI altogether.

There is also the possibility that we cannot modify the parent classes of the objects we are interested in. This could be because the specific class is in a library for which we have no source code, or even that it is in our own code base, but we cannot change it due to compatibility issues with other projects. Inheriting from that class to add our functionality might also be out of the question, sinceobjects of that type might be created directly inside the library, and we have no way to force it to use our new class instead. In a situation like this, using RTTI to detect specific classes and add some functionality or interaction with other objects based on their type might be the only possible solution.

Serialization is another situation where RTTI is essential (see Chapter 13, Object Creation and Management). Serialization is the process of saving and restoring an object. It can be done on disk, memory, or even over the network. During the serialization process, an object is asked to write itself to a stream. One of the first pieces of data written to the stream is the type of the object that is about to be saved. This can be the class name of the object or some unique ID that identifies it. This is exactly the type of information we will get from an RTTI system. To restore the object at a later time, or from the other end of the network, we first look at the object type stored in the stream, create one object of that type, and then read all the appropriate information.

STANDARD C++ RTTI

How exactly do we find out what class an object belongs to? Or, in a more general sense, how do we find out whether an object derives from a particular class? The first solution we will cover is the standard C++ RTTI system. Then we will present a custom runtime type information system.

dynamic_cast Operator

The first and most important part of the standard C++ RTTI system is the dynamic_cast operator. Its syntax is like any of the other C++ casting operators (see Chapter 3):

```
newtype * newvar = dynamic_cast<newtype *>(oldvar);
```

The concept behind `dynamic_cast` is very simple: it will cast the pointer or reference to the new type, but only if it is legal to cast the real type of the object to the type we want to cast it to. If `dynamic_cast` succeeds, it returns a valid pointer of the new type. If it fails because the attempted casting was illegal, it returns a `NULL` pointer.

What does it mean that the casting is legal? A dynamic casting is legal if the pointer type we are converting to is the type of the object itself, or if it is one of its parent classes. It does not have to be its direct parent class; any ancestor class will be considered a correct casting.

So `dynamic_cast` really does two things at once for us. It first checks whether the casting we are attempting is legal, which is the primary question. Then it actually converts the pointer to its new type. Most of the time, if we want to know whether a particular object derives from a certain class, we then want to manipulate that object through a pointer to the class that we just checked against, so `dynamic_cast` does all of this in one step and saves us some typing. Here are some examples of how `dynamic_cast` can be used with the inheritance hierarchy shown in Figure 12.1:

```
GameCamera * pCamera = new GameCamera;
// This works fine
GameActor * pActor = dynamic_cast<GameActor *>(pCamera);
// This is also fine
GameEntity * pEntity = dynamic_cast<GameEntity *>(pCamera);

// The next cast will fail because the object is of type
// GameCamera, which does not inherit from GamePlayer.
// The variable pPlayer will be NULL after the cast.
GamePlayer * pPlayer = dynamic_cast<GamePlayer *>(pCamera);
```

In the previous code snippet, all the conversions were done from a lower class type to a higher one. That type of conversion is called an *upcast* because it moves the pointer up the class hierarchy.

A more common type of casting in most applications is a *downcast*, which moves the pointer down the class hierarchy. This is particularly common when using polymorphism and when trying to get more specific information about a particular object.

```
// pEnt is of type GameEntity, but points to a
// GameActor object
GameEntity * pEnt = new GameActor;

// This is fine
GameActor * pActor = dynamic_cast<GameActor *>(pEnt);
```

```
// Not OK. This is a downcast, but the cast is not
// legal because GameUnit is now an ancestor of
// GameActor, which is the type of the object we
// are manipulating.
GameUnit * pUnit = dynamic_cast<GameUnit *>(pEnt);
```

You might have noticed that so far, `dynamic_cast` looks remarkably similar to `static_cast` (see Chapter 3, Constness, References, and a Few Loose Ends). It seems they both catch whether the upcast or downcast is legal, except that `static_cast` reports the problem at compile time instead of returning a `NULL` pointer at runtime.

The main difference is that `static_cast` has no idea about the actual type of the object pointed to by the pointer we are trying to cast, while `dynamic_cast` does. The `static_cast` will let any conversion go, as long as they are within the same inheritance hierarchy: up or down, it does not care; they will all be accepted. The `dynamic_cast` will check the type of the object and only allow valid casts to happen.

In addition to upcasts and downcasts on a single-inheritance hierarchy, `dynamic_cast` will also perform casting on a multiple-inheritance hierarchy, including *crosscasts*. Consider the class inheritance hierarchy shown in Figure 12.2:

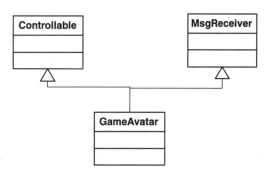

FIGURE 12.2   Class hierarchy using multiple inheritance.

Given a pointer to a `GameAvatar` object, we can correctly cast it up and down any of the branches of the hierarchy:

```
// Going up
GameAvatar * pAvatar = new GameAvatar;
Controllable * pCont = dynamic_cast<Controllable *>(pAvatar);
MsgReceiver * pRec = dynamic_cast<MsgReceiver *>(pAvatar);

// Going down
```

```
Controllable * pCont = new GameAvatar;
GameAvatar * pAvatar = dynamic_cast<GameAvatar *>(pCont);
```

You might remember from the chapter on multiple inheritance that casting up and down the hierarchy with multiple inheritance requires some runtime fix-ups. To make sure we are always accessing the correct class type, dynamic_cast takes care of adding or subtracting the correct offset from our pointer. We can also do crosscasts, going horizontally on the inheritance hierarchy:

```
// Crosscast
Controllable * pCont = new GameAvatar;
MsgReceiver * pRec = dynamic_cast<MsgReceiver *>(pCont);
```

typeid Operator

The dynamic_cast mechanism gave us information about the inheritance relations of a particular object, as well as allowed us to cast between the different types. C++ also offers another mechanism for finding out more information directly about one object.

The typeid operator returns information about the type of the object it is applied to. Going back to the class hierarchy of our previous example, we can use typeid in the following way:

```
Controllable * pCont = new GameAvatar;
const type_info & info = typeid(*pCont);
```

All the information about the object we asked about is contained in the type_info object returned by typeid. It turns out there is not a huge amount of information contained in type_info, and by far the most important piece of information is the class name (in its user-readable format as well as its C++-mangled version).

```
std::cout << "Class name: " << info.name();
// The output of running the above statement is
Class name: GameAvatar
```

One of the other uses of type_info is for comparing class types. If we wanted to make sure that two objects were of the exact same class, we could write:

```
const type_info & info1 = typeid(*pObj1);
const type_info & info2 = typeid(*pObj2);
```

```
if (info1 == info2)
    // They are the same type. Do something...
```

Notice that we are comparing the `type_info` structures themselves, not just their pointers. It turns out that it is possible for objects of the same class to return identical `type_info` structures in different memory locations, so we must compare their contents, not their addresses.

The `typeid` operator also works with type names, not just with objects. This allows us to check whether an object is of a particular class by comparing the `type_info` structure returned from the object and the `type_info` from the class we want to check against.

```
if (typeid(*pEntity) == typeid(GameAvatar))
    // The object *pEntity is of the class GameAvatar
```

Something to keep in mind when using `typeid` is that it can only be meaningfully applied to polymorphic types—that is, classes with at least one virtual function. If we use it on a nonpolymorphic class type, it will return the information for the type of the reference, not the type of the object. This should never be a problem, though, since we should never have nonpolymorphic objects for which we do not know their real type.

C++ RTTI Analysis

The standard C++ RTTI system is certainly adequate for most tasks. It answers the question of whether an object inherits from a particular class, it supports casting between different parents in a multiple-inheritance hierarchy, and it even returns the name of a class. We get all that automatically, without any extra work on our part. So why would we ever need anything else?

One of the main drawbacks of the standard RTTI system is that it is always on, or always off if your compiler has a switch to turn it off completely (most compilers do). This means that every class with a virtual function (i.e., polymorphic classes) will have runtime type information associated with it, whether we want it or not. On the positive side, notice that only classes that already have a virtual function (and therefore a vtable) will become part of this system. So all our simple, lightweight classes, like points, vectors, and colors, will remain unchanged.

What are the costs of all the polymorphic classes having runtime type information associated with them? It is not that bad. Remember, the information is per class, not per object, so it is not going to increase the object size any. As usual, the specific details are up to the implementation of each compiler; but usually a pointer to class information is stored in the vtable, and the class information itself should be big enough to contain the class name, a few pointers and counters, and that is about it. So the cost is usually on the order of 30–50 bytes. Even if you have 1,000 classes (classes, not objects), which is on the high end, that will only amount to about 50 KB. This is a cheap price to pay for what we get in return with typical computers and game consoles, but it might be significant in the case of handheld devices with extremely limited memories.

What about the restriction of only being able to do `dynamic_cast` and `typeid` on polymorphic types? Even though it might appear restrictive at first glance, it really is not an issue. The only objects we need to get information from at runtime are ones of a polymorphic type; otherwise the type would be known at compile time, so there is no need for runtime type information for them.

The biggest drawback of the default C++ RTTI system is its performance: if nothing else, for its lack of consistency across platforms and compilers. On some implementations, `dynamic_cast` will do all sorts of checks to verify that the cast is valid, but under other implementations it will be reasonably fast. Performance also depends on whether the object in question is using multiple inheritance or not.

For a well-designed program that has minimal reliance on RTTI, the potential performance hit is probably not an issue. If it is used very sparingly during the game execution, or its use is restricted to serialization operations, then the C++ RTTI system is perfectly appropriate.

Unfortunately, we are not in an ideal world. There are games out there that, either for legacy reasons or simply because they were designed that way against common wisdom, make extensive use of RTTI operations during runtime. If every game entity performs several RTTI operations per frame, and we have on the order of 1,000 game entities, this would result in tens of thousands of RTTI operations per frame. Efficiency is now critical, and using a custom RTTI system will be a necessity.

Finally, another reason to use a custom RTTI system is simply to have more control over it. As it will turn out, a custom RTTI system is not particularly complicated. It is rather easy to write, actually, and it involves very little code. So for very little effort, we can have a guaranteed operation across platforms and compilers (and compiler versions; do not underestimate the changes in implementation from version to version of the same compiler), and we know what to expect from it in terms of performance.

CUSTOM RTTI SYSTEM

By this point, we have decided we want to have a custom runtime information system. We really must ask ourselves: what, exactly, do we need from it? There is very little point in writing our RTTI system if we are just going to duplicate the standard C++ one. Let's start with a very simple approach and build our way up from there as our needs increase.

The Simplest Solution

The simplest possible RTTI query is to find out the exact type of a class. If that is all we need, it is really easy to do. If you are expecting some high-tech approach that uses all of the latest C++ language features to autodiscover the object type, then you are going to be disappointed.

Using Strings

The simplest approach is to write a function by hand that returns the name of the class:

```
class GameEntity
{
public:
    virtual const char * GetClassName() const
                            { return "GameEntity"; }
    // ... Rest of the class goes here
};
```

This is very simple. We just wrote a function in a class that we are interested in that returns the class name. That is it. Actually, there is a little trick and an unspoken assumption in the code above. The trick is that the function is virtual. The function needs to be virtual because we asking what is the name of the class of object, not what is the name of the class of the pointer. And that is exactly what virtual functions allow us to do—call the functions of the class of the object, not the class of the pointer.

```
GameEntity * pEntity = new GameEntity;
pEntity->GetClassName(); // OK, returns "GameEntity"

GameActor * pActor = new GameActor;
pActor->GetClassName();  // OK, returns "GameActor"
```

```
GameEntity * pObj = new GameActor;
pObj->GetClassName();    // Will only return "GameActor" if
                         // GetClassName is virtual!
```

The unspoken assumption is that the function that returns the class name has to be named the same for all classes. If it were not, then we would not know what function to call, since we do not know the type of the object, which is what we were trying to find out in the first place.

To make sure the function name is the same everywhere, and to save a bit of typing, we can create a macro to add that function automatically to any class:

```
#define RTTI(name) \
    public: \
        virtual const char * GetClassName() const\
            { return #name; }
```

Using the macro is extremely simple:

```
class GameEntity {
public:
    RTTI(GameEntity);
    // ... Rest of the class
};
```

This approach is extremely simple and flexible. It will work with any class, whether it is using single or multiple inheritance. Of course, it still does not answer the question of whether an object inherits from a certain class; but we are leaving that for later.

The main drawback of this approach is its use of character strings. In order to do anything useful with the results we get from the function GetClassName(), we are forced to use strings. Strings are great for printing and reading in the debugger, but they are not particularly fast to compare, which is what we are likely to do in this situation. If on top of that we throw in a case-insensitive comparison, then things are even slower. A program that relies heavily on finding the class type of objects will quickly notice the hit of all the string operations.

Using Constants

One alternative that trades flexibility for performance is to return a constant or an enum instead of a string for identification. This is particularly handy when we have a small number of subclasses, and we are not planning on letting other parts of the program extend it. We do not have to worry about creating new constants in the future or letting the users create new types, so there will not be a problem with the clashing of constants.

```
class GameUnit
{
public:
    enum UnitType
    {
        UNIT_PAWN,
        UNIT_RESOURCEGATHERER,
        UNIT_TANK,
        UNIT_PLANE
    };

    virtual UnitType GetUnitType() const = 0;
};

class GameUnitPawn : public GameUnit
{
public:
    virtual UnitType GetUnitType() const
                        {return GameUnit::UNIT_PAWN;}
};

class GameUnitTank : public GameUnit
{
public:
    virtual UnitType GetUnitType() const
                        {return GameUnit::UNIT_TANK;}
};
```

We have replaced returning the class name as a string with a much more specific constant that only applies to the game unit types. The advantage of this approach is that checking whether a unit is a tank is a very fast computation, requiring the comparison of two integers.

One major draw of this approach is in how clear the code is. We are not doing dynamic_cast, typeid, or even inquiring about the class name. We are merely checking what type of game unit this object is, which is exactly what we need to know in our code. Do not underestimate the power of a simple solution with extremely obvious code.

Using Memory Addresses

We can combine the best of the first two approaches and come up with a new implementation that is both completely general and very fast at checking the type of an object. To achieve this, we will use the memory address of a static class variable to uniquely identify a class. The variable itself will contain the name of the class. This allows us to have some of the best characteristics of the previous two implementations (although the second approach still wins in the category for self-explanatory source code).

```cpp
class RTTI
{
public:
    RTTI(const string & name) : m_className(name) {};
    const string & GetClassName() const { return m_className; }
private:
    string m_className;
};

class GameEntity
{
public:
    static const RTTI s_rtti;
    virtual const RTTI & RTTI() const { return s_rtti; }
    // ... Rest of the class goes here
};
```

We can use it in a very similar way to how we did it before, but now going through the RTTI object. If it looks like too much trouble just to keep a string, just wait a bit, because the next section will expand on this and make the RTTI class a bit more useful.

```cpp
GameEntity * pObj = new GameActor;
pObj->RTTI.GetClassName(); // Will return "GameActor"
```

We can check whether two RTTI objects are the same by comparing their addresses, since we are guaranteed to only have one per class because it is a class-static variable.

```cpp
// Comparing pointers directly
if (&pObj1->GetRTTI() == &pObj2->GetRTTI())
    // They are of the same class...
```

```
if (&pObj1->GetRTTI() == &GameActor::s_RTTI)
    // pObj1 is of type GameActor
```

This works. It is very fast because it is just a pointer comparison. But having to take the address of the RTTI object and compare it directly is quite awkward. Wouldn't it be better if it could all be encapsulated and if we could just ask if two RTTI objects are the same?

```
class RTTI
{
public:
    RTTI(const string & name) : s_ClassName(name) {};
    const string & GetClassName() const;
    bool IsExactly (const RTTI & rtti) const
                    { return (this==&rtti); }
private:
    string s_ClassName;
};
```

Now that we have hidden the pointer comparison under wraps, we can rewrite the previous code in a much simpler way.

```
// Comparing RTTI objects
if (pObj1->GetRTTI().IsExactly(pObj2->GetRTTI()))
    // They are of the same class...

if (pObj1->GetRTTI().IsExactly(GameActor::rtti))
    // pObj1 is of type GameActor
```

If you are really enamored of the idea, you could even provide an operator== for the RTTI class and use that instead of the IsExactly() function. It is just a matter of personal preference. The one good thing about using operator== is that it makes the code look more like the C++ RTTI system, so it might be a more familiar approach for programmers already familiar with it.

We can update our macro to make adding runtime type information to our classes a snap. Unfortunately, we run into a minor snag with this new RTTI class: we need to provide both a declaration of the class static and a definition in the .cpp file. This means that if we want to use the convenience of macros, we need to create two macros: one for the header file and one for the .cpp file:

```
#define RTTI_DECL \
    public: \
        static const RTTI s_rtti; \
        virtual const RTTI & RTTI() const { return s_rtti; }

#define RTTI_IMPL(name) \
    const RTTI name::s_rtti(#name);
```

Adding Single Inheritance

So far our simple RTTI system has no concept of inheritance. We can ask whether an object is of a particular class, but we do not know anything about its parents.

If we are going to use RTTI as a part of our code, it is much more robust to think in terms of inheritance than in terms of specific classes. For example, imagine we write a function that, in every frame, goes through all the game entities in the world and puts aside those that are cameras, so we can use them for rendering later on.

```
// Shaky code checking for exact class
GameEntityList::iterator it = entities.begin();
while (it != entities.end()) {
    GameEntity * pEnt = *it;
    if (pEnt->GetRTTI().IsExactly(GameCamera::rtti))
        cameras.push_back(pEnt);
}
```

What happens if at a later time we introduce several types of cameras that inherit from GameCamera? Our code would ignore them. What we are really after are all the objects that are, or inherit from GameCamera, since anything that inherits from GameCamera "is a" GameCamera (see Chapter 1, Inheritance). So, we would really like to write something like this instead:

```
// More robust approach using derivation
GameEntityList::iterator it = entities.begin();
while (it != entities.end()) {
    GameEntity * pEnt = *it;
    if (pEnt->GetRTTI().DerivesFrom(GameCamera::rtti))
        cameras.push_back(pEnt);
}
```

We can extend our RTTI class to give it some knowledge of its parent. We can accomplish this by adding a pointer to the parent's RTTI static ob-

ject, which gets initialized in the constructor, at the same time that we
pass the class name. Our improved RTTI class looks like this:

```
class RTTI
{
public:
    RTTI(const string & className) :
        m_className(className), m_pBaseRTTI(NULL) {}
    RTTI(const string & className, const RTTI & baseRTTI) :
        m_className(className), m_pBaseRTTI(&baseRTTI) {}

    const string & GetClassName() const
                                { return m_className; }
    bool IsExactly(const RTTI & rtti) const
                                { return (this == &rtti); }
    bool DerivesFrom (const RTTI & rtti) const;

private:
    const string m_className;
    const RTTI * m_pBaseRTTI;
};
```

With the new changes, we can easily answer the question of who its
parent is. But what about previous ancestors? We can find that from the
parent's parent, and from its parent, and so on until we reach a class that
does not have a parent. If we have not found the class we were checking
along the way, then we know that the object does not derive from that
class. This is how the implementation of DerivesFrom() looks:

```
bool RTTI::DerivesFrom (const RTTI & rtti) const
{
    const RTTI * pCompare = this;
    while (pCompare != NULL)
    {
        if (pCompare == &rtti)
            return true;
        pCompare = pCompare->m_pBaseRTTI;
    }
    return false;
}
```

We can wrap the latest changes in a macro again to make things simple. The only difference is that now we need two different macros: one
for classes with no parent and one for classes with a parent. Actually, we

could have made it with just one macro and passed NULL if there is no parent, but what follows is a bit cleaner:

```
#define RTTI_DECL \
    public: \
        virtual const RTTI & GetRTTI() { return rtti; } \
        static const RTTI rtti;

#define RTTI_IMPL_NOPARENT(name) \
    const RTTI name::rtti(#name);

#define RTTI_IMPL(name,parent) \
    const RTTI name::rtti(#name, parent::rtti);
```

The most interesting part is the RTTI_IMPL macro. At first glance, it looks a bit odd. We are passing the parent's RTTI static object as a parameter. But all this is happening at static-initialization time, before the game's main function has been called, so how do we know that the parent's RTTI object has been initialized? After all, there are no guarantees about the relative order of static initialization across different files. The answer is, we just do not know; but we do not care, either. All we are doing is storing that memory address for later; we are not trying to read any data from the parent's RTTI object or trying to call any of its functions. The memory address has been fixed since we compiled the program, so this turns out to be totally safe, even if a bit unorthodox.

At this point, every class that has RTTI information also knows about its parent and (potentially) all of its previous ancestors. Even though our RTTI system is still very simple and small, it has become full-featured. The only thing missing from the picture is multiple inheritance, and sometimes that will simply not be necessary if we are either sticking with single inheritance or just using abstract interfaces, which have their own QueryInterface functions. If that is the case, then this is good enough to put straight into your game.

If you need multiple-inheritance support, and you are willing to pay for a bit of extra memory and performance cost, then you should also read the next section of this chapter. The source code for the RTTI system supporting single inheritance is included on the CD-ROM in the folder \Chapter 12. RTTI\ (the Visual Studio workspace is rtti.dsw).

ON THE CD

One thing you should be aware of is the performance of the Derives-From() function. All the other RTTI queries were extremely fast, usually involving returning a single pointer or doing a simple comparison. The DerivesFrom() function is different because it needs to loop until it either finds the class we are looking for or until it reaches the root of that particular inheritance tree. Granted, it should be pretty fast: it is not calling any other functions, and it is just comparing pointers along the way. But it is looping, nevertheless.

Its worst case is when checking an object against a class that is not one of its ancestors. In that case, the RTTI query needs to loop through as many levels as there are in that section of the hierarchy. If somebody were to design a class hierarchy tens or hundreds of levels deep, then the hit would be significant. Of course, at that point they would have much bigger problems to worry about than the performance of this simple loop. Still, it is worth keeping in mind; this function should not be overused.

Adding Multiple Inheritance

To add multiple inheritance support, we just extend the single-inheritance implementation to allow for multiple parent classes. Then, the only change we need to make is to change the DerivesFrom() class to iterate through all the parent classes, not just the first one, as in the case of single inheritance.

Let's take things one step at a time. We will revisit the AI multiple-inheritance class hierarchy from Chapter 2. This particular hierarchy lends itself well to this RTTI approach, as opposed to the hierarchy from Figure 12.2, which is best implemented using abstract interfaces and a QueryInterface() method. The AI hierarchy is shown in Figure 12.3.

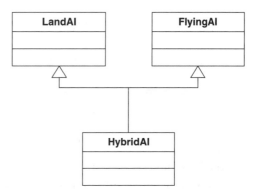

FIGURE 12.3 AI class hierarchy using multiple inheritance.

Adding support for multiple parent classes requires several changes. Before, we kept one pointer to the parent's class RTTI object. Now we need to keep one pointer per parent. Using an STL vector of points sounds like a good idea, but this is such a low-level construct that we want to avoid using any more memory than we absolutely have to, and we also want to keep tabs on all the memory we are allocating. In addition, the number of parent classes is not going to change at runtime, so a vector is definitely overkill here.

Instead, we will keep a dynamically allocated array of pointers. We will allocate the array in the constructor, which is when we know how many parent classes there are. In the case of no parent classes or just one parent class, this is how the constructors look:

```
RTTI::RTTI(const string & className) :
    m_className(className),
    m_numParents(0),
    m_pBaseRTTI(NULL)
{}

RTTI::RTTI(const string & className, const RTTI & baseRTTI) :
    m_className(className),
    m_numParents(1)
{
    m_pBaseRTTI = new const RTTI*[1];
    m_pBaseRTTI[0] = &baseRTTI;
}
```

There is nothing special here; it is just a bit more bookkeeping than we had before.

We also need another constructor that lets us specify as many parent classes as we want. We could create a constructor that takes two parent classes and another one that takes three. Chances are this will cover most cases with multiple inheritance, but it might not be sufficient in case someone takes multiple inheritance to an extreme. Instead, we can use a constructor with a variable number of arguments and avoid imposing any limits on how our class is used.

This constructor needs to allocate enough memory, parse the variable list of arguments, and copy the right pointers to the array.

```
RTTI::RTTI(const string & className, int numParents, ...) :
    m_className(className)
{
    if (numParents < 1)
    {
```

```
            m_numParents = 0;
            m_pBaseRTTI = NULL;
        }
        else
        {
            m_numParents = numParents;
            m_pBaseRTTI = new const RTTI*[m_numParents];

            va_list v;
            va_start(v,numParents);
            for (int i=0; i < m_numParents; ++i)
            {
                m_pBaseRTTI[i] = va_arg(v, const RTTI*);
            }
            va_end(v);
        }
    }
```

One unfortunate consequence of having a variable number of parameters in the new constructor is that we cannot wrap it neatly in a macro like we did with the other two constructors. C (and C++ for that matter) does not have widespread support for macros with a variable number of parameters, and the little support there is does not allow the parsing of each individual parameter. We could provide a few macros for the cases of two and three parent classes if we really wanted to. For now, you would have to set it up explicitly. It is not that much more typing, but the code is not as clear as the macros at first glance.

Also notice that in this case we need to pass pointers to the RTTI objects of the parent classes, not references like we did before. That is also due to how functions with variable number of parameters are handled in C, which does not allow those parameters to be references.

```
// In the HybridAI.cpp file
const RTTI HybridAI::rtti("HybridAI", 2, &LandAI::rtti,
                                         &FlyingAI::rtti);
```

Classes with a single parent or with no parent at all can use the same macros as before. In this case, both of our AI classes have no parent, so they can use the RTTI_ROOT_IMPL macro:

```
RTTI_ROOT_IMPL(LandAI);
RTTI_ROOT_IMPL(FlyingAI);
```

The only thing left is to implement the new version of the function `DerivesFrom()`, which checks through all its parents.

```
bool RTTI::DerivesFrom (const RTTI & rtti) const
{
    const RTTI * pCompare = this;
    if (pCompare == &rtti)
        return true;

    for (int i=0; i < m_numParents; ++i)
        if (m_pBaseRTTI[i]->DerivesFrom(rtti))
            return true;

    return false;
}
```

The version presented here uses recursion to iterate through all the parent classes, which has the disadvantage of multiple functions calls and the need to unwind the stack whenever we finally find a match. It is possible to write a more efficient version that replaces recursion with a stack and avoids doing any extra function calls.

Even the improved version using a stack will be slower than the equivalent function in the single-inheritance case. This is because of the extra checking and indirections that need to be done to traverse through the parent classes. It is for this reason that this version of the RTTI system is included separately on the CD-ROM in addition to the single-inheritance version (it is available in \Chapter 12. RTTIMulti\rtti.dsw).

ON THE CD

If we know we are going to be limiting our design to single inheritance, then we should choose the single-inheritance version. We can always switch to the custom version if we decide to use some multiple inheritance. The change will be totally transparent, and there will be no need to modify any existing code.

CONCLUSION

In this chapter, we saw that when we are manipulating objects polymorphically, sometimes it is necessary to find more information about them. That information is called runtime type information because it is gathered while the program is running, not at compile time. More importantly, we also saw how there are often better design alternatives that do not require any specific information about objects, and we can continue treating them polymorphically. We then saw what provisions the C++ language has for runtime type information, and we learned their uses and limitations.

Finally, we developed a custom RTTI system from scratch that can be dropped into any existing game with minimal effort. We saw several versions of this system, in increasing order of complexity, including one that supports multiple inheritance at the cost of a bit more memory and performance.

SUGGESTED READING

This is a good reference for the standard C++ RTTI system. It covers all of the details and even some advanced uses.

Stroustrup, Bjarne, *The C++ Programming Language*, 3rd ed., Addison-Wesley, 1997.

There is not much information on custom RTTI systems. These are some of the few references that cover it in any detail.

Eberly, David H., *3D Game Engine Design*, Morgan Kaufmann, 2001.
Wakeling, Scott, "Dynamic Type Information," *Game Programming Gems 2*, Charles River Media, 2001.

OBJECT CREATION AND MANAGEMENT

IN THIS CHAPTER

- Object Creation
- Object Factories
- Shared Objects

Most of the time when we envision a program running, we visualize the function calls between objects, the transfer of data, and the modification of memory. That aspect is called the *steady state* of the program. However, that is only part of it. Another, equally important part of program execution deals with the creation of objects, and this is called the *dynamic state* of the program. After all, a C++ program starts out with only the statically declared objects, and everything else has to be constructed from scratch.

This chapter will examine effective ways of creating different types of objects through the use of factories. These factories will allow us to be much more flexible with how we create objects than a plain new call would. They will also offer us the opportunity to extend our program more easily in the future.

Then, we will examine the thorny problem of what to do once we have created the objects. Typically, more than one part of the code has a pointer or a reference to an object. How do we go about deleting those objects without breaking the program? The last part of the chapter will offer different methods for doing this, including handles, reference counting, and smart pointers.

OBJECT CREATION

Every game needs to create objects at one point or another. Whenever we load a new level, we need to create all the objects in that level. If we exit back to the main menu, we destroy those objects and create the objects that represent the user interface.

Object creation is not limited to loading new levels, though. It can also occur during gameplay: a shot is fired and a projectile object is created; the projectile hits the wall and an effect is created that displays some sparks and creates a sound effect; a person walks through a pool of water and splash effects are created; your units finish creating a new type of building, so that object has to be created. There are also more subtle forms of object creation: you push the gamepad button, and a message is created that gets passed to the input-processing system; another player takes control of the ball, and a network packet is created and sent to you through the network. In other words, object creation is everywhere.

When "new" Is Not Enough

What is wrong with using new whenever we want to create an object? This is how we have most often done it. Usually there is nothing wrong with this method, but the type of object we created is determined at compile time. If we write the code as follows, the program will always create an object of type GameCamera. There is no way around it.

```
// This will always be a game camera
GameEntity * pEntity = new GameCamera;
```

In C++, we can manipulate objects in a polymorphic way, which (as you should remember from Chapter 1) means we can work on an object without knowing its specific type and refer to it through a pointer, or a reference of the type of one of its parent classes. The key to polymorphism is virtual functions.

Unfortunately, C++ does not allow a similar type of polymorphic access for the creation of objects. On the other hand, because C++ is so flexible, we can come up with acceptable solutions, but we have to write them ourselves.

What are some circumstances where using new is not good enough? The best example is during the loading of a level. We have a file that contains all the information we need to restore the state of a game that was previously saved. That file contains information about what types of objects there are in the game as well as all the data each object needs. (We will see this in much more detail in Chapter 14, Object Serialization.) Consider the following pseudocode to see the need for dynamic creation of objects:

```
// Pseudocode for object loading
for (each object in the file) {
    ObjectType type = LoadObjectType();
    GameEntity * pEntity = CreateEntity(type);
    pEntity->Load();
}
```

The LoadObjectType function returns what type of object we need to create, and the next function creates the correct type of object. That is exactly what we are after.

Big Switch

How can we vary the behavior of the code at runtime without using virtual functions? This is achieved in the ways we are used to: if statements, switch statements, or even function pointers. Here is how the loading code looks with a switch statement:

```
// Pseudocode for object loading
for (each object in the file) {
    ObjectType type = LoadObjectType();
    GameEntity * pEntity;
    switch (type) {
        case GAMEENTITY: pEntity = new GameEntity; break;
        case GAMECAMERA: pEntity = new GameCamera; break;
        case GAMEPLAYER: pEntity = new GamePlayer; break;
        case GAMEACTOR: pEntity = new GameActor; break;
        case GAMEENEMY: pEntity = new GameEnemy; break;
        // Add *all* the other possible types of game
        // entities here
        default: // Error entity type unknown
    }
    pEntity->Load();
}
```

If you feel a bit uncomfortable writing code like this, then you have the instincts of a good object-oriented programmer. It has all the usual problems of writing code that explicitly depends on object types. The more immediate problem is that it needs to be updated every time a new object type is introduced, or an existing object type is removed or changed.

Another problem is that it requires the program to know about all the specific types of objects. This is a theme that keeps coming up repeatedly in this book; the least amount of information about the rest of the program a particular section has, the better. It will be easier to test, maintain, and improve in the future. (We will see this in more detail in Chapter 15, Dealing with Large Projects, when we cover the physical structure of a program.)

A consequence of having all the information about object creation concentrated in this one function is that it will be very difficult to extend in the future. As we saw in Chapters 10 and 11, it is often desirable to be able to create new object types after the game ships, or at least without having to recompile and redistribute the original program.

For example, imagine we add a new level to our game that uses a new type of entity object, a dynamic weather entity that will add an extra level of realism and strategy to our game. With this approach, the only way we can create a new type of entity is by modifying the big `switch` statement and checking for the new type. If we cannot update the executable, we are out of luck. If we decentralize the responsibility of object creation, we will have a much easier time extending our program, and we will fix the other drawbacks of this approach at the same time.

OBJECT FACTORIES

An *object factory* is simply code that creates objects based on a parameter that indicates their type. That code can be something as simple as a function that takes an enum, or it can be a full-blown class that takes multiple parameters to describe exactly what type of object is created. Encapsulating all the object creation into a factory has several benefits:

- If any other parts of the code need to create the same type of objects, they can all use the same object factory.
- Only the factory needs to know about all the object types and include all the necessary headers. The rest of the program does not need to know anything else about them.
- Usually, we want to do more than just create objects. We often want to keep track of all objects of a particular type, or at least the number of them that are currently allocated. By having a single point of creation, we can keep track of these things more easily.

The way object factories are used, they often end up being needed at many different places. They also usually need to keep some bookkeeping data around, so they are a perfect match for the singleton pattern. There is only one object factory for each major object type, it keeps all its associated data with it, and it is easily accessible anywhere in the code.

A Simple Factory

In a way, the function with the big `switch` statement we saw in the last section was almost a very rudimentary type of object factory. We need to refactor it so the creation happens in a separate function from the loading, and then it really becomes an object factory function:

```
GameEntity * CreateEntity(ObjectType type)
{
    GameEntity * pEntity;
    switch (type) {
        case GAMEENTITY: pEntity = new GameEntity; break;
        case GAMECAMERA: pEntity = new GameCamera; break;
        case GAMEPLAYER: pEntity = new GamePlayer; break;
        case GAMEACTOR: pEntity = new GameActor; break;
        case GAMEENEMY: pEntity = new GameEnemy; break;
        // Add *all* the other possible types of game
        // entities here
        default: pEntity = NULL;
    }

    return pEntity;
}
```

This is very similar to the object factory we saw in Chapter 10 that allowed us to create different implementations of an abstract interface.

A Distributed Factory

Other than creating a more focused function, splitting that code into a function by itself and calling it a factory has not helped our situation any. We still have the same ugly code to maintain and too much centralized knowledge about all the objects types we can create. To really improve things, we need to create a distributed factory.

The idea behind a distributed factory is to avoid hardwiring the possible types of objects in the source code. By dynamically maintaining a list of possible object types, we can easily add more object types later on or change existing ones without any difficulty.

Up until now, we have been associating some sort of type ID with each class type. Whenever we passed that ID to the factory function, a new object of the correct type was created. That association was explicit in the code by using the switch statement.

Now we are going make that association dynamic. We would like to create a map, or some other type of data structure, that associates type IDs with the actual classes that will be instantiated. To accomplish this, we will create a set of very small creator objects whose only purpose is to create objects of a particular type. We need one of those objects per class type that we need to create. This is what a typical creator object looks like:

```
class CreatorCamera : public Creator
{
public:
    virtual ~CreatorCamera() {}
    virtual GameEntity * Create() const
                {return new GameCamera;}
};
```

Why go through this extra indirection? Because now we are dealing with terms we can work with more easily in C++. We are not associating type IDs with class types, which there is no way to do. Instead, we are associating type IDs with specific creator objects. Then, whenever we need to make a new object, we call the Create function on the creator object. Our factory class can implement the map and the object creation like this:

```
class EntityFactory
{
public:
    GameEntity * CreateEntity(ObjectType type);
private:
    typedef map<ObjectType, Creator*> CreatorMap;
    CreatorMap m_creatorMap;
};

GameEntity * EntityFactory::CreateEntity(ObjectType type)
{
    CreatorMap::iterator it = m_creatorMap.find(type);
    if (it == m_creatorMap.end())
        return NULL;

    Creator * pCreator = (*it).second;
    return pCreator->Create();
}
```

Notice that we are taking advantage of the STL map class. In just a few lines, we can create and use a complicated and well-optimized data structure. Refer to Chapter 8 if you want to refresh your memory on STL containers.

The entity factory class is in place. Now we can create objects dynamically without knowing anything about their specific class type.

```
ObjectType type = LoadTypeFromDisk();
GameEntity * pEntity = factory.CreateEntity(type);
```

Explicit Creator Registration

Of course, in order for everything to work, we need to tell the factory about what types of objects we support and pass one creator object for each of those types. That is exactly what the Register function in the factory will do. It lets us pass one object ID and one creator object, and the factory will keep track of this association and use it whenever an object of that type needs to be created.

```
bool EntityFactory::Register(ObjectType type,
                             Creator * pCreator)
{
    CreatorMap::iterator it = m_creatorMap.find(type);
    if (it != m_creatorMap.end()) {
        delete pCreator;
        return false;
    }
    m_creatorMap[type] = pCreator;
    return true;
}
```

Registering a new type of object is now simple. It just requires creating a new Creator class and calling the Register function.

When should we call the Register function? It depends on each project, but usually upon initialization of the system that needs to create those objects. In the case of game entities, a good moment would be as soon as the game is initialized, before we try to create or load any entities. The initialization function of the game could look something like this:

```
factory.Register(GAMEENTITY, new CreatorEntity);
factory.Register(GAMECAMERA, new CreatorCamera);
factory.Register(GAMEPLAYER, new CreatorPlayer);
factory.Register(GAMEACTOR, new CreatorActor);
// ... Register the rest of the entity classes
```

We have decentralized the information of the object types that can be created. A plug-in could add new object types just by calling the Register function whenever it is initialized. Whenever an object of that new type was loaded or created by any other part of the code, the correct factory function would be called.

Implicit Creator Registration

We can take this system a step further and make it even easier to use. If we do things just right, we can avoid even having to call the Register function explicitly. That would make the whole system even more transparent, and adding new types would just be a matter of creating new Maker objects.

We could write it so the constructor in the Maker object registers itself with the factory. Then, all we need to worry about is making sure that at least one creator object is instantiated so its constructor gets called. We can do that easily by declaring an object statically and letting the C++ initialization code deal with calling its constructor for us. The creator object would look like this now:

```
class CreatorCamera : public Creator
{
public:
    CreatorCamera() { GameFactory::Register(
                         GAMECAMERA, this); }
    virtual ~CreatorCamera() {}
virtual GameEntity * Create() const
                 {return new GameCamera;}
} instance;
```

Notice the new constructor that registers itself, and in particular, the variable instance created right after the class declaration. With this in place, we do not even need to call Register anymore. As it turns out, the extra convenience gained by not having to call Register might cause more problems than it is worth.

The first thing to keep in mind is that the creator class will be created at static initialization time. Unfortunately, C++ makes no guarantees about the order in which static variables are initialized if they reside in different files, so we have to make sure that all the initialization code does not depend on other objects being already initialized. If we need other objects, then we should probably use explicit initialization instead, which happens whenever we want.

The second problem is that we do not have very much control over what creators get registered. As long as they are processed by the compiler, they will be registered, whether we want them or not. This might be fine for game entities, but it might not be acceptable if we are registering creators for graphics resources. We probably want different creator types for different platforms, or even for different graphics APIs in the same platform. If so, we want to be able to choose whether we are registering the OpenGL creators or the Direct3D ones at runtime, based on the user's hardware or some configuration file.

Even if none of the previous drawbacks are a problem for you, there is one more annoyance about implicit registration of creator objects. Some compilers will perform some very aggressive dead-code elimination steps at link time. They consider dead code any code that is not actively called from anywhere else, with the goal of keeping the executable as small as possible. As commendable as this is, it has some unfortunate consequences when the compilers are too overzealous about dead-code elimination. For instance, look at the `CreatorCamera` class. Nowhere in the rest of the program is that class used directly, and neither is the static variable instance that we created. So, much to our annoyance, some compilers will eliminate the instance variable altogether, which will prevent the creator class from being registered at all.

You will quickly find out if your compiler falls in this category. Sometimes this problem only appears if the creator class is in a static library, which is often the case in large projects. You might be able to find ways around it and force your compiler to include the code, but this process is generally unpleasant and will change from platform to platform. It might be enough to force the compiler to use some other variable in the same file, and some compilers provide a compiler-specific `#pragma` directive to force all the symbols in the file to be linked. We might be able to turn off the dead-code removal optimization, but that might cause the executable size to grow too large in size. So in the end, unless you are sure that none of these drawbacks are going to affect you, it might be best to simply be explicit and call `Register` by hand.

Object Type Identifiers

Thus far we have totally glossed over the specifics of how we specify the object type. We have been using variables of the type `ObjectType`, but what are they exactly? As usual, it depends on your specific needs.

The easiest way to specify object types is to use a string that contains the class name. Strings are very easy to debug, since it is possible to read their contents from the debugger, and it is easy to come up with unique strings for each class. You could even use the string for the class name returned by the RTTI system (either the standard C++ one or your own custom one). On the other hand, strings take more memory to store (although you only need one per class type in the factory, so the cost is not exorbitant), but more important, their comparison operation is slower than that of an integer or an enum.

If objects are mostly going to be created at level-load time, then this should not be a problem. Any performance losses are going to be totally overshadowed by IO access to the hard drive or the CD-ROM. On the other hand, if we intend to use the factory to create many objects at runtime, then that extra performance loss might start to add up and become noticeable.

The alternative is to use some sort of integer or enum. Using an enum seems like an attractive idea: it is small, fast to compare, yet it is just as easy to read from the debugger as a string. This is true, but it is not possible to extend enums once they have been defined. Remember, we want to add new object types through plug-ins, so using an enum to describe all the object types returns us to the original problem of hardwiring all the possible types in one place.

So we are left with the option of using integers or some other lightweight object to uniquely describe object types. To make them unique, we cannot just increment the identifier for every object type, because we do not know how many other object types are out there, especially not from the perspective of a plug-in. The best solution is to attempt to generate a pseudo-unique ID based on the class, such as using the CRC of the class name or the memory address of a class static variable. If we need a bomb-proof solution, we can generate full UIDs, which are numbers that are guaranteed to be unique.

Using Templates

What if we have several totally different types of objects that we want to create through a factory—for example, game entities like we have seen so far, but also resources, or animations, or anything else that does not share a base common class with the game entities? We just create one factory for every one of those groups. Game entities can have their own factory and so will resources. We need to register the creator objects with the correct factory and call Create on the correct factory.

Suppose that after we write one factory, we realize that the code for the second one is not all that different. As a matter of fact, it is probably exactly the same, but it uses a different base class. The same holds true for all the Maker objects. Does this sound like a familiar situation?Itis a good situation to use templates. We need the same code, but we want to vary the class that the code works on. This is how the declaration of a templated factory would look:

```
template<class Base>
class Factory
{
public:
    Base * Create(ObjectType type);
    bool Register(ObjectType type,
                    CreatorBase<Base> * pCreator);
private:
    typedef std::map<ObjectType, CreatorBase<Base> *>
                                        CreatorMap;
    CreatorMap m_creatorMap;
};
```

The creator classes will also have to be templated. Previously, all creators inherited from a common Creator class, which is the type of the pointers that was stored in the factory. Since the Create function of the creator base class returns a pointer to the base class of the objects we are creating, we will also need to template the creator base class itself so that the type of the pointers returned match up in the proper way.

```
template<class Base>
class CreatorBase
{
public:
    virtual ~CreatorBase() {}
    virtual Base * Create() const = 0;
};

template<class Product, class Base>
class Creator : public CreatorBase<Base>
{
public:
    virtual Base * Create() const {return new Product;}
};
```

ON THE CD

The implementation of the factory functions is just like the nontemplated version presented earlier, but with the generic type parameters instead. Refer to the source code on the CD-ROM for the details on the templated implementation. The Visual Studio workspace is located in \Chapter 13. ObjectFactory\ObjectFactory.dsw.

With these templates, making new factories and creators is easy:

```
Factory<GameEntity> factory;
factory.Register(GAMECAMERA,new Creator<GameCamera,
                GameEntity>);
factory.Register(GAMEENTITY,new Creator<GameEntity,
                GameEntity>);
```

And using them is just as easy as it was before:

```
GameEntity * pEntity = factory.Create(GAMECAMERA);
```

As long as all your object types are created with a default constructor, and you do not need to do any extra processing or bookkeeping in the factory, then using templated factories and creators is probably a great way to go. However, it falls short if your objects need special ways of being created. Maybe they need a parameter passed on to their constructor, or maybe a function needs to be called right after they are created. These are things a templated solution will not do for you. Similarly, the templated solution will not allow you to keep a list of objects in your factory, or some statistics about them. In these situations, the nontemplated solution gives us the flexibility we need at the cost of some extra typing.

SHARED OBJECTS

Creating objects is only half the fun. Once they are created, we need to keep track of them, manage their life spans, and delete them correctly. This is more difficult that it looks, once more than one part of the code refers to the same object.

C++ does not have any sort of native automatic *garbage collection*, and instead, programmers need to manage the memory by hand. With automatic garbage collection, programmers are free from worrying about what memory is allocated and what memory is freed. Instead, the run-time code takes care of releasing all the memory that the program is no longer using. Of course, garbage collection has its own share of problems, such as taking time away from the processing of the program at an inopportune moment and making us miss the next vertical synch for a frame.

What the lack of garbage collection means is that we have to be very meticulous about the memory we allocate and the objects we create. We need to keep track of them, and when we no longer need them, we need to delete them. Unfortunately things are a bit more complicated than that. Consider the following code:

```
// Create a new explosion and point the camera to it
GameEntity * pExplosion= new GameExplosion;
camera.SetTarget(pExplosion);

//...
// Some time later, the explosion dies
delete pExplosion;
```

The camera class is keeping a pointer to the entity it is focused on. What happens if that entity is deleted? How is the camera going to know? The pointer still looks the same; it is just a memory address, and that has not changed. But now that memory address either does not belong to the process or is taken up by something totally different from the original entity to which it was pointing. This is called a *dangling pointer* because the memory location the pointer was referring to is gone or has totally changed.

This is the fundamental problem of shared objects. The rest of the chapter will present several approaches to dealing with shared objects in our programs.

No Object Sharing

As usual, one of the possible solutions to a problem is to not get in the situation in the first place. If we totally avoid shared objects, our problem is nonexistent. Unfortunately, it is not always possible or desirable to do without object sharing completely, but sometimes it might make sense.

In most games, if two game objects use the same expensive resource, it makes sense for them to share it instead of keeping two duplicate copies in memory. For example, all buildings of a certain type can share textures, and all tanks can share the same engine sound. It would be wasteful to create new copies of the same resource for each entity in the world.

In our previous example, the camera needs to point to a existing object in the world. It would not make any sense for the camera to have its own copy of the object, because the other object would move away, and the camera would stay pointed to its stationary copy. That is another case where some type of object sharing is necessary.

However, if object sharing is not necessary, then avoid it. It will keep the code a lot simpler, more efficient, and easier to maintain. There is no need to introduce complexity when a plain pointer will do just fine.

For example, a camera entity can keep a pointer to a rotation matrix as a private member variable. That pointer does not need to be exposed to the rest of the world. Only the camera knows about it, and it has full responsibility over it. Whenever it decides to delete the matrix, there will be no other pointers to it, so we will not run into any problems. The camera itself might set the pointer to NULL once the camera has been deleted, so it will know not to access that pointer anymore.

Ignore the Problem

Sometimes, for very simple problems and small projects, the ostrich approach works just fine; bury your head in the sand and ignore the problem. Granted, this approach could potentially lead to trouble, but since the project is small, we can probably foresee that nobody is going to access the shared pointer after it has been deleted. It is a bit like playing with fire, but if we do not get burned, then no harm is done.

This is definitely not an approach recommended for a project of any reasonable size—maybe a technology demo or a quickly produced, throwaway prototype, but that is about it. Also, if the team involves more than one programmer, this approach is bound to fail, because the other programmers will most likely forget the implicit rules governing deleted objects and accidentally introduce some bugs.

A game that has virtually no dynamic allocations at runtime might also be able to get away with the ostrich approach. If everything is allocated statically, then objects are never deleted and pointers remain valid. We always need to check that the object we are accessing through a pointer is active or valid before using it, though. If your game is architected that way, then this approach might be fine. (Refer to Chapter 7 for a comparison of static and dynamic memory allocation strategies.)

When problems arise with the ostrich approach, there are no easy fixes, either. The bugs are not simple to track down. Trying to find out who deleted some memory at some point in the past is not a pleasant task to do in the debugger, and even determining that the crashes are caused by a shared pointer being deleted is not simple.

When a project grows larger than expected, trying to change it from ignoring the shared object problem to implementing one of the other methods described in this chapter becomes quite involved; it is possible, but time consuming. Forethought and planning can save us a lot of time down the line, especially as milestones approach and time becomes more precious.

Leave It up to the Owner

A possible way to deal with the shared object problem is to designate a section of code, or in our case a particular object, as the *owner* of a shared object. A shared object can have many pointers and references to it from different objects, but only one of those objects is its owner.

The owner is solely responsible for creating, managing, and eventually destroying the shared object. Like the previous approach, there really is nothing preventing a nonowner object from deleting the shared object; it is more of a rule that the code needs to follow for everything to work correctly. Because it is more concrete than the previous approach, this is something that could be used in a larger team project without too much difficulty, as long as everybody is careful.

So the owner can now freely delete the object, but what happens to the pointers held by the nonowner objects? They have to know whenever the object is deleted so they can update their pointers to NULL or just change their state, so they do not attempt to use that pointer anymore.

This notification can be done by using an arrangement similar to the Observer pattern, where the nonowner objects are observers that subscribe themselves to notifications from the subject, which can be the owner or even the shared object itself. Whenever the shared object is deleted, all the observers receive a message with the news.

Just because something is the owner of a shared object, it does not have to remain this way forever. As long as all the objects involved agree, we can transfer ownership of an object as needed. For example, in a multiplayer strategy game, all the units a player controls can be owned by that player. If a player happens to get disconnected, we could create an AI player and transfer the ownership of all that player's units to it, so everybody can continue playing.

This method requires that we decide who the owner is, and how it is going to manage the lifetime of the shared object. It also requires that we write the nonowner objects in such a way that they can deal with the shared object being destroyed at any time.

Finally, if there are a lot of observers, and objects are created and destroyed very often, the performance costs of notifying every observer and the memory necessary to store all the observers in the list could be significant. This approach works best for relatively large objects that are not expected to be destroyed many times per frame.

Reference Counting

Another, more egalitarian approach is to use *reference counting*. In this method, there is no need for an owner of a shared object. Instead, that object will be kept around for as long as someone needs it. As soon as the last reference to that shared object goes away, we detect that nobody needs it anymore, and it is deleted. Reference counting is like a rudimentary garbage collection system.

Implementation

To be able to use reference counting, our shared objects need to implement two functions: `AddRef` and `Release`. Whenever any part of the code acquires a pointer to the object, `AddRef` is called. Whenever any part of the code is done with an object, instead of deleting it, it calls `Release`.

The reference-counted object will keep track of how many references it has. Every time `AddRef` is called, it will increase that reference count. Every time `Release` is called, the reference count will go down by one. If the reference count ever reaches zero, the object is deleted.

This is exactly how COM manages its shared objects. You will also use these calls often if you use the DirectX API, since it is based on a COM system.

To make things easy to use, we can place all the reference-counting functionality in a class and allow any class that inherits from it to automatically become reference-counted.

```
class RefCounted
{
public:
    RefCounted();
    virtual ~RefCounted() {};

    int AddRef() { return ++m_refCount; }
    int Release();
    int GetRefCount() const {return m_refCount;}

protected:
    int m_refCount;
};

int RefCounted::Release()
```

```
        {
            m_refCount-;
            int tmpRefCount = m_refCount;
            if ( m_refCount <= 0 )
                delete this;
            return tmpRefCount;
        }
```

To use it, a class just needs to inherit from the RefCounted class. If we want to make the class more foolproof, we could declare its destructor as protected; that way the only way the object is going to be destroyed is through its Release call. Any attempts by external code to destroy the object directly will result in compiler errors.

```
        class GameEntity : public RefCounted
        {
        public:
            // ...
        protected:
            virtual ~GameEntity();
        };
```

There are a couple of interesting aspects of the RefCounted implementation that are worth paying attention to. First of all, notice that the AddRef and Release functions return an integer. The returned value is the current reference count after the call takes place. This is sometimes needed by code that deals with reference-counted objects in order to beaware of whether an object is being destroyed or not.

The second interesting item is the Release call. You might not be used to seeing code that says delete this. It looks a bit dangerous to call it from within a member function, but it is quite safe. The object is deleting itself; it is no different than if somebody else had deleted it. What we have to be careful about is not to make any other function calls or touch any member variables after the delete call, which is why we have to go through some contortions to keep a temporary variable with the value of the reference count on the stack. If we attempt to return the value of m_refCount directly, everything would work fine until the reference count reaches zero; at which point the object would be deleted, and then we would try to read one of its member variables. As you can imagine, the program will then most likely crash. But if both that value and the memory address to return to are stored in the stack, we can safely return from the function without incident.

Recommendation

Are there any drawbacks to reference counting? Unfortunately, there are a few. It might appear that this method is totally foolproof. As soon as the reference count reaches zero, the object is deleted. Nobody has to remember to delete it in one place and notify other objects. Unfortunately, they have to remember to call `AddRef` and `Release` correctly. As soon as there is an unbalanced number of `AddRef` and `Release` calls, objects will either never go away because their reference count keeps going up, or they will be destroyed prematurely because their reference count accidentally reached zero. Tracking down unmatched `AddRef` and `Release` calls is not easy, and usually it only takes one unmatched call to break the system down.

Still, reference counting is a much more robust system than trying to ignore the problem, and it has the advantage that there is no need to designate an owner to keep track of the object. This method is best suited for situations where there is no strict ownership of the shared object. A perfect example would be graphic resources used by the game. Textures, geometry, and animations can keep a reference count of how many game objects use them. As soon as all game objects that use a particular texture are removed, the texture is also destroyed.

This brings us to the second drawback of the reference count approach; objects might get destroyed a bit too easily. Maybe we just released a texture, but we are about to create a new entity that needs that texture. Now we are forced to load it from the disk again, when we would have preferred that it had stayed in memory. You can work around that problem by having a resource manager that keeps one extra reference to all the textures. That way, even if there are no entities in the game that use a particular texture, it will stay around as long as the resource manager wants it to.

Finally, the last drawback of this approach is that it causes verbose, awkward code. Do not discount this problem as a capricious remark. It is similar to doing error handling by returning and checking error codes from functions. Your code might have more lines for checking error codes than for doing the actual work. The same thing can happen to reference counting. The code will soon be filled with `AddRef` and `Release` calls everywhere.

To make things worse, functions that fetch pointers to reference-counted objects will often take those pointers as parameters instead of returning them directly, which makes the code even more convoluted and verbose.

Consider the following code:

```
GameEntity * GameCamera::GetTarget()
{
    // We assume that the target always exists
    m_pTarget->AddRef();
    return m_pTarget;
}
```

Now, it would be too tempting for someone to write a line of code like this:

```
cout << pCamera->GetTarget()->GetName();
```

The `return` value of the `GetTarget` function was used directly from a temporary variable; and after that statement, we no longer have access to it. This means that the reference count to the target object was increased, but `Release` was never called. Instead, to avoid this problem, a function will typically be written this way:

```
void GameCamera::GetTarget(GameEntity *& pEntity)
{
    // We assume that the target always exists
    m_pTarget->AddRef();
    pEntity = m_pTarget;
}
```

and used this way:

```
GameEntity * pEntity;
pCamera->GetTarget(pEntity);
cout << pEntity->GetName();
pEntity->Release();
```

What should have been a single line is now four different lines. Still, sometimes it is worth paying that price to get a more robust way of managing shared objects.

Handles

The root of the problem of having shared objects is that there are multiple pointers to the same object. *Handles* prevent that situation from happening, so there are no longer any problems with objects being deleted and dangling pointers being left around.

The principle behind handles is to use some sort of identifier (a handle) instead of a pointer to a shared object. Then, anytime we want to work on a shared object directly, we ask the owner of the shared object to give us the pointer to the object that corresponds to a certain handle. We perform any operations on that object through the pointer, but when we are done, we throw the pointer away. We do not keep that pointer around.

This way there really is only one pointer to each shared object: the one of the owner of the object. Any]time someone else wants to use the object, they need to pass in the handle first. If the object has been deleted since then, we can return a NULL pointer. At that point they will know the object does not exist and can deal with it appropriately.

Handles can be just a plain integer. This is convenient, because they are small enough to be copied and passed around very effectively, but they also have a larger range of unique values they can cover. For this method to work, it is essential that we map every handle uniquely to each object.

How do we guarantee that we can give entities unique handles? Just using a 32-bit number and incrementing it every time we need a new entity gives us about 430 million different numbers. These should be more than enough for any game. Here is how we would use handles in a real situation when dealing with textures:

```
typedef unsigned int Handle;
Handle hTexture = CreateTexture("myTexture.tif");
// ...
Texture * pTexture = GetTexture(hTexture);
if (pTexture != NULL) {
    // The texture was still around, do something with it
    // ...
}
```

One side effect of dealing with 32-bit number handles is that it is impossible to tell a valid handle from any random number. This can be a problem if memory is being accidentally corrupted, there was a problem copying a handle correctly, or (a much more likely situation) a handle variable was never initialized, and it contains random data in it. Wouldn't it be nice if there were a way to tell valid handles from invalid ones?

We can sacrifice a few bits off the top and use them to store a 'unique' bit pattern. We could use the top eight bits, which would still leave us with 2^{24} different handles. We could even go with as many as 16 bits for the unique identifier, and we would still have over 60,000 handles for our entities. That should still be more than enough for most games, especially if you consider that we only need unique handles for each major type of shared objects. For example, all resources could use one handle system, but all game entities could use a different one. There really is no truly unique bit pattern, but the chance that a random number will match our bit pattern is pretty slim, and it gets slimmer the more bits we use.

Whenever we attempt to translate between a handle and a pointer, the program can first verify that the handle has the proper bit pattern and assert right away if it is invalid (see Chapter 16, Crash-Proofing Your Game, for the proper use of asserts). This verification is something we might only want to do in debug mode if performance is a problem, and bypass it completely in release mode.

Recommendation

Handles can be somewhat cumbersome because they require the translation step to get a pointer to the shared object. However, they can be quite effective for tasks for which we do not need to get to the underlying pointer very often. For example, there are not going to be many places in the code where we try to get a pointer to the texture of a mesh. That is probably only going to happen when we load the mesh and when we render it, so using handles in that situation is not going to be very painful.

Handles are also quite effective when the shared objects are deleted but need to be recreated at a later time. If we make sure that the newly created object maps to the same handle it used to have, then all previous handles become valid once again. This is perfect for situations where we are caching resources in and out during the game as the player moves to different locations.

The translation from handle to pointer should be implemented in a way that is very fast. Usually, a hash table or a map is a good implementation, but we could even consider using an array (or vector) of pointers so that each handle is just the index into the array. The main performance hit is going to be caused by the extra indirection level added by the translation table and its effect on the data cache.

Smart Pointers

Handles, reference counting, and all the different approaches that we have discussed for dealing with shared objects are trying to solve one problem: having dangling pointers if the shared object is deleted. Wouldn't it be great if either the pointer knew it was pointing to a deleted object or that the shared object would not be deleted as long as there were any pointers referring to it? This is what smart pointers can offer us.

C++ pointers are best described as 'dumb' pointers. They really do not do much. They point to a memory location, and they know what type of data we expect to find there. They are not aware of what is really going on at that location, and they do not seem to be aware of people using them or making copies of them.

It turns out we can tap into the flexibility and power of C++ to create objects that will look and feel like pointers, but that will do some extra work for us along the way.

There is really no single definition of what a smart pointer does. Different smart pointer can do different things: check that the memory is valid, keep reference counts, apply different types of copying policies when the pointer is copied, keep statistics, or even delete what they are pointing to when the pointer itself is destroyed.

We actually already saw some smart pointers in Chapter 5 when we dealt with exceptions. There is one type of smart pointer, auto_ptr, that when destroyed will delete the object it is pointing to. This ability is extremely useful for correctly freeing all resources, even in the face of exceptions and the unwinding of the stack.

For smart pointers to be effective, they have to behave like real pointers. That is, we should be able to use them in the way we have come to expect pointers to work in C++. We should be able to dereference them using -> and *, we should be able to copy them very efficiently, they should be type-safe, and they should be small and not take much memory. We will be able to accomplish all those goals.

There are two main different types of smart pointers that can help us with shared objects. They both implement two of the previous solutions we have discussed, but they wrap them in the convenience of a pointer-like object, which makes them more foolproof and actually helps to remove a lot of extraneous code when dealing with handles and reference counting directly.

Handle-Based Smart Pointers

A handle-based smart pointer is simply a wrapper around a handle. It does not need to have any other data. That is handy because it means that, on most platforms, we can make a handle-based smart pointer be just as small as a regular pointer.

The pointer will take care of doing all the leg work for us. Remember how in order to use a handle we had to first translate from the handle to the actual pointer? The smart pointer will take care of doing this under the hood. We just go ahead and use it as a regular pointer. To do so, we need to override some of the more esoteric operators defined in C++, such as `operator ->` and `operator *`. This is the skeleton for a handle-based smart pointer:

```
class EntityPtr
{
public:
    EntityPtr(Handle h) : m_hEntity(h) {}
    bool operator == (int n) {
            return (n == (int) GetPtr(m_hEntity); }
    bool operator != (int n) { !operator==(n); }
    GameEntity * operator->() { return GetPtr(m_hEntity); }
    GameEntity & operator *() { *return GetPtr(m_hEntity); };

private:
    Handle m_hEntity;
};
```

Notice how, thanks to the overridden operators, we can treat it as a real pointer.

```
EntityPtr ptr(GetEntity());
if (ptr != NULL) {
    cout << ptr->GetName();
    const Point3d & pos = ptr->GetPosition();
}
```

We are even able to check against NULL like we normally do with any pointer because we have overridden the `operator ==` function, which checks if a corresponding pointer exists and that it is not NULL.

The smart pointer above only works for pointers of GameEntity types, but we would really like to use it with any other pointer, including resource pointers or anything that uses handles. Since the only thing that changes is the type of the pointer, we use a template to create the type of pointer we want:

```
template <class DataType >
class HandlePtr
{
public:
```

```
        HandlePtr(Handle h) : m_hEntity(h) {}
        bool operator == (int n) {
                return (n == (int)GetPtr(m_hEntity); }
        bool operator != (int n) { !operator==(n); }
        DataType * operator->() { return GetPtr(m_hEntity); }
        DataType & operator *() { *return GetPtr(m_hEntity); };

    private:
        Handle m_hEntity;
    };
```

To use it, we just need to instantiate the template with the type we want to point to:

```
    typedef HandlePtr<Texture *> TexturePtr;
    TexturePtr pTexture = CreateTexture("smiley.tif");
```

Suddenly we have all the safety of handles with the convenience of pointers. That is all that smart pointers are about.

Reference-Counting Smart Pointers

Reference-counting smart pointers wrap the reference-counting approach into a smart pointer. Conceptually, every time a smart pointer is created to an object, the reference count is increased. Whenever that object is destroyed, the reference count is decreased. In a way, they are doing the calls to `AddRef` and `Release` automatically, based on the life of the smart pointer itself. As usual, if the reference count of the shared object reaches zero, it gets deleted.

In practice, things are a bit more complicated. We have to deal with the mechanics of copying smart pointers, as well as loops in reference-counting graphics, and we might even want to move the reference counting outside of the shared object and into the smart pointer itself. (See Suggested Reading at the end of this chapter for many more details on different effective implementations.)

The Boost smart pointer library provides different types of smart pointers for different purposes. One of them, the `shared_ptr`, implements exactly this reference-counting approach. Just as with the handle-based smart pointers, they are also templated for type-safe use with any pointer type.

Recommendation

Smart pointers can be the best of both worlds. If you are prepared to invest a bit of time and plan from the beginning how they will be integrated with the rest of the engine, they can be an ideal solution.

Implementing a smart pointer from scratch can be fairly simple and very enlightening. But if the mechanics it implements are complex, it can be difficult to make it work correctly under all circumstances (e.g., temporaries generated, copies in the stack versus the heap, etc.).

If what you need is already provided in one of the smart pointer types in the Boost library, then go ahead and use it. Just make sure you read carefully through the documentation to find out what its exact memory and performance cost is, and what its behavior is when copied, deleted, or passed around.

One of the situations in which smart pointers do not always behave exactly like a normal, dumb pointer is when casting to different types. The conversion from a pointer to a child class, to a pointer to its parent class happens automatically in C++. Unless you provide some special constructors, that same conversion will not happen with smart pointers. The most common way of dealing with conversions is to provide special templated functions just to perform the casting.

CONCLUSION

In this chapter, we have seen how we can use object factories to create any object type in a very flexible way. Object factories allow us to create objects of a type that is determined at runtime instead of at compile time. This allows us to create and load objects very easily, as well as to dynamically extend the types of objects in our game.

We then saw how having shared objects can be problematic in C++. If multiple objects are keeping pointers to a shared object, who is responsible for deleting it? And, most important, what happens when that object is deleted?

We covered several different techniques for dealing with shared objects. These included:

- Not sharing any objects
- Not worrying about object sharing and destruction
- Letting the owner deal with the destruction of the object and the responsibility to notify all the objects that kept pointers to the shared object

- Applying reference counting through the use of the `AddRef` and `Release` functions
- Using handles to avoid keeping any extra pointers around
- Using smart pointers to implement reference counting or handle usage, but in a pointer syntax.

SUGGESTED READING

These are some good references that deal with object factories. In particular, Alexandrescu's book goes in a lot of depth on the implementation details of a templated factory. The *Design Patterns* book also contains a good general description of the Observer pattern.

Gamma, Erich, et al., *Design Patterns*, Addison-Wesley, 1995.
Laramée, François Dominic, "A Game Entity Factory," *Game Programming Gems 2*, Charles River Media, 2001.
Alexandrescu, Andrei, *Modern C++ Design*, Addison-Wesley, 2001.

Here is a good article on how to use handles for resource management:

Bilas, Scott, "A Generic Handle-Based Resource Manager," *Game Programming Gems*, Charles River Media, 2000.

The following books explain reference counting in more detail and delve into the intricacies of implementing robust smart pointers.

Rogerson, Dale, *Inside COM*, Microsoft Press, 1997.
Eberly, David H., *3D Game Engine Design*, Morgan Kaufmann, 2001.
Meyers, Scott, *More Effective C++*, Addison-Wesley, 1996.
Alexandrescu, Andrei, *Modern C++ Design*, Addison-Wesley, 2001.
Hawkins, Brian, "Handle-Based Smart Pointers," *Game Programming Gems 3*, Charles River Media, 2002.

Finally, the Boost library provides several smart pointer classes, along with extensive documentation for each of them.

C++ Boost Smart Pointer Library, *http://www.boost.org/libs/smart_ptr/index.htm*.

OBJECT SERIALIZATION

IN THIS CHAPTER

- Game Entity Serialization Overview
- Game Entity Serialization Implementation
- Putting It All Together

S erialization is the ability to store an object into some medium and then restore at a later time. The medium can be any type of data storage: memory, disk, or even a network pipe.

Serialization is an essential component of games. At the very least, a game needs to load its levels, assets, and game state for the game to start. Most games also allow some form of in-game save, which can be later restored so the user can continue playing from that point.

Unlike other languages, C++ does not offer built-in serialization facilities, so we need to manually implement what we need. This chapter looks at how to effectively apply serialization to games, examines the challenges presented by serialization, and proposes solutions for dealing with both game entities and game resources.

Game Entity Serialization Overview

Just about every game needs to save the state of its game entities. Sometimes this is in the form of a mid-game save or a checkpoint to allow the user to come back later and continue from that point. Even if a game does not offer a mid-game save feature, it still needs to create an initial state for all the game entities at the beginning of each level. Most of the time, that initial state is generated by a level-editing tool with which the designers can place game entities in the world, set their parameters and the relationships between them, and save them to create a new game level.

Entities vs. Resources

Game entities are objects that represent the information about specific 'things' in the game. They are the objects we interact with: the enemies that shoot at us, the objectives we are trying to accomplish, and even the camera through which we are looking at the world. All these things can, and probably will, change during gameplay. We care about saving them in order to preserve the state of the game world.

It is important to distinguish between game entities and game resources. Resources are some of the parts out of which game entities are composed. Resources typically do not change during gameplay, and they do not have any information that is specific to a game entity. They just exist so entities can use them. Some examples of resources are textures, geometry data, sounds, and script files.

The key difference between entities and resources is that resources do not change once they are loaded (they might change under some rare circumstances, but we will explore that possibility later). We do not need to save the resources to capture the state of the game. They have not changed from the time they were loaded from the DVD when the level started. It also means that it is possible to load a previous state just by restoring all the game entities, since the correct resources are already loaded in memory.

Entities and resources present totally different challenges. Entities need to be both saved and loaded, while resources just need to be loaded. Entities tend to be relatively small objects, but they are made out of very heterogeneous data and are highly interconnected among themselves. Resources, on the other hand, are large, fairly homogeneous, and without many interconnections to other resources. This chapter deals only with the serialization of game entities, since they present very different challenges from resources.

The Simplest Solution that Does Not Work

Game entity serialization is one of those problems that seems very simple and straightforward at first, but becomes complicated and hard to get to work correctly once you start implementing it. At first the problem seems trivial; go through every entity in the world and save the object to disk. Then, to restore the game state, we just load that data back into memory. What is wrong with this approach?

There are many things wrong with it. The major problem is caused by pointers. The value of a pointer is just a memory address, but memory addresses change from one run of the game to the next. If we were to save the value of a pointer and later restore it, and try to use it, it would most likely cause the program to crash, since it would probably be pointing to some random memory location that the program is not using. It certain will not be pointing where it was when we saved it.

The second problem is how to restore the objects. Just saving the data from each entity is not enough. Later on, when we are loading that data to restore the game, how do we know what to do with it? How do we know whether we are reading data for a projectile entity or for a camera entity? We do not. We need some additional information to restore things correctly.

The third problem is that we probably cannot treat our game entities like plain C structures. It is not enough to create them and fill them with the correct data. We need to ensure that the initialization for each entity happens as it would normally happen. That means that its constructor gets called, and it receives any other initialization calls. That gives the entity the chance to register itself with some other manager class, or to acquire resources or anything else it might normally do.

What We Need

Given than we cannot just dump the bits on the hard drive and load them again, what is the ideal solution? Let's first examine what we want in high-level terms, and we will worry about the specific implementations of it in the next section.

We want to be able to save the state of any game entity at any time. We clearly want this system to deal correctly with pointers and relationships in general. If an end-of-mission trigger entity was supposed to go off when a certain entity was destroyed, we still want that trigger to be associated with the same entity when we load the game, even if they are each residing in totally different memory locations.

When we consider what to save, we need to make a distinction between instance data and type data. Type data is usually created by the designers, and it includes the general characteristics of all the objects of that type. For example, a particular enemy unit type can have maximum hit points, certain types of weapons, a maximum speed, and whether or not it has flying capabilities as part of its type data. If the type data never changes, then there is no need to save it. Otherwise, we still need to save it, but only once and not for every entity of that type. The instance data of our enemy unit, on the other hand, will include its current position and velocity, its current hit points, and how many rounds it has left in its weapons. It's the instance data that we care about saving.

When thinking about the data that we want to save, we also need to consider how important it is to save all the little details. Does our game require that every single detail be saved exactly right, or can we approximate things? For example, if a fire is burning in the fireplace when we save the game, it is important that the logs be still burning when we load the game; but does it matter whether the flames have the exact same number of particles as they did before? Do they have to be in the exact same position? Probably not. In this case, it is enough to say that there is a fire effect and that it has been burning for a while. On the other hand, it is important that we store the exact location, velocity, and maybe even acceleration of some other objects. If an arrow was in the air when we saved the game, we definitely want it to be there and to continue its trajectory as expected when we load it back up.

One aspect that is not particularly difficult, but would be great if our solution could support, is to be able to use different formats for saving and restoring the entity data. This would allow us to have a very fast binary format that we can use when the game ships, but also have a slower, but much easier to debug and read, text-based version. In general, this is a good approach to take with almost any type of serialization, especially if loading efficiency is important.

We also want to be able to serialize the entities to and from any type of storage media. At the very least, we want to be able to save them to and load them from disk and memory, while also having the flexibility to use other types of media, such as memory cards or even a network pipe. Being able to use different types of media, such as memory, can come in very handy when we have already loaded a file in memory, and we want to create the appropriate entities from its contents.

Serialization can also be used to transfer entities across a network. However, even though it might seem tempting to reuse this technology, do not expect to be able to create a fully network-enabled game just by supporting a network pipe as one of your media targets. This feature can be used to create new entities on other machines or to pass the data for a new type of entity that only the local machine knows about. It will definitely not be enough to support all the real-time updates necessary for a full multiplayer game. Updating of game entities is a difficult topic that requires a book all by itself.

We have not discussed the difference between a full game save and a checkpoint. Checkpoints are more often employed in console games; they store the state of the game world at a particular place in the level, but usually with most entities reset to their original states. Only a handful of states are preserved, such as the player's position and what objectives have been accomplished so far. Everything else, like doors, secret passages, enemies, and power-ups, are usually back at their initial states.

Checkpoints can be implemented using the same technique as game entity serialization, but only saving the state of a few selected entities. Whenever we need to revert the state of the game to one of the checkpoints, we can reset the level to its initial state and then serialize the few selected entities.

Size can be an important aspect of saved games. On PCs, or even on consoles with large amounts of permanent storage, the size of a saved game file does not matter very much. Hard drive space is cheap and fast, so taking 5–10 MB per file is not unheard of. However, sometimes we have to save our games to small devices, like memory cards, so saved games must be kept as small as possible. Keeping the saved game file size under control can make the difference between fitting dozens of saved games or taking up the whole card with just a couple of saves. Sometimes this is enough of an incentive for games to implement the checkpoint save system, since it requires much less data to be saved.

GAME ENTITY SERIALIZATION IMPLEMENTATION

So far, we have put together a sort of 'wish list' of what we want as far as serialization goes for our games. This section will turn those wishes into reality.

Streams

The concept of a stream will allow us to abstract out the media that we use for serialization. A stream is just a sequence of bytes in a particular order that can be read and written to. Additionally, we might want to provide other useful operations, such as rewinding or moving to a particular location.

The standard C++ library provides us with streams for general input and output with the `iostream` classes. It also provides a set of templated classes for input, some for output, and some that do both. Should we take advantage of these prebuilt classes for our serialization needs? It would depend on our specific situation. Most of the time, they are too heavy-weight for what we really want. We want something small and easily customizable to deal with unusual requirements and strange media types. Most of the time we have no need for the flexibility they provide with locales and character traits. Therefore, we will go ahead and create our own versions; but if it makes more sense to reuse the standard C++ ones in your project, go ahead and use their interfaces instead.

The `IStream` interface will describe all the operations that we will make available to streams. As we saw in Chapter 10, having an abstract interface will allow us to easily switch specific implementations of the streams at runtime without the rest of the code noticing the switch. This fulfills one of our wish-list items: being able to serialize entities to any media type. As long as we have a stream for that type of media, everything should work correctly.

```cpp
class IStream
{
public:
    virtual ~IStream() {};
    virtual void Reset() = 0;

    virtual int Read (int bytes, void * pBuffer) = 0;
    virtual int Write (int bytes, void * pBuffer) = 0;

    virtual bool SetCurPos (int pos) = 0;
    virtual int GetCurPos () = 0;
};
```

Then we can inherit from it, and provide specific implementations for memory streams, file streams, or any other type of media we need. We might also want to provide very platform-specific stream types that take advantage of all the functions available to that particular platform, in order to have the most efficient implementation possible. For example, a default file stream could be implemented with just `fopen` and `fread` operations, but we could write a special stream that is optimized to read from a DVD, taking into account goals such as reducing the number of seeks, or that is optimized to read from a hard drive in a specific console, using console API calls for low-level hard drive access.

The specific stream implementations would each have constructors or initialization functions that create the specific constructor with the correct parameters we want. For example, the file stream could take a file name and maybe another parameter indicating whether to open it in read or write mode. The memory stream could take a specific memory location and a size to use as its source, and a default constructor with no parameters that just creates the stream contents anywhere in memory. Alternatively, we can provide that functionality with the regular member functions of the stream classes, instead of constructors.

```cpp
class StreamFile : public IStream
{
public:
    StreamFile(const string & filename);
    virtual ~StreamFile();
    // ...
};

class StreamMemory : public IStream
{
public:
    StreamMemory();
    StreamMemory(void * pBuffer, int size);
    virtual ~StreamMemory();
    // ...
};
```

In addition to this minimal interface, we might also want to provide some helper functions so that common data types could be read more easily. Keeping with the spirit of trying to have the simplest possible interface, those kinds of functions would make more sense as nonmember functions. If you really like the C++ stream syntax, you can use `operator`

<< and `operator` >> to manipulate the streams. Otherwise, you can just use more straightforward functions, such as `Read` and `Write`.

```
int    ReadInt    (IStream & stream);
float ReadFloat (IStream & stream);
string ReadString (IStream & stream);

bool WriteInt    (IStream & stream, int n);
bool WriteFloat (IStream & stream, float f);
bool WriteString (IStream & stream, const string & s);
```

We could also implement special types of streams that read and write compressed data, for example. That way we would move the complexity of compressing and uncompressing the data out onto the specific implementation of the stream class, and any type of object could take advantage of it.

It is also possible to create more complex file types on top of a stream. For example, we could implement a binary chunk-based file format, .ini file format, or even XML file format on top of a stream.

As an example, here is how the integer read and write functions would be implemented:

```
int ReadInt (IStream & stream)
{
    int n = 0;
    stream.Read(sizeof(int), (void *)&n);
    return n;
}

bool WriteInt (IStream & stream, int n)
{
    int numWritten = stream.Write(sizeof(int), &n);
    return (numWritten == sizeof(int));
}
```

If you find yourself writing certain types of objects to a stream very frequently, such as points, vectors, or matrices, you could write helper functions for each of those types. This would make it easier for the rest of the code to serialize them.

Saving

When it comes time to save game entities, it is best if each entity decides for itself how to best save itself to the stream. To this end, we will make a pass through all the entities we are interested in saving and give them the chance to serialize themselves.

ISerializable Interface

We can call the `Write` function for each entity we want to serialize. We could just make that function part of the base `GameEntity` class, and everything would work fine. Entities that did not want to be serialized could just leave it blank, and all the others would implement the function, depending on its contents.

A better approach is to make the serialization-related functions part of an abstract interface, `ISerializable`. Then the `GameEntity` base class can inherit from it and everything would work the same way. However, splitting those functions into a separate interface allows us to easily serialize other types of objects that are not necessarily game entities. If we really need to 'discover' whether or not an object implements the `ISerializable` interface, then we could use the `QueryInterface` approach described in Chapter 10. For now, we will just assume that all game entities implement the `ISerializable` interface.

What does the `ISerializable` interface look like? The interface is very simply along these lines:

```
class ISerializable
{
public:
    virtual ~ISerializable() {};
    virtual bool Write(IStream & stream) const = 0;
    virtual bool Read(IStream & stream) = 0;
};
```

Clearly, we will also use the `ISerializable` interface during the load process. This is why it has a `Read` function as well.

Again, if we really prefer the C++ stream syntax, we could have used the `operator >>` and `operator <<` method. Or, if we wanted to be really fancy, we could have written two functions called `Serialize`, but with one of them being constant and the other nonconstant. The constant one can only do the writing, and the nonconstant one would do the reading. However, this is more trouble than it is worth, and it would make it unclear which function is being called when. Having terser interface cannot beat being explicit and clear about our intentions.

Implementing Write

Implementing the Write function for each entity is a very straightforward task. We need to decide what data we want to save. Then, for each member variable that we want to save, we serialize it to the stream.

For integers, floats, and other standard data types, we just stream them directly. But what if our entity contains a member variable of its own that we need to serialize? We simply have to ensure that the variable also implements the ISerializable interface, and we just call its Write function, which in turn will be implemented in the same way. This way we can save any number of nested objects without any difficulty. If the entity contains pointers or references to other objects, instead of the object itself, we need to deal with them in a different way (which will be covered in the next section).

If our entity classes use inheritance, we might want to let the parent classes deal with the serialization for their own data. Derived classes only have to worry about the new variables they add.

Here is some potential code for the Write function of a camera class:

```
bool GameCamera::Write(IStream & stream) const
{
    // Let the parent class write common things like position,
    // rotation, etc.
    bool bSuccess = GameEntity::Write(stream);

    // These are basic data types, serialize them directly
    bSuccess &= WriteFloat(stream, m_FOV);
    bSuccess &= WriteFloat(stream, m_NearPlane);
    bSuccess &= WriteFloat(stream, m_FarPlane);

    // This is an object that needs to be serialized in turn
    bSuccess &= m_lens.Write(stream);

    return bSuccess;
}
```

What we have implemented so far is a pure binary format—no headers, no extra information—just the raw data. It might be a fine format for whenever we need to load entities as fast as possible, such as in the released game, but it is not a very friendly format for game development. As soon as a minor change is made to an entity class, all the previously saved games become unusable. Worse, there is no way to detect something is wrong, and we will most likely read garbage data.

For this reason, it is a good idea to implement at least two types of formats: a fast one like the one we saw above, and a slower one that is easier to debug, which will still work when the format changes. We might even want to make that slower format text-based, so it is easier to debug and examine during development.

Unique Identifiers

We still have not solved one of the major problems: what to do about saving pointers. It turns out we have several choices.

The first possibility is to completely avoid pointers, or at least pointers to other game entities. Instead of a pointer, we could refer to any other game entities through unique IDs (or UIDs). If every game entity has a unique ID that is guaranteed never to be repeated, then we can just keep that number. Anytime we need to work directly with the entity, we ask the game entity system to give us a pointer to the entity corresponding to that number.

In addition to solving the problem of not having to save pointers, this approach also simplifies the bookkeeping necessary between game entities. If we keep direct pointers to entities, but one entity is removed from the world, what happens when another entity tries to access it? In theory, we could never delete any entities and always keep them around, just making sure they never get updated or rendered. If we use the UID method, and an entity does not exist anymore, we just get a NULL pointer back, and we know not to use it.

For example, the following code updates the position of a homing projectile that has locked on to some target, all using the UID method.

```
void HomingProjectile::Update()
{
    if (!m_bLocked)
        return;

    GameEntity * pTarget = GetEntityFromUID(m_targetUID);
    if (pTarget == NULL) {
        m_bLocked = false;
        return;
    }

    // Do whatever course correction is necessary here...
    // ...
}
```

This is exactly like the solution to the shared-object problem using handles that we saw in Chapter 13. The same comments about the construction of handles and how the translation is implemented also apply here.

Resources

What about pointers to resources instead of entities? Usually, this is less problematic. Entities point to resources because they were created that way, and their data was set up that way from the beginning. For example, one of the properties of a certain player avatar entity is the mesh it will use to be rendered, along with all its animations and textures. Usually entities will refer to resources by file name or by some resource ID, and that is all that we need. If the resource it points to is going to change during the program, the entity should save that file name or ID to be restored later on. Otherwise, it will always remain the same, so there is no need to save it.

Saving Pointers

There is an argument in favor of using pointers between game entities, which makes life simpler and code easier to write. We still need to deal with the problem of entities disappearing in the middle of the gamebut if that is not an issue, changing everything to use UIDs can be more trouble than it is worth.

It is also possible that our game entity system has been developed without plans for serialization, and saving the game was a feature that was left for the very end of the development cycle. Or maybe it was purposefully left out of the first release of the game, but we want to add it for the sequel while we reuse the same source code.

In that case, changing an existing code base from using pointers to using UIDs can be quite a task. Imagine wading through hundreds or thousands of classes, changing all the pointers and the code that uses them to UIDs. If all we want is a quick way of serializing entities, there is a better alternative. We can save the pointers straight to disk.

We know that the memory address contained in the pointer will not point to the correct memory location when we load the game again. Clearly, something has to be done to solve that problem when we load the game entities. For now, we will save the raw pointers and leave it at that. The next section covers what needs to be done at load time to get everything to work.

Loading

All we have done so far are preparations for being able to load the game entities and restore the game state. Now comes the actual game load, itself.

Creating Objects

A requirement when restoring different types of objects is to be able to create any object type based on the data we read from the stream. It is not enough to be able to read the data that should go in a GameCamera class; we need to know that it belongs to a GameCamera class, and we need to actually create an object of that type.

If the problem sounds familiar, it should, because we covered it in detail in Chapter 13. A good game entity factory should be able to create any entity type we want just by passing the class name or a type identifier. Then we can call Read on the newly created object in order to load all its data from the stream.

```
string strClassName = ReadString(stream);
GameEntity * pEntity = EntityFactory::Create(strClassName);
// ... Some bookkeeping here ...
pEntity->Read(stream);
```

Depending on what type of factory system we have, we can save full strings for the class name of our entities and create them again by passing the strings to the factory system. Using strings has the usual tradeoffs: it is easy to debug and very readable, but it is slower and takes more memory than using simple identifiers. Although they are more efficient, 32-bit identifiers will not immediately tell us what type of object we are trying to create when we look at the identifier in the debugger.

Loading Pointers

How do we deal with the thorny issue of pointers? As previously mentioned, we could just save them straight in the code, and they would restore correctly. Here is how to do it.

We know that every memory address is unique. By storing the memory address of an entity, we are uniquely identifying it. If along with every entity we also store its memory location when it is saved, we can construct a translation table at load time that can allow us to go from the old memory address to the new memory address.

For the translation to work correctly, it will need to be done once all the entities are loaded, otherwise we might try to look up a memory address that we have not loaded yet. The load process is as follows: first we load all the entities and construct a table mapping old addresses to new ones; then we make a 'fix-up' pass through all the entities, and give them a chance to fix any pointers they have to point to the new, correct memory locations.

To accomplish this fix-up of addresses, we need a bit more support from the loading system and the ISerializable interface. After we are done loading all the entities, we will give all the entities a chance to fix up their addresses in their pointers. To accomplish this, we extend the ISerializable interface to include a Fixup function.

```
class ISerializable
{
public:
    virtual ~ISerializable() {};
    virtual bool Write(IStream & stream) const = 0;
    virtual bool Read(IStream & stream) = 0;
    virtual void Fixup() = 0;
};
```

The same way that entities implemented their own Write and Read functions, they will implement a Fixup function that takes care of translating old pointer addresses to correct addresses for each saved pointer. If an entity saved no pointers, then it does not need to implement the Fixup function, since the base GameEntity class implemented an empty one. As with the other serialization functions, an entity must call its parent's version of Fixup in addition to doing its own pointer translations.

To make this fix-up step possible, each entity needs to be associated with its old address when it is loaded back in memory. This is done by simply saving the address of each entity when it is written out to the stream.

With all of this information in hand, we are ready to deal with pointers correctly. Whenever an object is created from the stream, we also read what its old address was and enter it in the translation table along with the new address. The class AddressTranslator will be in charge of

keeping track of all the addresses and providing us with a translation during the fix-up pass.

```
GameEntity * LoadEntity(IStream & stream)
{
    string strClassName = ReadString(stream);
    GameEntity * pEntity = EntityFactory::Create(
                                    strClassName);

    void * pOldAddress = (void *)ReadInt(stream);
    AddressTranslator::AddAddress(pOldAddress, pEntity);

    pEntity->Read(stream);
    return pEntity;
}
```

The AddAddress function puts the new address in a hash table, indexed by the old address, so it will be very efficient to translate from old
address to new address.

To implement the Fixup function, we need to use the other function
provided in the AddressTranslator, TranslateAddress. This function will
look through the hash table for an old pointer value and fetch the new
value. This is how the Fixup function for our HomingProjectile class
might look:

```
void HomingProjectile::Fixup()
{
    m_pTarget=(GameEntity *)AddressTranslator::
                        TranslateAddress(m_pTarget);
}
```

After the load is complete and all the pointer fix-ups are done, we
should reset the translation table to save memory, since it will not be
needed any longer.

One important thing to notice is that this method will only work
for pointers that we explicitly saved and then added to the table. In
this case, it happens automatically for all game entities. If we were to
attempt to do this with a pointer that had not been added to the translation table, it should assert or print a big warning to let us know
something went wrong in the translation process. Otherwise, the problem might go unnoticed, and the bug might not be found until after
exhaustive testing.

The problem is a little bit more subtle, though. We need to be very careful about saving the correct memory address of an object. That address must be the exact address that is pointed to by other game entities. If it is the slightest bit different, the translation step will fail. How could the address be 'slightly' different? Multiple inheritance could make it so. When multiple inheritance is involved (see Chapter 2), casting to the different parent classes could result in an offset to the value of the pointer itself. Fortunately in this case, GameEntity only inherits from IRenderable, so we have nothing to worry about. If it inherited from another abstract interface or from a separate base class, then we would need to be extremely careful to always save the pointer of type GameEntity.

PUTTING IT ALL TOGETHER

ON THE CD

The serialization example on the CD-ROM has source code for a fully-functional program that saves and restores the state of a game. The Visual Studio workspace for the project is located in Chapter 14. Serialization\ Serialization.dsw. It creates a simple tree of GameEntity objects, saves it to disk, deletes it, and loads it again. To verify that it indeed works as expected, it prints the contents of the tree before it is saved and after it is restored from disk

The program is only intended as a working example of how to apply the concepts in this chapter. It is not robust code that could be thrown into any development environment. It does not handle errors well, if at all, and the file format is too raw and basic. By keeping the code small and simple, it is easier to understand the concepts behind it, instead of getting lost in layers of complexity and error checking. For example, the game entity factory is just one function with hardcoded entity types. It is the simplest solution that works, but we saw much better ways of implementing it in Chapter 13.

Of particular interest is how all the pointers of all the entities are saved and restored correctly. All game entities have a vector of pointers to child entities. Those pointers are simply stored and then translated in the fix-up pass. Additionally, the camera has a pointer to another game entity that it uses to focus on. That pointer is treated the same way, and it is restored correctly. Figure 14.1 shows the structure of the game entity tree that is serialized in the sample code on the CD-ROM (\Chapter 14.Serialization\Serialization.dsw).

ON THE CD

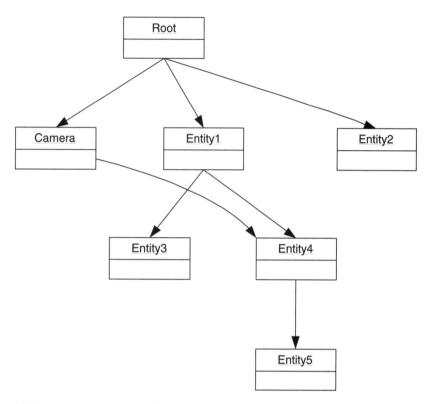

FIGURE 14.1   Simple game entity tree serialized in the sample code.

CONCLUSION

In this chapter, we have seen how something as simple-sounding as implementing in-game saves can be quite difficult to implement correctly. In-game saves are just one example of the problem of serialization: storing the state of an object in some data medium and being able to completely restore it at a later time.

Other languages offer better built-in facilities for serialization; but in C++, we have to take the hard road and implement them ourselves. In particular, when dealing with any complex object structure, we need to deal with the issue of saving and restoring pointers to memory locations.

This chapter presented several different variations on serialization. All of them rely on the use of streams, which allow us to abstract out the actual media to which we are serializing our entities. We can provide streams that work on disk files, memory, or even over a network.

We then saw how we could save the state of game entities by using the ISerializable interface, making each entity responsible for determining what to save. We also discussed the possibility of using UIDs instead of pointers to model relationships between entities. If the program has not been implemented this way from the beginning, changing it is a time-consuming task.

Finally, we saw how to restore the objects from a stream. We also learned how to translate raw memory pointers so they work correctly, even after the game entities have been loaded in different memory locations.

SUGGESTED READING

In-game saves is not as glamorous a subject as using the latest pixel shaders for photorealistic effects, so we are left without much literature in the subject. The following books have some short but interesting sections on object serialization in games:

Eberly, David H., *3D Game Engine Design*, Morgan Kaufmann, 2000.
Brownlow, Marin, "Save Me Now!", *Game Programming Gems 3*, Charles River Media, 2002.

The original factory pattern is described in the Gang of Four book:

Gamma, Erich, et al., *Design Patterns*, Addison-Wesley, 1995.

DEALING WITH
LARGE PROJECTS

IN THIS CHAPTER

- Logical vs. Physical Structure
- Classes and Files
- Header Files
- Libraries
- Configurations

S o far in this book, we have covered logical concepts of game programming: memory allocation, plug-ins, or runtime type information. That knowledge will be adequate for a small project or a quick demo, but it will fall short when dealing with a full-size game project. Even the best data structures or slickest algorithms in the world will not help when a full compilation of the game takes over an hour, or when the process of releasing a gold candidate becomes cumbersome and error prone.

This chapter deals with the realities of working with a large code base for a game project. We will see why excessive dependencies between files should be avoided as much as possible and present some rules to improve that situation, as well as speed-up compile times. We will also deal with how projects should be structured to be able to easily create different versions of the game or deal with targets in different platforms.

By the end of this chapter, you should have enough tricks in your portfolio to feel confident enough to tackle a large game project.

LOGICAL VS. PHYSICAL STRUCTURE

The *logical structure* of a program, which is the only subject covered in most C++ books, deals with classes, algorithms, data, and their relationships. Clearly, the logical structure is crucial for the success of a program; the choice of data structures will determine how efficient the program is, and the relationship between classes will make it easier or harder to maintain and debug.

The *physical structure* of a program, on the other hand, deals with more concrete items, like files, directories, and even project or make files. It is a much less glamorous topic, and one that does not get the attention it deserves, but it becomes almost as important as the logical structure as the project size grows. The exact same program can be implemented with many different physical structures, but some of them will allow for fast compile times, easy expansion, and building of different targets; while others will cause extremely long and painful build times, and difficulty in creating different versions of the program.

Just to put things in perspective, let's look at some real numbers. A normal PC or console game project can easily have a code base on the order of 4,000–5,000 different files, all of which need to be compiled to create the game. That does not even count behemoths like massively multiplayer online games, which can have a code base many times that of a regular game, plus all the code for their servers, billing, backup, and so forth. With a project of that size, the physical structure of the program becomes crucial. A well-structured project will have compile times of perhaps 5–10 minutes, and small changes will require almost no recompilations. On the other hand, a badly structured project can easily run into compile times of over an hour, and even a minor change could trigger a compilation that lasts for 10 to 20 minutes. Which project would you rather work on?

Physical structure is determined by which files need other files in order to compile. In C++, needing another file means including that file through the `#include` preprocessor directive. In an ideal world, every file would compile by itself, but this is clearly not possible, since a program is made up of interacting objects, so they need to know about each other to a certain extent. Minimizing the number of connections between files is a goal toward achieving an acceptable physical structure. The level of connections between a file and the rest of the source code is called *insulation*, and the fewer connections, the more insulated the file will be.

Fortunately, a good physical structure goes hand in hand with a good logical structure. A class that hides its implementation from the outside world is said to be well-encapsulated. The better encapsulated a class is, and the less other classes depend on it, the cleaner the logical structure will be, with all the usual consequences: ease of maintenance, clear debugging, and simpler testing.

As a general rule, whenever a file is modified, all the files that included it will be considered modified and will need to be compiled. Ideally, a change to a single file should result in the recompilation of only one or two files. A really tangled physical structure will cause most of the files in the project to be recompiled as a result of an innocent-looking change to one file. The turnaround time in these situations, from making a change to being able to run the game and test the results, quickly becomes unbearable, and it can result in lower quality work, untested features, and hacked shortcuts in the code to avoid major recompilations.

The rest of this chapter looks at different aspects of physical structure. We will explain some possible organizations and solutions for achieving a good physical structure and maximizing programmer efficiency in a large-project environment.

CLASSES AND FILES

At the core of the physical structure of a program, we have files. Organizing them correctly is the first step toward an effective physical organization. A lot of this information is available just by browsing through existing C++ code; some of it is not as common, though, so it might come as a surprise.

This section should give you a solid understanding of how and why classes are split into different files.

In general, a good rule to follow is to have two files for every C++ class: one header file (usually with the extension .h or .hpp) and one implementation file (with the extension .cpp). This organization has several advantages. First, it is convenient to browse through the files and easy to locate a particular class just by looking at the file names. Even with fancy IDEs and other source browsing tools, such a simple system is still very useful.

Second, it strikes a good balance for minimizing compile times, especially incremental compile times, which are the ones we are most concerned about because we do them many times a day while we are developing new code or fixing bugs. If we had packed several classes per file, compile times would be faster, but we would have to compile more code, even for a simple change to one class. Splitting a class into more files would not have given us any extra advantages, since most likely the whole class would have to be compiled when a change is made.

Finally (and this is very subjective), having the full class implementation in one file seems like a perfect unit to work with. A file should hopefully never be so long as to become unmanageable and cause us to get lost, but it should also not be so small that it becomes meaningless. If your class ever starts to get so large that you feel the urge to split it into more files, chances are it should really be split into multiple classes.

HEADER FILES

A header class is the window through which the outside world looks into a class. The information there lets other code know about our class and how to use it, nothing else. A header file is used by other parts of the code, by using the #include directive in their own files.

What Goes into a Header File?

So, what should go in the header file? The quick answer is that the header file should have the minimum amount of code that still allows everything to compile and run correctly. That is easier said than done, especially if you are coming from a C background where header files were used to dump everything that was not implementation code.

Preprocessor #include statements are extremely important to the structure of the program and deserve a whole section devoted to them, so they will be the subject of the next section. For now, we will carefully ignore them in our discussion of header files.

As a first step, move any nonessential information out of the header file and into the implementation file. Constants that are only used in the class implementation, or small private structures or classes are good candidates to move out of a header file. Always ask yourself, is this something other classes need to interact with this class?

Unfortunately, C++ muddies the water a bit by forcing us to put some things in the header file that would be best placed in the implementation file. The whole private section of a class is only of interest to the class itself, yet we are forced to declare all private member functions and variables in the header file. This has the unfortunate consequences of leaking out some extra information through the header file. We will see some possible solutions to this problem in the next section.

Something else to keep in mind when creating header files is how they will be used in the rest of the program. Class header files are reasonably straightforward. They get included everywhere that the class is used. This is usually not a problem, and only a small number of files include a particular header file. However, sometimes there are special classes that we seem to need everywhere: an error class with all the error codes for the whole program, a resource file, or a header file with a lot of the text IDs for the translation table.

Header files that become that ubiquitous are dangerous, but they can be tolerated if they hardly ever change. However, if they are likely to change during the program development, they should be avoided as much as possible. A file containing all the global error codes is likely to be included everywhere and updated frequently as we add more error codes. For example, we decide we want to add a new error code to indicate that one of the network clients has dropped out. We add it to the header file, do a quick recompile to test our changes and find out to our dismay that it has triggered a full project rebuild. Every library, every DLL, and every single source code file in the game needs to be rebuilt. This could take up to several hours on really large projects.

Instead, a file like that would be best split into several unrelated files, each containing error codes for different subsystems. The graphics renderer could have one, the network code another, the file IO another. Adding a new network error code would simply cause a recompile of the network subsystem and a full link, and drastically decrease our time for the change to about five minutes.

Include Guards

An `#include` is a preprocessor directive. That means it is interpreted by the preprocessor, which gets its chance to modify the source code before the compiler ever sees it. In this case, the preprocessor scans every single file for the `#include "filename"` directive, opens up the specified filename, reads all its contents, and inserts them where the `include` statement is.

There really are no rules about only using the `#include` directive for header files. We can use it for anything: header files, implementation files, parts of a file, or any random text file. However, traditionally, `#include` is used to include header files only, with either class declarations, function declarations, or global constants and defines, although you will see some other different uses from time to time.

Basically, the following code:

```
// Game.h
#define MAX_PLAYERS    16

// Game.cpp
#include "Consts.h"
Players players[MAX_PLAYERS];
```

is transformed by the preprocessor into something like this:

```
// Game.cpp
#define MAX_PLAYERS    16
Players players[MAX_PLAYERS];
```

which is what the compiler sees and proceeds to compile.

There are some potential problems that can be caused by `#include` directives, which are not all that obvious at first. Consider the following extra header file and modification to the previous example:

```
// FrontEnd.h
#include "Game.h"
// Rest of the front end declarations...

// Game.cpp
#include "Consts.h"
#include "FontEnd.h"
Players players[MAX_PLAYERS];
```

Just by looking at `Game.h`, nobody would think that there is a problem; yet trying to compile that code will result in a compiler error. In this case, the compiler will complain about attempting to `#define` the same constant twice.

The problem is that the contents of the file `Game.h` were included twice in the same file. This is how it looks after the preprocessor is done with it:

```
// Game.cpp
#define MAX_PLAYERS    16
// Rest of the front-end declarations...
#define MAX_PLAYERS    16
Players players[MAX_PLAYERS];
```

Now it becomes very obvious that we are trying to define the constant `MAX_PLAYERS` twice. Without us realizing it, the preprocessor included the same file twice. Not only was it a waste of compilation time, but it led to compiler errors.

To solve that problem we use *include guards*. Include guards are preprocessor directives that prevent the same file from being included more than once in the same compilation unit. Include guards are used extensively in most C and C++ programs, and are usually implemented in this form:

```
// Game.h
#ifndef GAME_H_
#define GAME_H_

#define MAX_PLAYERS    16

#endif // #ifndef GAME_H_
```

If every header file has guards around it, we can guarantee that it will never be included twice. The first time the preprocessor includes it, the guard symbol (`GAME_H_` in this case, but it should be different with each header file) is not defined, so it immediately defines it and proceeds to include the rest of the file. The next time that we try to include the same file, the guard symbol will already be defined, and the preprocessor will skip that file completely.

The choice of the actual guard symbol is not that important, unless you have such a large code base that you can get duplicate guard symbols in the same compilation unit. Usually, just making a variation in the header file name itself is the simplest solution and works perfectly well for most projects.

One related technique you might come across when looking through source code is the use of the preprocessor directive #pragma once. That directive prevents the preprocessor from ever including (or even opening again) the file that contained #pragma once in the same compilation unit. So it seems to do the same job as our more cumbersome include guards by preventing a file from being included multiple times, but also prevents it from even being opened a second time, which should speed up compilation times somewhat.

As it turns out, #pragma once is not a particularly good substitute for include guards. Its main advantage is that it is clearer and easier to type, but that is about all. The major blow against it is that it is not part of the C++ standard. There are a fair number of C++ compilers that will understand it and apply it correctly, but not all of them. If you are doing multiplatform development, you should take this into consideration.

What you will often see is both of them used in the same file at once—the include guards to prevent double inclusion in compilers that do not support #pragma once, and #pragma once to avoid opening the file multiple times in compilers that do support it. Since not all compilers understand the #pragma once directive, it is usually surrounded by conditional statements that only allow its processing in compilers that support it. The typical header file is written this way:

```
#ifndef MYHEADERFILE_H_
#define MYHEADERFILE_H_

#if _MSC_VER > 1000
#pragma once
#endif // _MSC_VER > 1000

// Contents of the header file here
// ...

#endif // MYHEADERFILE_H_
```

In this case, the _MSC_VER > 100 means we only want to use #pragma once on Microsoft compilers after a certain version. This certainly did not save us any typing or make things cleaner and clearer. If it at least helped with compilation times, it would be bearable, even at the cost of having to modify all of the header files every time we add a new compiler that supports #pragma once.

As it turns out, most of the time `#pragma once` is not even necessary. Most preprocessors that understand the `#pragma once` directive are smart enough to detect the pattern of include guards and automatically avoid opening the same file multiple times. So in the end, just adding include guards to our header files is the best solution.

If you ever find yourself trying to debug a problem that you think might be caused by the preprocessor, you might want to turn to your compiler's documentation. Most compilers have a handy feature for saving out the source code the way it is after the preprocessor is done with, so that you get to see exactly what the compiler will process and compile. This will allow you to debug macro expansions more easily, or detect any strange or out-of-order inclusions.

Another handy utility provided by some compilers is a switch that will force the compiler to print out every included file in the order in which they are included. Not only is this handy for tracking down include problems, but you may discover that your innocent-looking class is pulling in hundreds of other header files all by itself.

Include Directives in .CPP Files

The `#include` directives totally determine the shape of a program. If your code is lean, efficient, and streamlined, or if it is an ugly beast of a program with long tentacles reaching to every single source file it is all due to the `#include` directives.

We want to minimize the amount of header files that are included in each implementation file, not only the actual `#include` statements in the .cpp file, but also any `#includes` in each of the header files pulled in. In some extreme cases, compiling a .cpp file could cause the inclusion of hundreds of header files. Just the time to access and open all of those files will probably be quite significant (a second or two per .cpp file). Multiply that times the number of .cpp files in the project, and all of a sudden we are talking about compile times of half an hour or more.

The first step toward minimizing how many files are included, and consequently compilation times, is to untangle the `#include` web and organize it in such a way that we can make sense out of it.

Usually, .cpp files include several header files at the very top of the file. The number of files included can range from just a couple to many dozens. Each `#include` directive will literally bring in all the contents of the file it refers to and add them to the file that included them. Then the file, with all the `#include` statements expanded out to their file contents, is compiled as normal.

A key observation is that the #include statements are expanded in place in the same order they appear in the code. Compilation also proceeds from top to bottom, so by the time the code contained in the second header file is compiled, it will have the knowledge of the contents of the first header file, but not of what is coming up in subsequent header files. This means that if we are not careful about how we organized our includes, the same header file could compile perfectly fine in one .cpp file, but fail to compile in another, just because of the #include statements that were preceding them.

We can untangle this seemingly complicated situation by following a very simple rule: in a .cpp file that contains the implementation for a class, the first included file must be the header file corresponding to that class. We will make an exception for this when dealing with precompiled headers later on, but otherwise you should consider it a universal rule.

Following this rule, our source code should look like this:

```
// MyClassA.h
class A
{
    // ...
};

// MyClassA.cpp
#include "MyClassA.h" // <- First include is the
                      //    header file for the class
#include "MyClassC.h"
#include "SomethingElse.h"

// The rest of MyClassA implementation
// ...
```

What exactly have we accomplished? We avoid ever having the problem of header files depend on other header files that came earlier. We guarantee that our header file will compile correctly, even if it is the first one in the inclusion list. By following this rule for all the classes, the order of the rest of the header files should not matter.

One of the consequences of this rule is that some header files will have to include other header files in order to compile properly. That is fine. If they needed those files, we might as well put the #include in the header file and not have to remember to include them in every .cpp file that uses them.

Include Directives in Header Files

First in the list of things to remove are any unnecessary #include statements from the header files themselves. It sounds strange, but unfortunately, it is far too common to have unnecessary #include statements cluttering up your headers. For example, some header files might have been included at some point, but then things changed, and they were not needed any more, but nobody remembered to remove the #include statements. It does not matter whether they were needed or not, you will pay the price every time you compile the program—so out with them. Only #include statements that cause the compilation to fail should be in the header file.

Once we have removed all the useless includes, we can turn our attention to the ones that are necessary, but can be replaced by other means. The only reason we include a file in a header file is because the header file uses something that was declared in the included file. For example, when one class derives from another, we must include the header file for the parent class.

```
// B.h
#include "A.h"

// B inherits from A, so we must include A here.
// There is no way around it
class B : public A
{
 // ...
};
```

Inheritance is one of those cases where we only have to include the header file for the parent class. There is simply no way around it, because the compiler needs to have seen the full parent class to know how to build the derived class correctly.

However, there are times when the compiler does not need to see the full declaration of a class; all it needs to know is that there is a class with that name. This situation happens whenever we are only using pointers or references to a class. As long as we assure the compiler that there is a class of that name, we do not need to include that class declaration. Instead, we use a *forward declaration* with the class name. Consider the following two files describing the class GameCamera:

```
// GameCamera.h
#include "GameEntity.h"
```

```
#include "GamePlayer.h"

class GameCamera : public GameEntity
{
    GamePlayer * GetPlayer();
private:
    GamePlayer * m_pPlayer;
};

// GameCamera.cpp
#include "GameCamera.h"

// Rest of GameCamera implementation...
```

At first glance, it might appear that the two #include statements in the GameCamera.h file are necessary. Clearly, the first one is necessary, since GameEntity is the parent class. On the other hand, the only reason we had to include GamePlayer.h is because we use a few pointers to objects of that class in the functions and as a member variable. Since they are only pointers, we can use a forward declaration and avoid including the file altogether.

```
// GameCamera.h
#include "GameEntity.h"
class GamePlayer;      // Forward declaration is enough

class GameCamera : public GameEntity
{
    GamePlayer * GetPlayer();
private:
    GamePlayer * m_pPlayer;
};

// GameCamera.cpp
#include "GameCamera.h"
#include "GamePlayer.h"

// Rest of GameCamera implementation...
```

Notice that when we removed the #include statement from the header file, we had to add it to the implementation file. That is because GameCamera uses the GamePlayer somewhere in its implementation, and that requires that the compiler sees the GamePlayer class declaration.

Notice that we could have saved an #include statement in the header file, but we moved it to the implementation file instead. What kind of gain is that? It is a tremendous gain, actually. Imagine that 100 other classes need to include GameCamera.h. By removing the #include of Game-Player.h from GameCamera.h into GameCamera.cpp, we prevented the Game-Player.h file from being opened and included 100 times during the compilation of the program. If GamePlayer.h in turn included 10 other files, then we prevented the opening and reading of 1,000 files! Instead, now GamePlayer.h is only included in the GameCapera.cpp file, which gets compiled only once. Imagine applying that simple example across the thousands of files that make up a project, and you can start seeing the huge difference that proper use of forward declaration can make in the physical structure and compilation times of a large project.

Precompiled Headers

Even after all of our code follows the inclusion rules presented in this chapter, we might still notice how many of our files include the same headers over and over because a large section of our code depends on the C standard library header files, STL, Windows, OpenGL, or any other common API. So every file ends up including some of the same headers:

```
// MyClass.cpp
#include "MyClass.h"
#include <vector.h>
#include <list.h>
#include <algorithm.h>
#include <stdio>
#include <windows.h>

// Now we can start including the other files from our code
#include "MyClass2.h"
#include "MyClass3.h"
```

This is even worse than it seems, because those large APIs typically have really large and complex header files, which can in turn include many other files. The most frustrating part is that we know those header files are not going to change during development. Yet we keep including and processing them every time we compile any file. Compile times could slow to a crawl in a situation like this.

Fortunately, several compilers provide a solution: *precompiled headers*. Granted, precompiled headers is an option that is available only in specific compilers, so you cannot rely on it across multiple platforms. Still, it is such an incredibly useful feature, that it is well worth taking advantage of it whenever possible. If you are not sure about your specific compiler, check the documentation, and find out how to turn it on.

What exactly are precompiled headers? It is more or less what it sounds like. With this option turned on, some files will be compiled only once, and the results will be saved to disk for later use during the compilation of the rest of the program and subsequent compilations. This means that all the headers included by the files that are used to create the precompiled headers will only be loaded and processed once.

Additionally, every time the program is compiled, as long as none of the files used to generate the precompiled headers have changed, the same generated precompiled header file can be used without the need to compile it again. This is an ideal situation for those large, external API header files that just about every file in our program depends on. They get compiled once, and from there on, they are almost free as far as compilation time goes.

Different compilers will have different rules on how a file can take advantage of the precompiled headers. In the case of Microsoft's compilers, you have to make sure you include a specific header file as the first inclusion in your .cpp file. Check your compiler documentation for all the details. This is the only allowable exception to the inclusion rule that the first include statement in the .cpp file for a class must be the header file for that class. Using precompiled headers, a normal .cpp file would look like this:

```
// MyClassA.cpp
#include "precomp.h"  // Precompiled header files
#include "MyClassA.h" // First real include is the
                      // header file for the class
#include "MyClassC.h"
#include "SomethingElse.h"

// The rest of MyClassA implementation
// ...
```

The effects of precompiled headers can be dramatic, so it is well worth investigating their usage for your project if you are not doing so already. It is possible for a project to compile 10 times faster with precompiled headers than without it, depending on how the project was structured to start with and how much it uses other large header files. In a less extreme case, you might still expect compile times to be two to three times faster when using precompiled headers.

The major drawback of precompiled headers is that since including headers is pretty much free, the amount of headers included that way will grow over the course of the project. This means that every file that uses precompiled headers (which ends up being most of them) will automatically know about all the files that are part of the precompiled headers. This is not a bad thing in itself, because it does not increase compilation times, but it makes header files available to source files that were never intended to know anything about them.

For example, adding windows.h to the precompiled header section will cause every file that uses precompiled headers to know about all the Windows structures, constants, and functions. It will only be a matter of time before you start seeing functions and data types popping up all over the program. If you are doing multiplatform development, this will be a good way to break the build on other platforms; even worse, if you are not currently working on multiple platforms, whenever you decide to port your code, you might be in for a bit of a shock.

In addition to bringing in more information than necessary, the other drawback of relying on precompiled headers in is switching between platforms or compilers. The code will still compile fine without precompiled header support, since each file includes the precompiled header file pre-comp.h, which in turn includes all the needed header files. The problem is that precomp.h includes all the big header files that the entire program needs, not just the ones that each individual .cpp file requires. This means that if a project was laid out with the usage of precompiled headers in mind, compiling it without precompiled headers will probably result in significantly slower compilation times than if it had been laid out without precompiled headers from the start.

To alleviate this problem, we can substitute the inclusion of the precompiled header file with the minimum amount of inclusions necessary to compile that file in the case of platforms that do not support precompiled headers—something along these lines:

```
// Precomp.h
#include "LargeAPI1.h"
#include "LargeAPI2.h"
#include "LargeAPI3.h"
#include "LargeAPI4.h"
#include "LargeAPI5.h"

// MyClassA.cpp
#ifdef PRECOMP_SUPPORT
#include "precomp.h"
```

```
#else
// This file only needs LargeAPI3.h
#include "LargeAPI3.h"
#endif

#include "MyClassA.h"
#include "MyClassC.h"
#include "SomethingElse.h"

// The rest of MyClassA implementation
// ...
```

The Pimpl Pattern

If you have followed all the advice up to now, your header files should be self-sufficient (they do not rely on another header file being included for them), should only be included once, and should have the minimum number of includes that still allows them to be compiled correctly. In addition to all that, you should be using precompiled headers effectively if your compiler supports them.

It is possible that, even given all that restructuring of header files, a large project will still compile very slowly, or that small changes will often trigger long compilations. We really need to do something about these issues. Nobody likes working with projects that take several minutes to compile a minor change, or that require you to go out to lunch every time you do a full compile.

The problem is probably still caused by too many tangled headers. This might be a good moment to see if your compiler has a switch to display all included files in the order the preprocessor opens them. If every .cpp file ends up including dozens or hundreds of header files, we can probably improve on our design. If, on the other hand, only a handful of files are included per .cpp file, then the problem lies elsewhere. Maybe you just have a lot of code, and it simply takes a long time to compile it. In that case, upgrading your hardware to a faster CPU and faster hard drives might be more beneficial than any another solution.

Before attempting to improve the physical organization, have a good look to see if the project would benefit from a better logical organization. If the whole game is just one huge project with several thousand files, it will probably benefit from some subdivision into smaller, more self-contained systems. Some of the systems that should be able to be isolated are rendering, input, sound, AI, collision, and physics.

A project that is divided into several fairly independent subsystems has many advantages (which we will see in more detail later in this chapter). One of the major benefits is the reduced physical dependencies between files on different subsystems. In particular, if the subsystems use abstract interfaces or a facade patterns to hide their contents from the rest of the world, then the only physical dependencies we need to worry about are the ones between files within the same subsystem, which becomes much more manageable.

Assuming that the problem is still due to too many include files, the Pimpl pattern might help. Pimpl, which stands for Private IMPLementation, is also known as the Cheshire Cat pattern. Let's first look at an example of a situation that might be helped with a Pimpl. Consider a minor variation on our previous `GameCamera.h` header file:

```
// GameCamera.h
#include "GameEntity.h"
#include "CameraLens.h"
class GamePlayer;

class GameCamera : public GameEntity
{
    GamePlayer * GetPlayer();
private:
    GamePlayer * m_pPlayer;
    CameraLens m_lens;
};
```

The only difference from the previous `GameCamera` header file is that now we show an extra member variable, `m_lens`, which represents the camera lens that the camera is using. By default, it can just be a totally transparent lens, but we could use colored lenses to give the whole scene a specific tint, a black and white lens to filter out all the color, or even some sort of dynamic lens that we can use to flash the screen with red patterns whenever the player gets hit. Even better would be the ability to have multiple lenses at once, but we are restricting ourselves to one in order to keep the example as simple as possible.

A consequence of adding the `m_lens` variable to the header file is that now we are forced to include the header file that contains the declaration of the `CameraLens` class. We cannot just do a forward declaration, because we are dealing with a full variable, not just a pointer or a reference. The same thing will happen for every variable we add to the class.

This is particularly frustrating, because `m_lens` is a private variable. That means that only the `GameCamera` class will have access to it, so it is frustrating to have to include the header file for `CameraLens` in the `Game-Camera.h` file and force everybody that uses the camera to include it as well. We saw how the inclusion of files can proliferate if `GameCamera` is a 'popular' class that is used in many places in the code.

The Pimpl pattern allows us to avoid including files that are only required by private variables in our header file. We accomplish this by putting all the private implementation inside a simple structure and taking care of creating it and destroying it along with the object. This is how a Pimpl that contains the camera lens would look for the `GameEntity` class:

```cpp
// GameCamera.h
#include "GameEntity.h"
class GamePlayer;

class GameCamera : public GameEntity
{
    GamePlayer * GetPlayer();
private:
    GamePlayer * m_pPlayer;

    class PIMPL;
    PIMPL * pimpl;
};

// GameCamera.cpp
#include "GameCamera.h"
#include "GamePlayer.h"
#include "CameraLens.h"

struct GameCamera::PIMPL
{
    CameraLens m_lens;
};

GameCamera::GameCamera()
{
    pimpl = new PIMPL;
}

GameCamera::~GameCamera()
{
    delete pimpl;
```

```
}

        // Rest of GameCamera implementation...
```

Notice that now we were able to remove the inclusion of `CameraLens.h` from the header file, which was our goal. If we had any more private variables that would require including other files, we would add those to the Pimpl structure as well.

By using the Pimpl pattern, we have traded a reduction in the physical dependencies between classes for a bit of extra complexity and the dynamic allocation of the private implementation of the object. The extra complexity is not too bad. The Pimpl only needs to be created once, regardless of how many variables it contains, and accessing one of those variables just requires prefixing them with the name of the Pimpl object.

The more worrisome drawback is the dynamic memory allocation caused by every object that uses the Pimpl pattern. This might be perfectly fine for large objects with relatively few instances, but it might cause problems for small objects with many hundreds or thousands of instances. If we still want to use the Pimpl pattern in these cases, we might want to use a memory-pooling system like the ones described in Chapter 7.

LIBRARIES

The techniques that work with a small code base often break down when dealing with a large project. Most of the source code examples you will find with APIs, or those available on the Internet, are very small and are simply thrown together to demonstrate some particular feature or illustrate a point. Because of their size, these small projects are structured as a single system that compiles into an executable.

This approach works fine for a relatively small code base, but it quickly becomes inadequate for a larger project of the size of most games produced today. The dependencies between files quickly become unmanageable, compile times go up, things that should be simple become very complicated, and programmers suffer.

When dealing with large projects, it is usually a much better approach to break down the massive code base into relatively independent subsystems. Each subsystem is a set of related source code that has a logical, cohesive objective. It exposes the minimum amount of functionality to the outside world, but still allows everybody to use it to its full extent. Subsystems are compiled separately from the main executable and create a static or dynamic library. That library is then linked with the main executable to create the full program. Some of the perfect candidates that come up often during game development that can be split into separate libraries are memory management, graphics rendering, input handling, collision detection and physics response, animation, music and sound playback, user interface widgets, and generic AI functions.

The first advantage of separating subsystems into libraries in this way is the reduced dependency between classes and between files, so we improve both the logical and the physical structure of the project. Figure 15.1 illustrates how dependencies are reduced by separating a project into libraries, thus presenting a simple interface to the rest of the code.

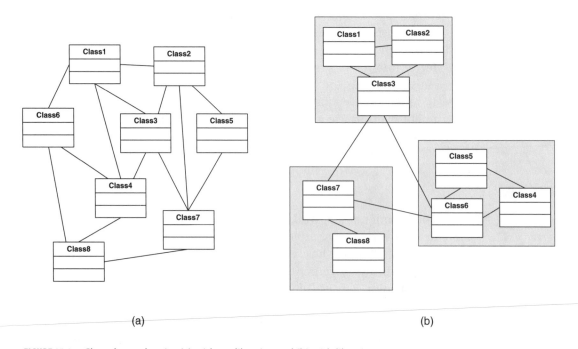

(a)   (b)

FIGURE 15.1   Class dependencies (a) without libraries and (b) with libraries.

The same effect can be achieved without a subdivision into libraries, but it will be much more difficult to maintain. Programmers have to be constantly aware of the artificial divisions they are trying to enforce, because in any real project, things will degenerate very quickly into a mass of chaotic dependencies. By explicitly creating subsystems, we are enforcing that subdivision and making sure no extra dependencies are introduced.

Now that we have a higher-level view of the project by looking at the libraries, it should be possible to determine which libraries depend on other libraries. One very desirable, but not absolutely necessary, property is to make sure that there are no cyclical dependencies between libraries. That is, libraries can depend on other libraries 'below' them, but no library shoulddepend on a library 'above' them. An example of correctly organized libraries is shown in Figure 15.2.

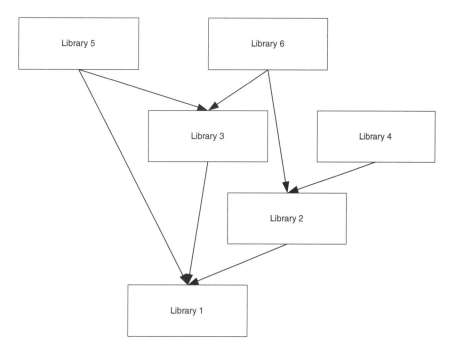

FIGURE 15.2   Library dependency without cycles.

When libraries are organized this way, we keep the code base from being a confusing mass. Instead, we can treat any section of the code independently of the rest by taking one library and including all the libraries it depends on, all the way to the bottom. There are many beneficial consequences of such an organization:

• We can test each library in isolation, working our way from the bottom up. This is particularly useful when trying to isolate a bug, and we have no idea whether it is being caused by a low-level library or something much higher up. We can even create simple test applications that rely on a small subset of the libraries to test certain behaviors.

- In-house tools can pick and choose what libraries they need. When dealing with a big mass of code, tools tend to either include all the game code (with the subsequent bloating, slowness, and restrictions) or not share any code at all with the game, which prevents us from seeing things exactly as they will behave in the game, and which requires us to write a lot of duplicate code. With a layered library approach, a tool that only needs the graphics renderer can include that library plus all the libraries all the way down, but no more. A more complex tool could include a few more libraries, and a tool that requires virtually all of the game functionality could include most libraries and the game code.

- It becomes easier to share already-built code. With a layered library system, it is possible to build some of the lower-level libraries and distribute them to the rest of the team. That way, programmers (as long as they are making localized changes) only need to build the libraries they are working with, not the whole project. By itself, this can mean considerable time savings. To take the idea even further, an automated build system could do a full build of all the libraries and game code every night, and make the compiled versions available to all the programmers every morning.

- Separating engine and game-specific code becomes easier. When code is structured in relatively independent libraries, the game-engine boundary becomes a natural separation point. As a consequence, with little effort, there will be some libraries that are completely game-independent, and some will be totally game-specific. That allows much easier code reuse across different projects and even makes it easier to start a new project with an existing code base, since it is very clear what code was game-specific and needs to be replaced.

- We can take a modular approach to the code. If the code is structured in separate libraries, it becomes relatively easy to replace a whole library with a new implementation. That allows us to customize many parts of the engine, as well as the game itself for the current project. For example, we could replace an portal visibility system with a quadtree-based one just by swapping libraries, and almost no other code changes would be necessary. It also makes multiplatform development a lot easier by allowing us to replace platform-specific libraries with new libraries for the new target platform.

CONFIGURATIONS

In a real project situation, it is not enough to be able to compile the game only one way. You will want to compile it with different settings for different uses. Each of these different settings is called a *configuration*. Each configuration will use different levels of error reporting, code optimizations, and debug facilities.

It is often a good idea to add a postfix to all the executables and libraries produced by each configuration, instead of all of them having the same name. That way, we can have several executables of the game in the same directory and run whichever one is appropriate.

It is fairly common to have at least two configurations per project: debug and release.

Debug Configuration

The debug configuration is usually intended to be used only by programmers when they are debugging the program or adding new features. Compiler optimizations are completely disabled, and all the debug information is included. That makes stepping into the program with a debugger very easy, and all variables are easily accessible from the debugger's watch windows.

This configuration can also have all sorts of guards and protections enabled, at the expense of performance, to catch whenever there is a logic bug in the code. For example, this version could automatically do bounds checking with every array access, or it could fill freed memory with a certain bit pattern to make it easier to find situations where pointers lead to memory that has been released.

Performance in this configuration is going to be poor, easily two to four times slower than the final product. This will make things slow enough that playing the game might not be particularly easy due to the low frame rate, but performance is not the focus of this configuration. Also, the debug configuration will typically require more memory to run, since it has extra code as well as all the debugging symbols.

Release Configuration

This is the opposite of the debug configuration. All the optimizations are on, all the debugging aids are removed, all the guards and safety tricks are gone. The executable that comes out of this configuration is what is usually sent to the manufacturer to create the CD-ROMs, DVDs, or cartridges of the final product. This is what the end user will get.

Performance is as good as it is going to get, but trying to debug this configuration is virtually impossible. Also, if all the debugging code has been removed and the game crashes, it might not report any useful information to help track down the bug.

Debug-Optimized Configuration

The debug and release configurations are opposite extremes. They are both useful, but we need some intermediate solution. This intermediate configuration strikes a balance between performance and debugging facilities, and chances are that most of the work with the game will be done using it.

This configuration often has code-debugging information, as well as all the debugging tools, like in-game consoles or full error reporting, but it also has all the optimizations turned on, which allows it to run at close to full speed. This configuration will use more memory than the release version, because it has all the debugging symbols.

Some projects will use another intermediate configuration, one without any debugging information, but which can still produce meaningful error reports whenever the game crashes. This version can be used to iron out any problems that appear only in the release configuration. Depending on your game and platform, sometimes the shipped version of the game is intended to have some level of error reporting; in which case, error reporting would be built into the release configuration, and there would be no need for an intermediate version.

CONCLUSION

In this chapter, we saw the difference between the physical and logical structure of the source code, and how it is possible to have a good logical structure yet still have a bad physical one. The physical structure refers to the relationship between files, not classes. A good physical structure will result in fast compile times, short recompilations for small changes, and easier testing and maintainability of the code. Physical structure plays a much more important role in large projects than in small demos.

We then saw the proposed organization of classes into two files: one for the class declaration and one for the implementation. The management of header file inclusions is at the heart of a good physical structure, so we saw several suggested rules to tame the potential tangle of includes, how to minimize the number of header files included, and how to avoid having header files that depend on other header files. We also covered two techniques that help with compilation times: precompiled headers and the Pimpl pattern.

Having a good higher-level organization of the project,with it divided into relatively independent libraries and with a clear dependency chain, can have many benefits, such as code reuse, replacement of libraries, ease of testing, or the potential to only use part of the libraries when building tools or running tests.

Finally, any project of a reasonable size needs to have multiple configurations that produce different executables or libraries. The most common are debug, optimized debug, and release.

SUGGESTED READING

The great majority of the C++ literature seems to only cover the logical structure of the program. These are a few of the books that actually cover the physical structure in any depth. John Lakos' book is especially detailed.

Lakos, John, *Large Scale C++ Software Design*, Addison-Wesley, 1996.
Stroustrup, Bjarne, *The C++ Programming Language*, 3rd ed., Addison-Wesley, 1997.

The following book is a true classic and has many useful patterns. Of relevance to this chapter is its discussion of the facade pattern, used to reduce the number of dependencies to files in one library or module.

Gamma, Erich, et al., *Design Patterns*, Addison-Wesley, 1995.

There are many articles and books that talk about Herb Sutter's Pimpl pattern. The following book offers several chapters on that topic.

Sutter, Herb, *Exceptional C++*, Addison-Wesley, 2000.

CRASH-PROOFING YOUR GAME

IN THIS CHAPTER

- Using Asserts
- Keep the Machine Fresh
- Deal with 'Bad' Data

A s you have most likely realized by now, C++ is not forgiving. We have to be very explicit about what we want it to do. Sometimes, against all principles of good software engineering, we even have to be redundant, such as when writing both the function name and arguments in the declaration and definition of the function.

C++ is just as unforgiving at runtime. A minor miscalculation on our part, and the program will at best crash with some cryptic message; at worst it will lock up the user's computer (and make it more likely for them to uninstall our game and return it to the store right away).

Obviously, we would like to avoid the latter situation as much as possible. This chapter deals with several techniques we can apply to crash-proof our game. We will see the most effective use of asserts to catch bugs as soon as they happen, how to keep the machine fresh to avoid bugs that creep up after running for a while, and how to deal with bad data in our own functions without wasting performance or sacrificing safety.

USING ASSERTS

The assert function is part of the standard C++ library and will soon become one of your favorite tools. Put simply, all it does is stop the program right away if the condition does not evaluate to true.

When to Use Asserts

If we are trying to crash-proof the game, why would we want to use asserts? In a way, we are 'crashing' the program ourselves in order to avoid having it crash by itself. The main difference is that we are doing it in a much more controlled manner, collecting useful information for debugging, and doing it as close as possible to the source of the problem. There is nothing more frustrating that tracking down a crash produced by something that occurred several frames ago and that went by completely unnoticed. By asserting often, we will know as soon as something goes wrong, and it will make debugging much easier.

These are the most frequent scenarios for an effective use of assert:

- **Stop the program if the parameters passed to a function are something that we cannot (or do not want to) deal with.** Not every function has to deal with all possible combinations of parameters, especially private functions of a class or functions that are not exposed to the final user. Catching the misuse of a function right away is much better than letting it follow the old adage of garbage in, garbage out.

This scenario is often called checking the preconditions of a function. Each function has a set of preconditions, and if they are not met, the function will not be executed.

For example, consider a function that adds an object to the player's inventory. This function takes a pointer to a game object. To make things simple, we decided early on that it is illegal to pass a NULL pointer to that function, since it makes no sense, and we would never want to do that. Using assert at the top of the function makes sure that the pointer is not NULL.

```
void Inventory::AddItem (Item * pItem) {
    assert(pItem != NULL);
    // Add it to the inventory here, since now we
    // know for sure it's not NULL
    // ...
}
```

- **Check that the program is in a consistent state.** Sometimes before we do an operation, we want to make sure that it is safe to go ahead and perform that action. By using an assert in that situation, we catch a problem before it even surfaces. This is also useful as a future safeguard: we know what we are doing right now, so the checking might be unnecessary, but chances are the code will be updated in the future. At that point, having those extra asserts could make a huge difference in finding problems early on.

  Take as an example the function that handles a game entity's death. We know from past experience that sometimes several kill messages can sneak through, but it is not supposed to happen, so we guard against that eventuality. That way if it happens, instead of either ignoring it or having something unexpected happen, we can just deal with it right away and fix the bug.

```
void GameEntity::HandleKillMessage (const Msg & msg) {
    assert (!IsDead());
    SetIsDead (true);
    // Do the rest of the killing process here...
}
```

- **Check that a complicated algorithm is working the way we expect.** These are also commonly referred as "sanity checks." We know that something should be in a certain state after we perform a set of operations, but because it is somewhat complicated, it is hard to say for certain that it will always be true. To make really sure, we can insert an assert call, and we will know right away if it ever fails.

These are postconditions, the counterparts of preconditions. Like preconditions, they check that certain conditions are true, but unlike preconditions, they happen at the end of a function or a code segment instead of the beginning. Checking them is not as crucial as checking the preconditions, but they will help catch bugs during development and will make us feel more confident that the code is working as it should.

The following function processes all the messages in the queue. However, as a message is processed, more messages may be sent. A postcondition for this function states that there should be no more messages in the queue when the function finishes. We can express that postcondition with an assert.

```
void MsgQueue::ProcessAll() {
    // Do all the processing here. Maybe from different
    // queues, so it isn't a straightforward process
    // ...

    // Before we finish, double check that there are no
    // messages left.
    assert (IsEmpty());
}
```

- **Stop the program if a function fails and we cannot recover.** Something bad has happened—really bad. We have tried to allocate a block of memory, and a NULL pointer was returned, or we tried to move an enemy entity only to realize that that entity does not exist anymore. Obviously, there is a major problem in the code. Now is the time for an assert so the problem can be fixed right away.

Sometimes we would like our programs to detect parts that fail and recover gracefully. That is a nice goal, but often unnecessary for games. It does not mean we never want to recover, though; see the next section for advice on when not to use asserts.

When Not to Use Asserts

So far, it seems that we should use asserts as soon as something unexpected happens. That is generally true, but there are some situations in which we want to handle errors gracefully.

A good rule of thumb is that a designer or an artist should never be able to trigger an assert (or even worse, crash the program outright) unless they come up against a code bug. In other words, someone using our game or tools should not be able to crash it. If we follow that rule, we will make everybody happier and will minimize the downtime caused by nonfunctional games and tools. What does this mean? It means we should not assert in the following situations:

- **Trying to open or load a file that does not exist.**
- **Trying to load a file of the wrong format or an older version.** This does not mean we have to support old versions forever, just that we should handle them without stopping the program.
- **Entering 'bad' data.** For example, if the users can specify a near and far plane for the camera settings, and they enter a smaller number for the far plane than for the near plane. The best method would be to prevent the user from doing that to begin with through the user interface, rather than through `assert`.
- **One of the objects in the game did not load correctly.** If it is not a required object to run the game, we should put in a warning message and then run the game as usual. If it is a required one (like a player camera), then we should print a message explaining the problem and stop. That will still be better than an assert when the level designers see it come up.

On the other hand, if a tester manages to make his character walk into a room that doesn't exist, this is a perfect time to assert, since it is something that should not be possible to do. What it all boils down to is that asserts are messages by programmers for programmers. If ever an assert is triggered, it should be up to a programmer to fix it, and right away.

Custom Asserts

It is great that `assert` is part of the standard C++ library. It is a very handy function that we can use right away. However, once we start using it extensively in a large project, it becomes clear that it is too simple, and we would like to get more functionality out of it. It is time to roll our own `assert`.

What we want is more information and more flexibility. Remember that asserts are messages for programmers. If they happen while we are running the game from the debugger, we do not need much more than what the default assert function already gives us. However, if they happen while the testing department is hammering on the game, then we need all the information we can get to try to identify the problem. Even if they are running the game from the debugger, there might not be any programmers around that can look into the crash right away, so displaying all the relevant information becomes even more important.

Specifically, these are some of the options we might want to consider having in a custom `assert`:

- **Gather and display more information on the screen.** The default `assert` will stop the program, show the failed condition, and perhaps display the file and the line number where the error occurred. This is not bad for a start, but we might want more, such as the ability to see the call stack, the register state, or the build version.
- **Save information to a file.** Not only do we want to display information, but we probably want to save all that information and more to a file so it can be easily e-mailed to the right person or added to the bug database to be fixed later. In the file, we want to have the same information as it was displayed on the screen, and maybe a code and memory dump of some potentially interesting places (e.g., stack, instruction pointer, etc.) to investigate.

  This can be taken a step further: do a core dump, or the equivalent, in our working platform. A core dump is a binary snapshot of the state of the machine that allows a programmer to restore that state in a different machine later on for debugging purposes.
- **E-mail information directly.** A nice touch is to enable all the assert information to be e-mailed right from the assert display. This is usually only feasible from a PC, and not a game console, but it is very handy and worth considering. Alternatively, if you have a bug database, you can provide the option to enter it directly in the bug database, along with the comments from the testers, describing the situation that led to the assert.

An option that often comes up when considering custom asserts is the ability to continue even after an assert goes off. The argument for adding that option is that sometimes it is possible to continue running the game, even though one assert was triggered, so why force people to stop? This is typically a bad idea for several reasons.

First of all, asserts are indicating absolute conditions that must be true in order for the program to continue. The code will rely on that for its proper execution, so continuing if an assert condition is not met is an almost guaranteed failure. In the presence of nonstopping asserts, people will stop relying on the conditions that have been asserted, and are forced to check for them in the code. That will make the code messier, more bloated, slower, and much harder to maintain.

Another consequence of nonstopping asserts is that they will inevitably be used to flag errors and warning messages. For example, if a file does not exist, or an object is not initialized correctly, instead of coming up with a correct error-reporting scheme, programmers under pressure might instead choose to put in a nonstopping assert and let people press the "continue" button to move on. This causes numerous problems. Error messages are not batched, so there might be hundreds of assert boxes to wade through before we can play the level. The errors might not be reported and saved correctly, or real asserts might be lost in the shuffle among all the meaningless ones.

Finally, the worst problem of all. If the program crashes some time after a nonstopping assert was bypassed, it will be very hard to determine whether it was because of a bug in the code or whether it was because the testing continued after an assert was triggered.

What to Do in the Final Release?

Typically, all the `assert` calls are automatically removed in the final build. The reasoning is that all the bugs have been ironed out, and leaving the asserts in will only slow down the game and make its memory footprint larger (due to all the `assert` statements and messages associated with them). In other words, it would be best to have the game act unusually or crash, rather than show an assert message to the player.

Unfortunately, the issue is not that straightforward. What we decide to do will depend on our target platform and our development plans.

The big problem is that no matter how much testing we have done on the game, somebody is going to come across a situation that will trigger an assert. If you find that hard to believe, consider this possible scenario: imagine we have a large testing department, and we have 40 people hammering on the game for 20 weeks, 40 hours per week. (We will gloss over the fact that the game will be changing over those 20 weeks, and will consider this a best-case scenario.) That is a total of 32,000 man-hours of testing, which translates to about three and a half years.

After we are confident we have removed all the bugs, the game is released and becomes an instant hit: one million copies are sold in the first month. Now we have one million people playing the game on an average of one hour per day for two weeks. That works out to 14 million hours, or 1,639 years of testing—three orders of magnitude more time than was spent in our exhaustive testing. That is only in the first month. These numbers are very conservative; they could in reality be much higher, depending on sales and how much people play. In addition, those assumptions do not take into account different user configurations, incompatible hardware, or defective media.

Things might be improved a bit by doing open beta tests, but that is not always feasible (e.g., with console games). Also, with beta tests, you will probably only be testing a small fraction of the game; so bugs are bound to show up in other parts that did not receive the same attention.

In other words, it is virtually impossible to ship a game without bugs. So let's accept it, get over it, and do our best to deal with it.

We need to think about how we are going to deal with the bugs once the game has been released. Just because we admit that we are going to ship a game with bugs does not mean we have an excuse for not fixing them or for shipping a game that we know has bugs. We still want to do everything in our power fix every single bug; but we have to accept the fact that we will not find them all.

As previously mentioned an all-too-common way of dealing with bugs is simply to ignore them. All the `assert` calls are removed, and we hope for the best. However, if something goes wrong, it might simply cause some weird behavior, but it can also freeze the game, which is not a good experience for the player.

As an alternative, especially for the PC platform where patching games is very common, we could leave the asserts in, along with the ability to e-mail all the crash information to us, including information about the user's system configuration and driver versions, with the click of a button. After the first few weeks of the game's release, we can process all these reports and iron out most of the problems. This is a particularly attractive option for PC games, because there is so much variation in user configurations that it is completely impossible to test even a good sample of them before the game ships.

Console configurations are much more limited, so hardware testing can be much more thorough. Besides, in the console world, patching is not as accepted, even if it is possible, so patching is probably not a viable option.

If we do not want to report the assert to the player, but at the same time we do not want a crash, what can we do? There is no obvious answer. Here are some possibilities that you should consider:

- **Recover from the error.** If we have an assert in the graphics subsystem, we can try shutting it down completely, restarting it, and continuing the game from there. This is a very difficult option to implement, since once we get an assert, the state of the system could already be compromised.

- **Restart the console.** We could try saving the game (assuming that the assert does not affect the integrity of the game-save data), reboot the console, and reload it as quickly as possible. The player will get an interruption of a few seconds, but this is clearly a much better option than crashing.
- **Finish the level.** If something bad happens, we could just finish the level and bring them back to the front end. We could even make up an in-game reason for ending the level early.

An intermediate solution is to remove the asserts completely in the final release, but deal with all uncaught exceptions. By removing the asserts, we hope for the best. Maybe a situation will arise that would have triggered an assert, but it does not cause the game to crash. However, if something really bad happens, depending on your platform, there is a good chance that it might result in an exception (e.g., accessing an incorrect section of memory, using the hardware incorrectly, etc.). We can then catch that exception and try to do the best we can with it.

Sample Custom Assert Implementation

Whichever method we end up choosing for dealing with errors once the game is released, it is clear that having a custom version of assert is very useful. We also want to be able to change the actual implementation of assert depending on the type of build, with the option to disable it completely and totally remove all performance costs.

This sample implementation is only enabled in debug builds, and it is totally turned off in release builds. We have the flexibility to turn it on and off independently of the build type, through the preprocessor define DO_ASSERT.

```
#ifdef _DEBUG
#define DO_ASSERT
#endif

#ifdef DO_ASSERT
#define Assert(exp,text) \
    if (!(exp) && MyAssert(exp,text,__FILE__,__LINE__)) \
        _asm int 3;
#else
#define Assert(exp,text)
#endif
```

The way the macro works is that it always evaluates the expression, and if it is `false`, it calls our own function `MyAssert` with the expression that failed, the explanatory text, and the file and line where the assertion occurred. If the function wants to stop the execution of the program and break into the debugger, it can return `true`, otherwise it can return `false`, and the program will continue executing as normal. That is the purpose of the `_asm int 3` line after the `if` statement. In a PC, this will cause the program to break into the debugger. If there is no debugger hooked up, the call will be ignored and the program will resume execution. Other platforms have similar functionality that will allow you to break the debugger execution. By having the `_asm int 3` line in the macro itself, the debugger will break at the line with the `assert` call itself, not in some internal implementation file like the standard `assert` function does.

What the `MyAssert` function does is totally up to us. It can simply print the explanatory text to the debug channel, along with the file name and line number, or it can bring up a fancy dialog box with that information, or it can simply save it to a file for future processing.

Keep the Machine Fresh

This situation is not uncommon: the game will run without any problems for quite a while; then testing starts, reporting crashes after five, six, or even more hours of continuous playing. What is going on?

These can be some of the most frustrating and difficult bugs to fix, because they are not easy to reproduce. They only happen after a lot of continuous play; maybe a few hours if we are lucky, maybe after a few days if we aren't. These errors are can be caused by several reasons.

Memory Leaks

Memory leaks are unfortunately all too common in C++. Some bytes are allocated dynamically and are never released. The big offenders are usually caught pretty quickly during development, but sometimes there are just a few bytes that sneak through. They have no ill effect in the short term, but once they start accumulating, they can bring a system to its knees. The system will eventually run out of memory and crash, or it will start swapping out virtual memory and suffer a major performance hit.

Imagine that we are leaking 200 bytes every second (maybe as the AI is refreshing its pathfinding information). That is a leak of 4.5 MB in five hours. This might not be much for a PC with a large amount of RAM, but it will certainly be a big problem in a console with much more limited resources. If the leak happens not once every second but once per frame, even a small amount of bytes can be a huge problem for even a PC in just a few hours.

Memory Fragmentation

Dynamic memory is allocated from a heap. At first, all memory in the heap is available for allocation in one large, contiguous block. As requests to allocate and free memory blocks are made, the heaps will become fragmented, meaning that the free memory blocks will be interleaved with many blocks of used memory. In the end, this can have an effect similar to a memory leak, because we might request an allocation of a certain amount of memory, and there will be no single block that large, so the memory allocation will fail.

This problem is much more of an issue in consoles than in PCs, since PCs typically have much larger memories. Sometimes developers will completely give up on dynamic memory allocations to prevent this problem (and memory leaks along with it). However, that is a very drastic measure; it is inefficient with resources and is very limiting. Other solutions, like memory pools, are usually preferred. (See Chapter 7 for details on memory-allocation techniques.)

Clock Drift

Sometimes elapsed game time will be implemented as a float in the game code. In principle, this sounds like a fine idea; unless we are careful, it can have some unfortunate side effects down the line. Because of the nature of a float number, the larger the number becomes, the less precision it will have. Up to one second, it will have all 32 bits dedicated to subsecond precision. After two hours, the precision dedicated to subsecond time is reduced to 11 bits, and after 18 hours of running time, it will be down to eight bits, which means that the smallest time increment is roughly eight milliseconds. At this point, things start to become dangerous. Time steps are not reliable anymore, and strange effects can occur in the game, especially with some of the more time-sensitive systems, like physics or collision detection.

Another common representation for time is as a 32-bit integer containing the number of milliseconds since the start of the game. The integer will not have any loss of precision, but it will eventually run out of bits after 49 days. That is usually long enough for most games (other than game servers that need to be on all the time).

Error Accumulation

Another type of error caused by running the game for a long time is the accumulation of mathematical imprecision. Sometimes we are not calculating a new value from scratch, but instead, we are always adding to it or concatenating it with a new value. This can happen with the camera position and orientation, the location of game objects, or many other things. Sometimes the mathematical error will accumulate, and it will show up as strange effects after several hours of play.

What to Do?

We have seen that running the game for a long time has its own set of problems, aside from the fact that it is also more likely to uncover some normal bugs. Is there some way that we can avoid these types of problems?

The answer is to keep the machine 'fresh.' Keep it in a state as close as possible to how it was when the game started. In a console game, the best way to do this is by doing a reboot of the machine between levels. Usually, consoles will have a fast reboot mode, and the user will not even be able to tell that the machine was rebooted. Doing so is the perfect solution to all these problems, since technically your game will only be running for the duration of one level. Everything, including the memory systems and the clock count will be completely reset.

Unfortunately, not everybody can reboot between levels. We cannot do it on a PC, and maybe we cannot do it on a console, either, given the particular circumstances of the game (e.g., having to keep the network connection open). In that case, we have to do much more work by hand.

Between levels or at convenient moments (e.g., when the game is paused or the system is not loaded at 100%), we should take care of resetting as many systems as possible—at the very least, the memory and clock systems. The memory heaps should be compacted, and we might even want to run some form of garbage collection or do a pass through all the memory to identify memory leaks. The clock should also be reset at certain intervals. We might also want to completely reset the graphics system, sound system, physics, or AI to avoid any accumulated errors. This is not as ideal as rebooting the machine, but it will help prevent, or at least delay most of the above problems.

If rebooting is not an option, we should also consider tearing down whole levels at once. At the end of the level, instead of freeing every single dynamically allocated object, we could instead just reset all the memory that was used by the level data itself. As long as we took precautions so there were no pointers or other code that depended on anything in that area, totally wiping that memory could prevent any fragmentation and be much more efficient. This is particularly easy to do if we are using memory pools (see Chapter 7) to hold a lot of our level data.

DEAL WITH 'BAD' DATA

What is 'bad' data, and why is it a problem? Let us consider the following simple function that normalizes a vector:

```
void Vector3d::Normalize() {
    float fLength = sqrt(x*x+y*y+z*z);
    x /= fLength;
    y /= fLength;
    z /= fLength;
}
```

Your programmer alarm bells are probably going off—we might divide by zero! That is true; if someone calls `Normalize` on a zero-length vector, our code will attempt to divide by zero. That is 'bad' data, because it makes no sense from the function point of view. To normalize a vector is to set its length to exactly one unit, but leave its direction unchanged. What exactly does it mean to normalize a zero-length vector? It does not really have a direction to start with. It is pretty meaningless.

One of the aspects that makes bad data difficult to deal with is its tendency to propagate. If a function like the one above goes ahead and runs with bad data, either an exception will be triggered (if the system is set up to trigger that particular type of exception) or the values computed will be NAN (Not A Number). NAN is a special float value that indicates an invalid result. The problem is that doing any operations on a NAN always will result in a NAN, so those values will propagate throughout all of the calculations. This was originally designed this way in the IEEE 754 standard, but it had standardization of floating point computations for scientific purposes in mind, not game programming. So, how do we deal with this problem? There are two main opposing views.

Assert on Bad Data

We apply what we learned in the first section of this chapter and we do not allow any bad data in any function, through the use of asserts. This approach has the advantage of flagging bad data as soon as it happens, so it can be fixed right away. The drawback is the same as for the general use of asserts: if we leave them in the final build of the game, somebody will most likely come up with a situation when it will be triggered; if the asserts are removed, then the function will return NAN, with unexpected results to the rest of the game. Specifically, this is how the normalize function would be implemented:

```
void Vector3d::Normalize() {
    float fLength = sqrt(x*x+y*y+z*z);
    assert (fLength != 0);
    x /= fLength;
    y /= fLength;
    z /= fLength;
}
```

Something that makes math functions particularly susceptible to this problem is the nature of the problem itself. Unlike most other functions, there is not a range of good data and a range of bad data; things are a bit fuzzier. For example, the normalize function above can deal with any vector of any length, except for a vector that is all zeros. Similar situations happen with other math functions that cannot handle exactly parallel vectors or two points that are in the exact same place in space. For instance, a game might run without any problems until the player aligns the camera exactly with some other object, which causes both the camera vector and the alignment vector of that object to be exactly parallel, causing a function to fail. Reproducing that case might be very difficult, and it might be rare enough to go unnoticed even during internal testing.

Cope with Bad Data

The opposite view claims that we should make sure our function does not crash, does not trigger an assert, and returns the most meaningful values possible. What can we do in the case of normalizing a zero-length vector? We can detect that situation and leave the vector alone. Unfortunately, the resulting vector will not be of unit length. An alternate approach would be to return a unit vector along some arbitrary axis; that would satisfy the postcondition of the function, even if the direction of the vector is not meaningful. This is how the normalize function would be implemented to cope with bad data:

```
void Vector3d::Normalize() {
    float fLength = sqrt(x*x+y*y+z*z);
    if (fLength > 0) {
```

```
            x /= fLength;
            y /= fLength;
            z /= fLength;
        }
        // Return a unit vector along the x axis if
        // this is a zero-length vector
        else {
            x = 1.0f; y = 0.0f; z = 0.0f;
        }
    }
```

The advantage of this approach is that the functions become much more robust. It should be impossible to pass any data that will return NAN (other than passing NAN in the first place as a parameter). There is no need for asserts, so even if something unexpected happens, the functions will be able to handle it reasonably well without crashing the game.

This approach is not without drawbacks, however. These functions are all at a fairly low level, and they can get executed many times per frame (easily thousands of times). By adding the extra logic, we are making them slightly slower—and even worse, slightly larger, which could prevent them from being inlined. The performance hit could be noticeable.

Another drawback is in the data returned. At least it is not NAN, but it might not be particularly meaningful and could cause strange behavior in the game. In this case, imagine we are normalizing the normal of a collision between the player and an object. For whatever reason, that normal was zero-length, but we went ahead and attempted to normalize it anyway. This function will now return a vector along the *x*-axis, which is clearly incorrect and could cause the player to get stuck in a wall.

Finally, probably the greatest drawback of all is the reliance on the fixed results. Once all the math functions that fix bad data are in place, people will start using them without a second thought, relying on their implementation as part of the game. We will be normalizing zero-length vectors, doing square roots of negative numbers, dividing by zero, and so forth. If at some point that behavior changes (e.g., when porting the game to another platform or when optimizing a function), it might be extremely difficult to fix all the code that relied on that behavior.

Interestingly, this is the approach that some of the standard math libraries included for some consoles' use. They realized that there was no point in doing exceptions or creating NAN, because we are developing a game; instead, try to deal with the data in the best way possible. For example, in those consoles, dividing a number by zero results in zero. The problems come when a program that was developed for that console needs to be ported to a different platform, since it will typically result in continuous crashes until all the logic has been straightened out.

A Compromise

Neither of the two options we have seen so far seem particularly promising for games. They both have some major drawbacks. Instead of offering a third solution, a good option is to do a compromise of the two approaches described above.

To get the best of both worlds, one possible approach is to alternate between both approaches. By default, we take the second approach and deal with the bad data the best way we can. That will guarantee that the game does not crash, but it will make the code rely on the meaningless returned values. The key is, every so often, to switch to the first method and assert as soon as bad values are passed in. This will help you find as many bugs as possible and fix them. Doing this once every few weeks should help you catch most of the bad data being passed around. To switch back and forth easily, it is best to surround those specific asserts with an #ifdef statement, and only compile them in when needed.

```cpp
void Vector3d::Normalize() {
    float fLength = sqrt(x*x+y*y+z*z);
    #ifdef ASSERTBADDATA
    assert (fLength > 0);
    #endif
    if (fLength > 0) {
        x /= fLength;
        y /= fLength;
        z /= fLength;
    }
    // Return a unit vector along the x-axis if
    // this is a zero-length vector
    else {
        x = 1.0f; y = 0.0f; z = 0.0f;
    }
}
```

The advantage of this approach is that it discourages passing bad data to math functions (and therefore relying on their meaningless results); at the same time, it ensures that the game works correctly if that situation every happens once the game has been shipped.

The main drawback remains the potential performance hit for all the extra conditionals and lack of inlining. Therefore it might be worthwhile to provide two functions for the same operation: one that is safe and does all the checking, and another one that is very fast and does no checking at all. The difficult part is in deciding which one to use, and that might require some discipline. It is very important that the fast version should only be used if it is called from a function that is already guaranteed not to contain any bad data. Otherwise, we are back to square one, with anybody potentially calling the unsafe versions with bad data. A potential solution might be to only make the unsafe versions available within the math library and not expose them to the rest of the game. This will help remedy the problem, but it will prevent the use of the faster functions from a few places where their use was justified. Our normalize functions would look like this:

```
void Vector3d::Normalize() {
    float fLength = sqrt(x*x+y*y+z*z);
    #ifdef ASSERTBADDATA
    assert (fLength > 0);
    #endif
    if (fLength > 0) {
        x /= fLength;
        y /= fLength;
        z /= fLength;
    }
    // Return a unit vector along the x-axis if
    // this is a zero-length vector
    else {
        x = 1.0f; y = 0.0f; z = 0.0f;
    }
}

inline void Vector3d::NormalizeUnsafe() {
    float fLength = sqrt(x*x+y*y+z*z);
    assert ( fLength != 0 );
    x /= fLength;
    y /= fLength;
    z /= fLength;
}
```

CONCLUSION

The focus of this chapter was on techniques to avoid having the game crash in the hands of the final user, thus ruining their experience (and our reputation). The first part dealt with how to use `assert` effectively in our programs. We saw when it is appropriate to use `assert`, and when it is better to handle the error in a different way. We debated the merits of the different possibilities of what to do with asserts once we release the game and presented a very basic custom assert that we can use in our own programs.

The next section dealt with the problems that creep up when the program has been running for a while. Memory leaks, memory fragmentation, and clock drift are some of the problems that can occur in that situation.

Finally, we suggested some solutions to the problem of dealing with bad data. Bad data is when meaningless data is passed into a function. On the one hand, we do not want our program wasting time so that every low-level function can accept any parameter; on the other hand, we want to make sure that our game does not crash if this ever happens. A good compromise is to switch between reporting every instance of bad data with an assert for a few weeks, and then ignore it for a few more weeks. That way, hopefully, the code will develop a resilience to bad data, but we will still manage to catch most of the bugs that cause the bad data in the first place.

SUGGESTED READING

This is one of the few books that discusses how `assert` calls should be used and why using them is a very good idea. It seems that most other books have decided to ignore `assert` as a simple 'implementation detail.'

McConnell, Steve, *Code Complete*, Microsoft Press, 1993.

This article explains in great detail how to set up your own custom assert.

Rabin, Steve, "Squeezing More Out of Assert," *Game Programming Gems*, Charles River Media, 2000.

ABOUT THE CD-ROM

The CD-ROM included with this book contains the source code for several programs that demonstrate some of the more complex concepts in this book. All the programs have been kept to a minimum size to allow you to concentrate on the point they are trying to illustrate; but at the same time, they are fully functional programs that show how all the different ideas interrelate and come together.

Instead of boring you with page after page of program listings in the book, only the most important sections are included in the chapter text; you can refer to the source code on the CD-ROM for the rest of the details. If you prefer to have a lot of source code, then you might open the source code files and have them by your side while you are reading the chapter.

The best way to use the source code is to compile the program and verify that it works. Step into it with the debugger if you want to verify a particular sequence of operations, or make modifications to it to see how you can extend them or improve them.

Each program is in a separate folder with all of its source code and project files.

- **Chapter 07: MemoryMgr.** A fully implemented memory manager and a small test application.
- **Chapter 11: Plugins**. A simple Win32 application with plug-ins. The application displays the currently loaded plug-ins, and the plug-ins themselves add some menu entries to the main application. Plug-ins can be loaded and unloaded dynamically.
- **Chapter 12: RTTI**. A custom runtime type information system, this one is intended to work only with single inheritance.

- **Chapter 12: RTTIMulti**. This is a variation on the previous custom runtime type information system. It supports multiple inheritance at the cost of some extra performance.
- **Chapter 13: ObjectFactory**. This is a templatized object factory for game entities.
- **Chapter 14: Serialization**. A very simple implementation that serializes a full game-entity tree to disk and loads it back. it uses a custom stream class and the pointer fix-up method.

All the programs were compiled using Visual Studio C++ 6.0 and were tested under Windows 2000. However, except for the plug-ins example, they should all be platform and compiler independent, so they should be easy to compile and run in your favorite environment.

The executable for the plug-ins example program is also provided. You can experiment with it without having to compile it first.

INDEX